WASHINGTON

COMMANDER IN CHIEF

BY THOMAS G. FROTHINGHAM
Captain U.S.R.

WASHINGTON COMMANDER IN CHIEF

A GUIDE TO THE MILITARY HISTORY OF THE WORLD WAR

A TRUE ACCOUNT OF THE BATTLE OF JUTLAND

THE NAVAL HISTORY OF THE WORLD WAR

THE AMERICAN REINFORCEMENT IN THE WORLD WAR

WASHINGTON

COMMANDER IN CHIEF

THOMAS G. FROTHINGHAM

CAPTAIN U.S.R.

WITH ILLUSTRATIONS

BOSTON AND NEW YORK
HOUGHTON MIFFLIN COMPANY
The Riverside Press Cambridge
1930

The Riverside Press
CAMBRIDGE · MASSACHUSETTS
PRINTED IN THE U.S.A.

Foreword to the Reader

THE object of this work is to set forth in its true light, and with its right perspective, the military record of George Washington, American Commander in Chief throughout the Revolution. The many biographies of Washington have not approached their subject from the military point of view, with the account of the actual military operations as the inflexible basis for the text.

There is an urgent need for such a book, because, especially of late, the character of Washington has been distorted out of all semblance of reality. There has been a constant stream of books filled with petty and personal comment, and with *ex parte* treatises that have blurred the great issues and the great events. The recent biographers of Washington have made the mistake of controversial argument, to an extent that has colored their statements of his career.

At this approaching two-hundredth anniversary of his birth, it is fitting that we should study the actual facts of the case — and that we should allow these facts to shape the verdict, without special pleadings. In a book which deals with the course of military events, the narrative of facts must be the main theme, and adhering to this is the only sound method of treatment. For, in the military field of action above all, *res ipsa loquitur*. In this work every effort will be made to give a true statement of the military events,

v

and, as the character of George Washington was bound up in these events, the writer believes that a true picture of the character of Washington will be reflected in the following narrative.

Contents

CONTENTS

Illustrations and Maps

WASHINGTON
COMMANDER IN CHIEF

Chapter I

SELF-TUITION IN BOYHOOD

IN THE first place, it must be evident at once to the reader that, in a work of this nature, any long or detailed account of the boyhood and youth of George Washington would be out of place and useless. But, in order to give a true picture, it is necessary to study briefly certain phases of Washington's young days, because there were unusual circumstances and influences present in his boyhood which undoubtedly moulded his character at an early date, and in a way that affected his whole future career.

There is no need to go to any length in describing his origin. As is well known, the Washingtons were of good English stock. Although they were not distinctively a military family, there had been many soldiers among them. In the civil war which brought about the deposition and execution of Charles I, Sir Henry Washington, a cousin of that generation, commanded the Royalist forces which made a desperate defense of Worcester (1646) against greatly superior numbers. The following was Sir Henry Washington's reply to a summons to surrender, and Irving

I

has justly noted that this was prophetic of future qualities in George Washington: 'Sir, It is acknowledged by your books and by report of your own quarter, that the king is in some of your armies. That granted, it may be easy for you to procure his Majesty's commands for the disposal of this garrison. Till then I shall make good the trust reposed in me. As for conditions, if I shall be necessitated, I shall make the best I can. The worst I know and fear not; if I had, the profession of a soldier had not been begun, nor so long continued by your Excellency's humble servant, Henry Washington.'

The other Washingtons in England were also Royalists. In 1657, two brothers, John and Andrew, came to Virginia, as did many of the Cavalier party. George Washington's father, Augustine Washington, was a grandson of the immigrant John. Augustine had large holdings of land in the Colony of Virginia, and there was no pinch of poverty or hardship for his children. But he died in 1743, when his son George (born February 22, 1732, of his second marriage with Mary Ball) was only eleven.

Before his father's death, the young George Washington had only received instruction at a small local school. His brother Lawrence, fourteen years older than George, had the advantage of being sent to a school in England, where he had remained until George was over seven. On his return to Virginia, Lawrence showed a warm fondness for George, and soon gained a strong influence over the boy. By a strange chance, this influence of George Washington's eldest brother was cast in a military direction. For it happened that, at this very time, the Colony of Virginia became absorbed in the military activities of raising troops to be sent against the Spaniards in the West Indies. Lawrence Washington had offered his services at once, and thus the young George was thrown into a military atmosphere. He saw his brother Lawrence commissioned a captain in the new levies, which sailed in 1740 to take part in the joint expeditions of Admiral Vernon and General Wentworth. It was natural that the imagination of the boy should be excited by these unusual surroundings — by the drilling and preparations, and by seeing his much-admired brother depart for active service. The result was an enthusiasm for military affairs, which filled his thoughts in work and play. This became much more than a passing boyish fancy in its effects upon the young George Washington, and gave to his mind an actual military bent.

Of course this would have worn away in the ordinary course of events. He was only a little boy, although impressionable beyond his age. But the young George's military hero, and the model he desired to imitate, returned in 1742, to kindle anew the boy's enthusiasm and to bring him again into a military atmosphere. And this time his mentor stayed near him. On his return, Lawrence Washington had promptly fallen in love with Miss Anne Fairfax, and for this reason he had resolved to remain in Virginia. But he continued zealous in military affairs and became Adjutant General of his district in Virginia, with the rank of Major. Consequently, the boy George was growing up in the same military surroundings and under the same influence of his brother's example.

In July, 1743, three months after his father's death, Lawrence Washington married Miss Fairfax. He took up his residence on the lands on the banks of the Potomac River, which were his share of the property distributed by his father's will. This beautiful estate Lawrence called Mount Vernon, in honor of Admiral Vernon. In the division of his father's property, George Washington was to

3

receive, on coming of age, the house and lands on the Rappahannock River.

Young George was left under the guardianship of his mother, Mary Washington, but he was much at Mount Vernon with his brother Lawrence. This settling of Lawrence in Virginia and his connection by marriage with the Fairfax family exerted a marked influence upon the future of George Washington.

He had been sent to a better school. However, it must be stated unequivocally that his actual schooling never went beyond the 'plain and practical.' What he learned from his teachers would never have accounted for the abilities he soon displayed. But there was another factor that made all the difference in the world, a personal characteristic innate in the boy, which made his education more effective than could have been thought possible under the circumstances. It was successful, only because the young George Washington was actuated by that intense passion for self-education and self-improvement which has been recognized as a potent force and spur in the careers of many who have made their marks in history. In this respect he was like Lincoln — not that he was obliged to lift himself out of similar disadvantageous surroundings. For the associates of the Washingtons were the best in the Colony. But there was the same absorbing desire for self-tuition, which was so notable a trait in Lincoln and set him apart from his fellows. In the case of Washington there was the same cause, and there was the same effect.

As the Washingtons and their like were all landowners on a large scale, and as the development of their lands was the most important thing in their lives, it was not surprising that the young George Washington's ambition followed this trend. In fact, he concentrated his craving for self-educa-

4

tion upon hard study that would fit him to be a surveyor of land. Of this there is a record that all may read.

Washington's books of exercises, written before he was sixteen, have been preserved. In one of these there is proof of a truly astonishing grasp of mathematics. So good an authority as Charles Moore has written: 'The one devoted to mathematics exhibits a wide range of subjects, combined with sureness, and accuracy in working, and clearness and neatness of presentation. Few graduates of colleges to-day, unless they specialize in mathematics, become as well trained in that subject.'

In itself, this is high praise. But its real significance lies in its being the just estimate of achievement due to the ardor for self-tuition, which this unusual boy threw into the studies that would advance his own ambition. As in the case of Lincoln, self-education had won knowledge for George Washington that never could have been gained by any other means.

In addition to this precocious excellence in mathematics, another exercise book of the same youthful period has preserved a record of George Washington's comprehensive study of the forms of all kinds of mercantile and legal papers. Of these his knowledge was shown to be so extensive, that Irving declared it 'gave him through life a lawyer's skill in drafting documents.' It is needless to emphasize the value of this special ability in Washington's future career.

In one of the same books were preserved the one hundred and ten 'Rules of Decent Behaviour in Courtesy and Conversation.' These were written out in George Washington's handwriting. And it should be noted, as another significant measure of his progress, that, even at this youthful stage, his writing had already taken on the extraordinary character

5

which ever afterwards so distinguished it. His 'Rules' were not merely the perfunctory copybook texts of the ordinary schoolboy. On the contrary, they were his carefully chosen maxims, for daily guidance in the paths of his ambition. And, with his unusual powers of concentration and self-control which formed so strong a part of his character, he actually modeled his conduct upon them.

All through this formative period, George Washington's interest in military affairs remained active, and always stimulated by his brother Lawrence. At Mount Vernon there was also a flavor of the Navy. Lawrence Washington was an admirer of both services. He had personal knowledge of the Navy as well as the Army, because he had served in the joint military and naval expeditions in the West Indies. For this reason, when George Washington was about fourteen, Lawrence had encouraged the idea of putting his young brother into the British Navy. It almost came to the point that George was to go on board a British man-of-war as a midshipman. But, at the last moment, his mother could not face the parting, and the boy was kept at school, with the result that has been described.

There can be no question of the fact that at sixteen George Washington had acquired a precocious training which was most unusual. At that early age he actually was prepared in every sense to take up his chosen profession as a surveyor of land. This was astonishing enough in itself. But, in addition, it must be evident that all his early training had been along the very lines that would be of the most practical value in the destined military career, then hidden behind the veil of the future. It is only common-sense for us to recognize this unmistakable element in his development. Among the conglomerations of anecdotes and controversies, this broad condition has been obscured. But it is merely

Rules of Civility & Decent Behaviour
In Company and Conversation

1 Every Action done in Company, ought to be with Some Sign of Respect, to those that are present

2 When in Company, put not your Hands to any Part of the Body, not usualy Discovered

3 Shew nothing to your Friend that may affright him

4 In the presence of Others Sing not to yourself with a humming Noise, nor Drum with your Fingers or Feet

5 If You Cough, Sneeze, Sigh, or Yawn, do it not Loud but Privately; and Speak not in your Yawning, but put Your handkerchief or Hand before your face and turn aside

6 Sleep not when others Speak, Sit not when others stand, Speak not when you Should hold your Peace, walk not on when others Stop

7 Put not off your Cloths in the presence of Others, nor go out your Chamber half Drest

8 At Play and at Fire its Good manners to Give Place to the last Commer, and affect not to Speak Louder than Ordinary

9 Spit not in the Fire, nor Stoop low before it neither Put your Hands into the Flames to warm them, nor Set your Feet upon the Fire especially if there be meat before it

10 When you Sit down, Keep your Feet firm and Even, without putting one on the other or Crossing them

11 Shift not yourself in the Sight of others nor Gnaw your nails

12 Shake not the head, Feet, or Legs rowl not the Eys lift not one eyebrow higher than the other wry not the mouth, and bedew no mans face with your Spittle, by approaching too near him when you Speak

FIRST PAGE OF YOUNG GEORGE WASHINGTON'S 'RULES
OF CIVILITY & DECENT BEHAVIOUR'

a statement of fact to write that the self-tuition of the boy of sixteen had given to George Washington an almost uncanny basis for building up, from his experiences which were soon to follow, a preparation for his future great tasks.

Chapter II

GRADUATION TO MANHOOD

JUST after George Washington had reached his sixteenth birthday, the occasion arose which at once proved that his determination for self-improvement had truly equipped him to play a man's part. He had left school in 1747, and he was living with his brother Lawrence at Mount Vernon. Consequently, it was natural that George should see a great deal of the family of his brother's wife. Belvoir, the estate of William Fairfax, Lawrence's father-in-law, was not far from Mount Vernon. At Belvoir the young George soon attracted the special attention of Lord Fairfax, who became George Washington's first patron. Lord Fairfax was William Fairfax's cousin, and he had come to reside in Virginia, where he had large possessions in lands inherited from a grant of Charles II to Lord Culpepper.

At this time George Washington was a tall, well-developed, athletic youth, who appeared much older than his years, and showed the good effects of his early self-training in his speech and conduct. He was still actively pursuing his studies, and was constantly practicing surveying in the neighboring fields. This good-looking, well-mannered, and able youth was as different from the usual hobbledehoy of his age as can be imagined. Added to this, he was a bold and skillful horseman and fond of fox hunting, of which

8

Lord Fairfax was a devotee. In the hunting field, Lord Fairfax found that George Washington was one after his own heart. But the youth was not relegated to the position of being merely a protégé as a companion for the chase. On the contrary, Lord Fairfax had soon perceived that George Washington possessed qualities which fitted him for the important things of life.

Lord Fairfax wished to have a survey made of his lands beyond the Blue Ridge, and he chose George Washington for the task. This selection of a youth of sixteen, for a mission that implied responsibilities usually thought to be beyond the ability of any one so young, was a first instance of the truly extraordinary impression George Washington produced upon those who came in contact with him. This is one characteristic of Washington that has never been disputed. Admirers and detractors alike have borne testimony to the invariably favorable effect of George Washington's personality and presence. It was an attribute that remained throughout his life — and it is most interesting to perceive the beginning of its influence in this first designation of the young George Washington for a man's task.

For him it was actual graduation into manhood, and his performance of the work assigned to him proved the wisdom of Lord Fairfax's choice. In March, 1748, he set out on this expedition with George William Fairfax, a brother of Lawrence's wife. They were accompanied by James Genn, a surveyor, and other assistants. Washington's diary of the 'Survey' has been preserved, and this journey was evidently one that demanded all his vigorous physique and fitness to cope with the hardships of the wilderness, aside from his knowledge of surveying. This was the beginning of an extensive practice of his profession that was remarkable for one so young. After Washington's report of the results of

9

his first survey, Lord Fairfax moved across the Blue Ridge and resided there. George Washington received the appointment of public surveyor, and this gave a standing of authority to his surveys. Consequently, for the next few years he was busily engaged in surveying the vast tracts of land which included the Shenandoah Valley.

He remained in high favor with Lord Fairfax, was still his companion in the chase, read his books, and saw much of the Fairfax family. As a surveyor he was greatly in demand, and his earnings were large — all of which he invested in purchases of land. For this last he had a great advantage, as his profession gave him an expert knowledge of land. But more important was the knowledge acquired through this early maturity of Washington — his experience of the rugged life of the regions beyond the settled districts, of hardships, expedients, and the development of self-reliance in all emergencies.

The great colonization scheme of the Ohio Company was then being launched, of which his brother Lawrence was one of the prime movers. Altogether, while he was yet in his teens, George Washington was receiving a broad training in resource. If he had been restricted to the wilderness, or if he had been confined to the settled areas, it would have been different. But Washington was gaining the invaluable experience of being active in both. He was also in touch with the most important people of the Colony and with public affairs of magnitude — and this before he was twenty.

Besides all this, there was a new outbreak of the military spirit in the Colony of Virginia. For it had become evident that the French would resist the aggrandizement in the region of the Ohio. In this scheme the Virginians were deeply interested, and the Colony began to make military

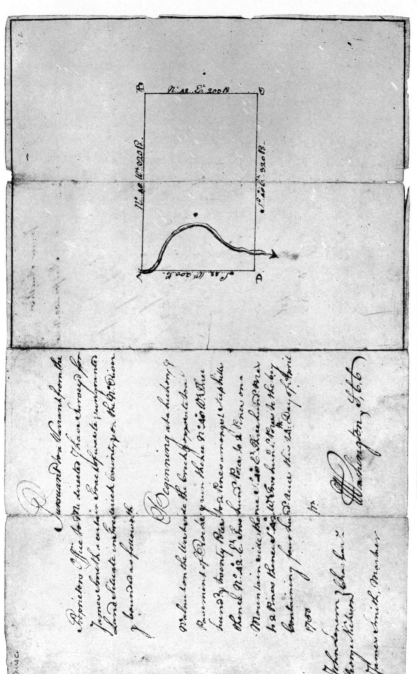

SURVEY MADE BY GEORGE WASHINGTON, 1750

preparations. Under the tutelage of Lawrence, George Washington again became active in military affairs. At Mount Vernon the two brothers studied tactics, evolutions, and the practice of arms, with two ex-officers who had served with Lawrence. In 1752, when he was but twenty, George Washington was appointed one of the district adjutant generals with the rank of Major.

But their military studies had been interrupted, when suddenly it became evident that Lawrence's lungs were seriously threatened. And in September, 1751, the two brothers sailed for Barbados to seek a cure for Lawrence. At first the malady seemed curable, and George returned to Virginia in February, 1752. Lawrence finished the winter in Barbados, but only came back to die at Mount Vernon (July 26, 1752). He left a daughter, who did not long survive him. And, as he had bequeathed Mount Vernon to George in case of her death, this beautiful estate became the lifelong home of George Washington, of whom it remains a perpetual memorial.

The situation in the region of the Ohio had grown serious, as the attitude of the French became more hostile. They were gathering military forces and arousing the Indians to take the side of the French in the impending dispute. In 1753, in response to inquiries from England, Governor Dinwiddie of Virginia was very anxious to get a letter through to the Commandant of the French forces, to ascertain his intentions in regard to the Ohio Valley. The Governor also wished his messenger to make a report of the general situation as to the French and Indians in that region. This was a mission of the greatest difficulty and danger. One chosen messenger had been sent, who was so daunted by the threatening aspect of affairs on the frontier that he did not dare to attempt to penetrate to the French Commandant, and returned without accomplishing any part of his errand. After this failure, Governor Dinwiddie turned to Washington, as the one who had shown himself qualified to carry out this dangerous mission.

The mere statement of this fact is enough to show the standing that Washington had already attained in the estimation of the rulers of the Colony. There is no room for argument. All that is necessary is to cast aside anecdotes and controversies, and to ask ourselves why this young man of twenty-one was chosen. It was the highest proof of what has been written as to the tested qualities of the young Washington. In spite of his youth, he had won a wide recognition of his abilities and judgment. His military appointment had been renewed as Adjutant General of the Northern District, and Governor Dinwiddie wrote that he had sent 'a person of distinction' [1] on this difficult mission.

George Washington showed himself worthy of this high confidence. It was again a task that tried to the utmost his physical hardihood and the resourcefulness he had acquired from his experiences in the wilderness. He had set out on October 30, 1753, and, after many hardships and adventures, on January 16, 1754, he brought to Governor Dinwiddie at Williamsburg the letter of the French Commandant, with a full report of the situation, which was much more important. Washington's report of his mission Governor Dinwiddie ordered printed, and it was widely circulated in the Colonies and in Great Britain. This report was written by Washington himself, using his journal of events, and it was a clear account of the performance of his mission and of his shrewd observations of the situation.

As the main interest in the early events of Washington's life, for the purposes of this book, must lie in tracing the in-

[1] Letter to Governor Hamilton, November 24, 1754.

12

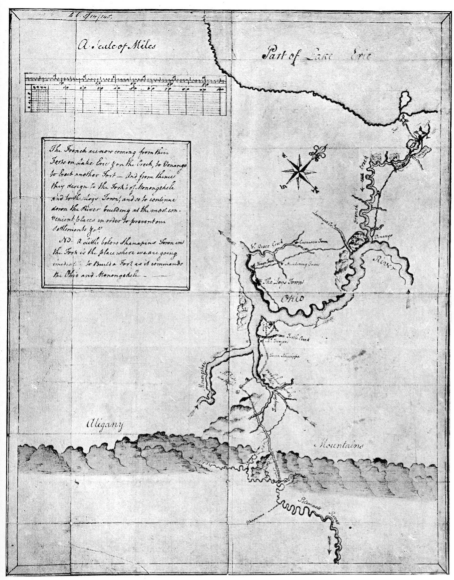

WASHINGTON'S MAP OF THE OHIO VALLEY WITH HIS COMMENT
ON THE SITUATION AT THE END OF 1753

fluences that moulded his future career, we should note that the text of this report showed a great stride toward the ability to express his thoughts in writing, which afterwards became so notable a characteristic of Washington. The true significance of Washington's extraordinary ability in writing has never been sufficiently recognized. We forget that it is universally acknowledged that the greatest help to clear thinking is putting the thought into writing. In this George Washington was already becoming practiced.

It is altogether an amazing story, when calmly considered without being drawn aside into petty details — this sudden graduation of George Washington into the full estate of manhood. For that is the only term to describe it. Here was no case of a premature assumption of a place that could not be held, neither was there anything spectacular or sensational. Washington's assured position in Virginia was well won by qualities acquired through his efforts to fit himself for ambitious tasks. His successful grasp of these tasks, whenever he encountered them, must be attributed to the intense self-tuition which has been described. But there is no escaping the conclusion that Washington, at twenty-two, had become in the true sense of the words 'a person of distinction' as described by Governor Dinwiddie. This distinction, so early attained, was founded on the fact that George Washington already stood out in the eyes of the Colonists as one whose ability and judgment had been tested and proved.

Chapter III

FIRST MILITARY ADVENTURES

AFTER the receipt of the letter of the French Commandant, St. Pierre, brought to Governor Dinwiddie by George Washington, and after the publication of Washington's report of the situation on the Ohio, there could be no longer any doubt as to the intention of the French to seize the Ohio Valley. But the preparations to resist them can only be called feeble and futile. Great Britain at first stood aloof, and the Colonies took no united action. In fact, Virginia was the only one to do anything at all. And what was done was only on so small a scale that failure was preordained. The Ohio Company was to build a fort at the fork of the Allegheny and Monongahela, which was an advanced and isolated position. The only support for this venture was to be a regiment of Virginia militia, which was to be raised by Governor Dinwiddie. This bare description of the Virginian plans will show how inadequate was their conception of what must be done.

Washington was ordered to Alexandria to recruit for this militia force. From that time on, he was absorbed in military duties. On March 20, 1754, he received a commission as Lieutenant Colonel from Governor Dinwiddie, and he was designated second in command to Colonel Joshua Fry for a proposed expedition of these levies to the new fort at the fork of the rivers. Recruiting was slow, and, in April,

14

THE
JOURNAL
OF

Major *George Washington*,

SENT BY THE

Hon. *ROBERT DINWIDDIE*, Esq;
His Majesty's Lieutenant-Governor, and
Commander in Chief of *VIRGINIA*,

TO THE

COMMANDANT

OF THE

FRENCH FORCES

ON

O H I O.

To WHICH ARE ADDED, THE

GOVERNOR's LETTER,

AND A TRANSLATION OF THE

FRENCH OFFICER's ANSWER.

WILLIAMSBURG:
Printed by WILLIAM HUNTER. 1754

TITLE–PAGE OF WASHINGTON'S REPORT TO GOVERNOR
DINWIDDIE. PUBLISHED 1754

1754, Washington was ordered to advance to the Ohio with all that were available, only about one hundred and fifty men. The plan was to reinforce him later by sending on the main body under Colonel Fry. But, in that same month, before Washington's little force could get anywhere near the fork, the French had appeared in strength and had ejected the men of the Ohio Company from their newly built fort. Of these there were less than forty, and of course they could not hope to make any defense of the place. The French took possession, strengthened the fort, and called it Fort Duquesne.

Washington was thus left footloose and isolated. He was never reinforced beyond a total of about three hundred and fifty. Needless to say, he could not possibly win any results against the superior numbers of the French. Under these circumstances, his weak force became an easy prey. He was soon cooped up in an extemporized entrenchment on the Great Meadows, called by him Fort Necessity. All Washington could do was to put up a strong enough fight to gain terms of marching out with colors flying, and with arms, effects, and stores (July 4, 1754).

This was, indeed, a reverse of fortune for the ambitious young Virginian. But it was so evident that he could not have accomplished anything with the means at his command that the failure did not in the least injure his prestige. On the contrary, he was given a vote of thanks by the House of Burgesses.

After the expulsion of Washington's little force, the French were left in full possession of the disputed territory. But this seizure of the Ohio was a call for action, both in America and in Great Britain. The Colonies began to consult together as to what was to be done. But the British Ministry at once assumed the leading rôle by ordering a force of British Regulars sent to America. General Braddock, who had been chosen to command the British force sent to America, arrived in Virginia in February, 1755. He was a disciple of the school of the Duke of Cumberland, and his monumental unfitness for his task can best be described by stating that he was utterly unable to admit the possibility of anything on earth that could affect the perfected parade-ground tactics of Europe. From his point of view, it was enough that he was to command an expedition of British Regulars against Fort Duquesne. The affair he considered ended. He said to Franklin, 'After taking Fort Duquesne, I am to proceed to Niagara, and, having taken that, to Frontenac.' In answer to warnings against ambuscades, he only replied, 'The savages may be formidable to your raw American militia; upon the King's Regular and disciplined troops it is impossible they should make any impression.'

Much dissatisfaction had been aroused by a royal order which made all Colonial commissions inferior in rank to any commission from the King. But General Braddock had invited Washington to become a special aide 'in his family, by which all inconveniences of that kind will be obviated.'[1] To this offer Washington replied, frankly avowing 'an inclination to serve the ensuing campaign as a volunteer; and this inclination is not a little increased, since it is likely to be conducted by a gentleman of the General's experience. But, besides this, and the laudable desire I may have to serve, with my best abilities, my King and country, I must be ingenuous enough to confess that I am not a little biased by selfish considerations. To explain, Sir, I wish earnestly to attain some knowledge in the military profession, and

[1] Letter of Robert Orme, aide-de-camp of General Braddock, to George Washington, March 2, 1755.

16

believing a more favorable opportunity cannot offer, **than** to serve under a gentleman of General Braddock's abilities and experience, it does, as you may reasonably suppose, not a little contribute to influence my choice.' [1]

This letter of George Washington is most interesting. It not only revealed his military trend, but also showed that he shared the implicit faith in the British Regular troops which was prevalent at the time. In this regard, it was true that Washington was about 'to attain some knowledge'; but it was to be a 'knowledge' altogether different from anything he had expected.

What followed is too well known to need any description. Its bitter lesson of disillusionment has been best expressed in Washington's caustic letter to Governor Dinwiddie,[2] giving his first account of Braddock's defeat (July 9, 1755): 'We continued our march from Fort Cumberland to Frazier's (which is within 7 miles of Duquesne) without meeting any extraordinary event, having only a straggler or two picked up by the French Indians. When we came to this place, we were attacked (very unexpectedly) by about three hundred French and Indians. Our numbers consisted of about thirteen hundred men, chiefly Regulars, who were immediately struck with such an inconceivable panick, that nothing but confusion and disobedience of orders prevailed among them. The officers in general behaved with incomparable bravery, for which they greatly suffered, there being near 60 killed and wounded — a large proportion out of the number we had. The Virginia companies behaved like men and like soldiers; for I believe out of three companies that were on the ground that day scarce

[1] Answer of George Washington to Robert Orme, aide-de-camp of General Braddock, March 15, 1755.

[2] Written July 18, 1755.

17

Chapter IV

THE LESSONS OF THE FRENCH AND INDIAN WARS

THE unexpected defeat of Braddock by so inferior a force of French and Indians [1] was ruinously decisive in every sense of the word. It brought failure to the other expeditions which had been planned. The Northern Colonies had quickly raised a surprising number of troops (Massachusetts 4500, the rest of New England and New York 3000). These were to be used in coöperation with the expected victorious advance of Braddock. But the French, 'warned by papers captured from Braddock of the design against Crown Point,' [2] had reinforced the place to a strength that balked the expedition of Johnson, in spite of his defeat of Dieskau (September, 1755). And they had also strengthened the forces defending Niagara, so that the expedition of Governor Shirley was compelled to limit itself to throwing a strong garrison into Oswego.

But, in the immediate area of the defeat on the borders of Virginia, there was a collapse more tragic in its consequences. The part of Braddock's army left behind under Colonel Dunbar at Fort Cumberland had not been involved at all in the disaster, and, after the retreat of the remnants

---

[1] 'Of thirteen hundred and seventy-three non-commissioned officers and men, but four hundred and fifty-three came off unharmed.... The loss of the French was trifling.... It was in fact a total and crushing defeat.' (Fortescue: *History of the British Army.*)

[2] Fortescue: *History of the British Army.*

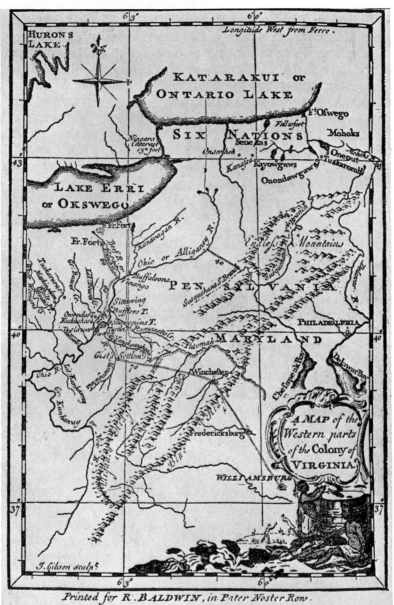

HURONS LAKE

Longitude West from Ferre.

KATARAKUI or ONTARIO LAKE

SIX NATIONS

Ft. Ofwego

Mohoks

Niagara Cataract 137 feet

Senekas

Onanghek

Kanelso

Kayowgraws

Onondawgraw

Oneout

Tuskarorahl

LAKE ERRI or OKSWEGO

Fr. Fort

Fr. Fort

Kanawagan R.

Ohio or Alligany R.

Buffaloons

Venango

Susquehana St Branch

PEN

SYLVANIA

Endless Mountains

Sittaning

Buffters T.

Onoydot T.

Kuskuskus

Shaxopins T.

The Lawns

Turtle

Roxanetto G.

PHILADELPHIA

Gist's Settlem.

Patomak

MARYLAND

Ohio R.

Gr. Kankanau

Gr. Kanhanau

Winchester

Chefopeak Bay

Delaware Bay

Fredericksburg

A MAP of the Western parts of the Colony of VIRGINIA

WILLIAMSBURG

J. Gibson sculp.

Printed for R. BALDWIN, in Pater Noster Row.

from the battlefield, was still superior to any force the French could have brought against it. However, Colonel Dunbar did not want any more of such warfare, and he withdrew these British troops in a retreat from the frontier to Philadelphia. His act left the whole border exposed to raids of the French and Indians.

At the call of this emergency, Governor Dinwiddie convened the House of Burgesses of the Colony of Virginia on August 4, 1755. They promptly voted forty thousand pounds and authorized raising a regiment of one thousand men. At once Washington was given a commission as Commander in Chief of all the forces raised, or to be raised, in the Colony of Virginia. This commission was in response to a general demand for the services of George Washington, as the one who had shown that he possessed the qualities needed at this crisis. It must be considered a remarkable tribute to the young man of twenty-three, and a convincing testimony of full confidence in his military ability and judgment.

For Washington, it meant the beginning of endless struggles to organize a military defense for the border — without ever possessing adequate means. His plan was, to gather a force strong enough to operate from one central fort, to be built at Winchester in Virginia, with other coordinated posts in the outlying areas. This would have enabled him to strike promptly in force against any incursions of the French and Indians. His scheme was sound and showed a clear military vision. But Washington was never given the opportunity to progress beyond the construction of the central fort, which was called Fort Loudoun after the new British Commander in Chief for the American Colonies.

So far as Washington's plan was concerned, its execution

21

5743

stopped short at this. Instead of attempting to carry out the rest of his scheme, the Virginia authorities restricted Washington to a dictated policy of a chain of small fortified posts, so slenderly manned that they could not hope to protect the adjacent territory from the raids of the Indians. These were all the time harassing the unfortunate inhabitants, and the list of atrocities grew — to wring the heart of the young Virginian commander.

Washington's letters of that period have been preserved, and they certainly gave him a wide practice of letter-writing. They were a record of remonstrance against adverse conditions, with protests, arguments, entreaties, invectives, scoldings — every method tried to induce the powers in control to grant him the means to protect the unfortunate settlers on the borders.

In these letters Washington showed depths of feeling that found eloquent expression: 'I see their situation know their dangers and participate their sufferings, without having it in my power to give them further relief, than uncertain promises. In short, I see inevitable destruction in so clear a light, that, unless vigorous measures are taken by the Assembly, and speedy assistance sent from below, the poor inhabitants that are now in forts, must unavoidably fall, while the remainder of the country are flying before the barbarous foe. . . . The supplicating tears of the women, and moving petitions from the men, melt me into such deadly sorrow, that I solemnly declare, if I know my own mind, I could offer myself a willing sacrifice to the butchering enemy, provided that would contribute to the people's ease.' [1]

The Virginia authorities made efforts to remedy these evils, but, under the new administration of Lord Loudoun,

[1] Letter to Governor Dinwiddie, from Winchester, April 22, 1756.

Virginia was not only left to its own defense, but the Colony also was required to send four hundred Virginian troops to the aid of South Carolina. This left Virginia even worse off than at first, for recruiting was very slow, as it was hard to induce the men to leave their own families and homes. Consequently, Washington had a long and arduous service in trying to defend three hundred and fifty miles of frontier with less than a thousand men.

This hopeless state of affairs continued through 1756 and 1757. In these two years, under the command of Lord Loudoun, there was nothing but a succession of British failures. He was recalled, but it was the accession of William Pitt as Prime Minister that turned the tide of the war in America. Under his able and energetic administration, the British began to throw strong military forces into America, with adequate naval forces to supplement them. There was no corresponding move on the part of France, and the French forces in America were abandoned to their fate.

It was not until 1758 that this change of affairs brought relief to the hard-pressed Washington. The young Virginian commander had always urged that there should be an expedition against Fort Duquesne, to destroy that nest of depredations on the border. But always his hopes had been disappointed. At last, in 1758, this expedition was made a part of the energetic military programme for the year. It was to be under the command of Brigadier General Forbes, and Washington was to lead the Virginian troops, then increased to a total of two thousand.

There were long delays in preparing for this expedition, and it is interesting to note that, at this time when there was a great shortage of regimental clothing, Washington conceived the idea of fitting out his command in the light Indian hunting garb. This was a first departure from the cumbersome uniforms of the day. Washington pointed out, not only the great gain in comfort, but also the great reduction of impedimenta to be transported. This serviceable costume, derived from the Indians, soon proved its utility, and Washington was, all unconsciously, introducing an equipment which was to be of great value to the Americans in the Revolution.

The long delays were not at all the fault of Washington. If he could have had his way, the expedition would have moved forward in short order, using the road already hewn out for Braddock. Washington urged this course in the strongest terms. But his resultant detention in Virginia brought about a most important event in his life, his short courtship of the young and attractive widow of Daniel Parke Custis. She had been Martha Dandridge, and was to become the Martha Washington of history. Before General Forbes' expedition was ready to start on its march, they had promised one another that they would be married as soon as Washington returned from the Fort Duquesne campaign.[1]

Before Washington's departure, he was also elected representative for Frederick County in the House of Burgesses of Virginia. His military duties had prevented his appearing at the polls, but he was chosen by a large and enthusiastic majority of the electors. Consequently, the young Virginian

---

[1] Washington's farewell letter to Martha Custis is one of the few written to her that have been preserved, as his widow destroyed his letters. It is quite a little masterpiece of English composition, that could have been put together only by a writer of ability:

'we have begun our march for the Ohio. A courier is starting for Williamsburg, and I embrace the opportunity to send a few words to one whose life is now inseparable from mine. Since the happy hour when we made our pledges to each other, my thoughts have been continually going to you as another self. That an all-powerful Providence may keep us both in safety is the prayer of your ever faithful and affectionate friend.'

Suggesting a Plan for a Line of March

Camp at Raystown, 8 October 1758

Sir,

In consequence of your request of the Colonels assembled at your lodgings, the 13th instant, I offer the plans (on the other side) to your consideration. I hey express any thoughts on a line of march thro', a country covered with woods, and how that line of march may be formed in an instant into an order of battle. The plan of the line of march and order of battle, on the other side, is calculated for a forest march with field-pieces only, unincumbered with waggons. It represents, first, a line of march; and, secondly, how that line of march may in an instant be thrown into an order of battle in the woods. This plan supposes four thousand privates, one thousand of whom (picked men,) are to march in the front in three divisions, each division having a field-officer to command it, if the necessary precautions are observed, must always be in front.

The first division must, (as the second and third ought likewise to be,) subdivided for the captains; the se subdivisions to be again divided for the subalterns, and the subalterns again for the serjeants and corporals. By which means every non-commissioned officer will have a party to command, under the eye of a subaltern, as the subaltern will have under the direction of a captain, &c.

N.B. I shall, altho' I believe it unnecessary, remark here, that the captains, when the subdivisions are again divided, are to take command of no particular part of it, but to attend to the whole subdivision. As the subalterns are to do, with theirs, each captain and subaltern acting, as commandant of the division he is appointed to, under the field-officer, visiting and encouraging all parts alike, and keeping the soldiers to their duty. This being done, the first division is, as soon as the van-guard is attacked, (if that gives the first notice of the enemy's approach,) to file off to the right and left, and take to trees, gaining the enemy's flanks, and surrounding them, as described in the second plan. The flank-guards on the right, which belong to the second division, are immediately to extend to the right, followed by that division, and to form, as described in the aforesaid plan. The rear-guard division is to follow the left flankers in the same manner, in order, if possible, to encompass the enemy, which being a practice different from any thing they have ever yet experienced from us, I think may be accomplished. What Indians we have, should be ordered to get round, unperceived, and fall at the same time upon the enemy's rear. The front and rear being thus secured, there remains a body of two thousand five hundred men to form two brigades, on the flanks of which six hundred men must march for the safety of them, and in such order as to form a rank, by only marching the captains and subalterns, guards into the intervals between the serjeants' parties, as may be seen by plan the second. The main body will now be reduced to nineteen hundred men, which should be kept a corps de reserve to support any part, that shall be hard beset or forced.

The whole is submitted to correction with the utmost candor, by

Sir, &c.

WASHINGTON'S LETTER TO GENERAL FORBES
Submitting a Plan for a Line of March

Sir,   Camp, at Raystown, 8 October, 1758

In consequence of your request of the Colonels assembled at your lodgings, the 15th instant, I offer the plans (on the other side) to your consideration. They express my thoughts on a line of march thro' a country covered with woods, and how that line of march may be formed in an instant into an order of battle. The plan of the line of march and order of battle, on the other side, is calculated for a forced march with field-pieces only, unincumbered with wagons. It represents, first, a line of march; and, secondly, how that line of march may in an instant be thrown into an order of battle in the woods. This plan supposes four thousand privates, one thousand of whom (picked men,) are to march in the front in three divisions, each division having a field-officer to command it, if the necessary precautions are observed, must always be in front.

The first division must, (as the second and third ought likewise to be,) subdivided for the captains; these subdivisions to be again divided for the subalterns; and the subalterns again for the sergeants and corporals. By which means every non-commissioned officer will have a party to command, under the eye of a subaltern, as the subalterns will have, under the direction of a captain, &c.

N.B. I shall, altho I believe it unnecessary, remark here, that the captains, when the subdivisions are again divided, are to take command of no particular part of it, but to attend to the whole subdivision, as the subalterns are to do with theirs, each captain and subaltern acting as commandant of the division he is appointed to, under the field-officer, visiting and encouraging all parts alike, and keeping the soldiers to their duty. This being done, the first division is, as soon as the van-guard is attacked (if that gives the first notice of the enemy's approach), to file off to the right and left, and take to trees, gaining the enemy's flanks, and surrounding them, as described in the second plan. The flank-guards on the right, which belong to the second division, are immediately to extend to the right, followed by that division, and to form, as described in the aforesaid plan. The rear-guard division is to follow the left flankers in the same manner, in order, if possible, to encompass the enemy, which being a practice different from any thing they have ever yet experienced from us, I think may be accomplished. What Indians we have, should be ordered to get round, unperceived, and fall at the same time upon the enemy's rear. The front and rear being thus secured, there remains a body of two thousand five hundred men to form two brigades, on the flanks of which six hundred men must march for the safety of them, and in such order as to form a rank entire, by only marching the captains and subalterns' guards into the intervals between the sergeants' parties, as may be seen by plan the second. The main body will now be reduced to nineteen hundred neb, which should be kept a *corps de reserve* to support any part, that shall be found weak or forced.

The whole is submitted to correction with the utmost candor, by Sir, &c.

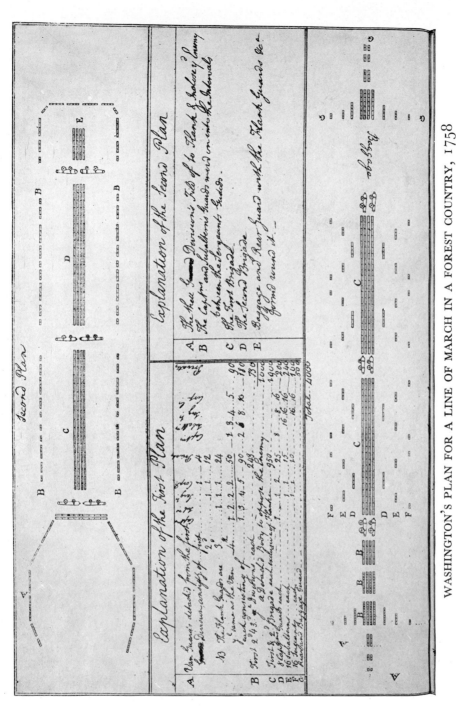

WASHINGTON'S PLAN FOR A LINE OF MARCH IN A FOREST COUNTRY, 1758

was leaving behind him important commitments for the future.

It was not until September, 1758, that General Forbes' expedition was on its way against Fort Duquesne. He had adhered to the plan of making a new road from Pennsylvania, and this was retarding his advance. Although the distance was shorter than the Braddock trail advised by Washington, the labor of making the new road involved greater delays.

At this stage, General Forbes asked Colonel Washington to submit a plan of a tactical formation for marching through the forest country. In response, Washington offered a scheme for 'a line of march thro' a country covered with woods, and how that line of march may be formed in an instant into an order of battle.' [1] The diagram drawn by Washington himself for this proposed order of march, with his own written explanation of its tactics, is included in this chapter.

Here was a milestone that marked the progress of the military education of George Washington. And this is something else that has not been estimated at its real value. Its true significance will be evident, if only we take a clear look at the sequence of events. In the first place, when the British Regulars came to America in 1755, there never was any intention of asking advice from the American militia officers. Above all things, it was then inconceivable, to General Braddock and his staff, that any of these militia officers would be able to offer the slightest improvement in any detail of the supposedly perfected European tactics of the day. But, in 1758, there was this extraordinary reversal. A British General was asking a young Virginian Colonel of twenty-six, not merely for a suggestion as to some detail of

[1] Washington to General Forbes, September, 1758.

25

tactics, but for a tactical scheme for the conduct of an expeditionary force of four thousand men.

And, when we hark back to the military forms of the time, it was equally astonishing to find that the young Virginian officer was fully prepared to offer a right solution of the problem, with flexible tactics that would change quickly the line of march into a line of battle, in case of an attack. The advantages of this scheme of tactics were so obvious that it was adopted.

The foregoing is merely a statement of fact, and the result proved that George Washington had acquired a grasp of military affairs, which can only be called extraordinary. It is, therefore, important that, in a study of his military career, this convincing evidence should be cited, as proving his clearness and originality of conception. The testimony in black and white, that George Washington possessed these qualities, must be taken into account in explaining his career in the American Revolution.

General Forbes' expedition advanced with painful slowness. Colonel Bouquet, the advocate of the new route from Pennsylvania, worked with great zeal and efficiency, but the making of this new road through the wilderness was very difficult, and the approach to Fort Duquesne was delayed until there was danger of its being halted by the weather. But, most fortunately, the fate of Fort Duquesne was settled in advance by the capture of Fort Frontenac. After the disastrous defeat of General Abercromby's attack on Ticonderoga (July 8, 1758), Fort Frontenac had been left garrisoned by only a little over a hundred men. It was, therefore, easily captured in August by a brilliant dash of Colonel Bradstreet, across Lake Ontario, with a force of twenty-five hundred Colonial troops.

The loss of this important post cut the French line of communications, and the weakened garrison of Fort Duquesne abandoned their thus isolated position, when at last the Forbes expedition appeared in force. The French garrison had routed a rash advance of a part of Bouquet's command, under Major Grant of the Highlanders, but they could not hope to make a successful resistance against the main body of their enemies. After burning the fort, the French garrison retreated up the Allegheny. It saved the situation for General Forbes, who was fatally ill at this stage, that the French were unable to attempt a defense of Fort Duquesne. For the long delays had kept him from getting near the fort until the last of November, and he had nearly given up the enterprise for that year. The ruins of the fort were patched up into a stockaded defense, and General Forbes renamed it Fort Pitt (afterwards Pittsburgh). Two hundred of Washington's Virginian troops were left as a garrison, and the expedition returned.

The downfall of Fort Duquesne ended the troubles on the border, as Washington had foreseen when he urged that the reduction of the fort was the one cure for the sufferings of the harassed settlers. Duquesne had been, in fact, the sustaining source of the power of the French over the Indians. It had been the base of supplies and the center of operations for the raids that had devastated the Ohio Valley. But the Indians at once read the writing on its abandoned and blackened walls. They saw that the day of the French was over.

Thereupon, the Indians hastened to align themselves with the victorious British, and in a short time there were treaties of peace with all the Indian tribes between the Ohio and the Great Lakes. This restoration of tranquillity on the border ended the war, so far as Virginia was concerned. The French had been driven far away, and the beginning of 1759 was to see the launching of the over-whelmingly superior British forces against the French troops, which had been left in America without any rein-forcement. The result was inevitable, and Canada was soon won from France. Consequently, the end of 1758 was the end of the military service of George Washington in the French and Indian War.

Chapter v

THE CLEAVAGE BETWEEN THE AMERICAN
COLONIES AND GREAT BRITAIN

UPON Washington's return from his military service, he at once performed the two acts for which he had pledged himself before his departure on the expedition against Fort Duquesne. He married Mrs. Custis and he took his seat in the House of Burgesses. These meant a complete change in his life.

His marriage with Mrs. Custis took place on January 6, 1759. This marriage brought to George Washington, in addition to the management of his own estate, the responsibility of the administration of the large estate of Martha's first husband, Daniel Parke Custis. In regard to this last, it became Washington's task to take control of the whole property. For the court had put in his charge the inheritance of the two Custis children, John (aged six) and Martha (aged four). Their youthful ages set a long term for the duties of this trust, which Washington discharged with the most judicious care. He gave these stepchildren the same place in his affections that would have been held by his own children, if any had been born to him. The care of these increased holdings of land welded Washington to an agricultural life — and indeed this was a life to his own taste.

He took up his residence at his much-loved Mount

Vernon, and began his personal management of these estates in the belief that his lot was cast there for life. Soon afterwards, in September, 1759, he wrote his farewell: 'I am now I believe fixed at this seat with an agreeable Consort for Life. And I hope to find more happiness in retirement than I ever experienced amidst a wide and bustling World.' [1] This final dismissal of the 'bustling World,' at the age of twenty-seven, was a far cry from any gaze into the crystal that would reveal Washington's destiny.

But his membership in the House of Burgesses of Virginia was to keep him in touch with public life throughout the ensuing years which led to the American Revolution. On the occasion of Washington's first taking his seat in this Assembly, the Speaker had been directed by a vote of the Burgesses to express the thanks of the Colony of Virginia for his distinguished military services. This was another proof of the universal approbation Washington had won, and, in the increasingly stormy years which followed, he always remained a man of great and widely recognized influence.

Any long account of the political controversies, which preceded the Revolution, must also be excluded from this book, as outside its field. But the one broad and ever-present situation, the cleavage between Great Britain and the American Colonies which made the break inevitable, must be described in unmistakable terms, for a double reason. In the first place, as will become evident to the reader in studying the course of the Revolution, its successive military situations were the direct result of this incurable cleavage. And, secondly, the description is necessary because this broad aspect of the Revolution has been too often lost to sight of late.

In recent years a great deal of valuable history has been

[1] Letter to Richard Washington, from Mount Vernon, September 20, 1759.

THE
FIELD
ENGINEER.

Tranflated from the FRENCH of

M. le Chevalier DE CLAIRAC,

BY

Captain CHARLES VALLANCEY.

To which are added,

REMARKS

ON

Marfhal SAXE's new Syftem of

FORTIFICATION,

Propofed in his REVERIES, or Memoirs on the

ART of WAR.

Fas eft et ab Hofle doceri.

D U B L I N :
Printed for JOHN SMITH, at the Philofophers Heads
on the Blind-Quay. MDCCLVIII.

TITLE-PAGE OF A MILITARY BOOK IN WASHINGTON'S LIBRARY
AT MOUNT VERNON

written, dealing with the controversies which led to the American Revolution. This type of history has done much good in making clear the arguments on both sides. But, on the other hand, these many discussions of the details of the controversies, and of the pros and cons of the various measures, have perhaps obscured the truth as to the main issue, the irreconcilable difference between the two systems of government, which became the cause of the revolt. This one impelling cause of disruption was no new thing, but it was the product of an unusual course of events which had moulded the structures of the Colonies, after their first settlements.

The American Colonies were of different origins and of differing populations. Yet one extraordinary thing had happened throughout the group. By one means or another, as a result of their enterprising make-up and their early distribution of the land, there was from the first the trend towards self-governing communities. Consequently, the germs of representative government were innate. As the Colonies grew from the first straggling coast settlements into larger communities, these germs quickened into life, and ripened into the actual establishment of representative government in the various Colonies. This was an origin and development utterly unlike anything else in history. And this gave the American Colonies, in spite of their differences, one strong bond in common.

They had a common belief, which had become a common article of faith, in representative government, which they had tested and found efficient. This was what gave them the united strength that prevailed. And we must now recognize that they had whole-heartedly committed themselves to the cause of a form of government that has prevailed over all other governments in the world.

It was another story in the Great Britain of that day. Representative government was then at a low ebb in the mother country. The House of Commons was not in any sense representative. Its electorate was restricted to an extent almost inconceivable to-day. Its seats were a matter of patronage. In this regard, it is enough to state that Pitt, the great Prime Minister who turned British defeat into victory, only obtained his seat in the House of Commons through the patronage of a great lord. Under this abnormal system, the government of Great Britain had become vested in the King's Ministers. And these Ministers were merely attempting to apply to America the system in vogue at home.

That was the reason for the complete misunderstanding of the attitude of the Americans. To the minds of the King's Ministers, their own course was perfectly normal. It was natural for them to remain unable to see that what was being done in Great Britain might be a mistake in America. The remonstrances of the Colonies seemed unreasonable to the King's Ministers, who thought themselves justified in their acts. There was no intention of exercising any special tyranny in America. They swept aside the legislative assemblies of the Colonies, because these were beyond their ken. There was nothing of the kind in Great Britain, and they were merely trying to apply their own system to a situation they could not comprehend.

A modern British historian has expressed this situation in terms that could not be made more clear. The following from Sir George Trevelyan's 'The American Revolution' has put in a nutshell the question of the point of view as to the remonstrances of the Americans: 'The most admired speech was that of young Lord Caermarthen, who denied the right of Americans to complain that they were taxed without being represented, when such places as Manchester — and he might have added Leeds and Sheffield and Birmingham — had no members of their own in the British Parliament. It was indeed a magnificent anticipation of the calling in of the New World to balance the inequalities of the old.'

This last sentence described an element that underlay the whole situation. The future was to prove that the New World was thus destined to do away with 'inequalities of the old.' Even at the time, Americans fully realized that it was not a quarrel with Great Britain, but with the King's Ministers. This was in evidence from the beginning, for the Americans called the British troops in the Colonies 'the Ministerial forces.' As a result, the American alignment was not against the British, but always against the King's Ministers.

We must never forget this fact, that the Americans took up arms to fight the Ministerial régime, which was attempting to destroy the established American system of representative government vested in the elected legislative assemblies of the Colonies. For this reason, the American Revolution was different from the other revolutions of history. It was fought to defend and maintain an existing form of government — not to overthrow a government. Consequently, it is almost a misnomer to call the American Revolution a revolution at all. Its success did away with the arbitrary rule that threatened to overthrow by force American representative government, and American independence perpetuated this representative government.

This sentence sums up the case of the American Revolution. So well defined was its object, that it was unique in being free from upheavals and anarchy, which have followed in the train of other revolutions. Throughout its course, there was never any change of purpose, never a question of any result other than the maintenance and firm establishment of the American representative government of the people.

It was thus fought out for a just cause. The truth was, the Americans were fighting the battle of English liberty for Great Britain, as well as for America. The agitation for this common cause had begun in Great Britain. There was already a political faction with the same aims, but they were in a helpless minority at the time of the outbreak in America. However, they were constant in their support of the Americans, as standing for the same principles they were striving for in Great Britain. They declared in Parliament that our fight was their fight. And, although the attainment of their object was delayed long after the American Revolution, the success of the American test of representative government was the precursor of the reforms of the nineteenth century, which made Parliament a truly representative body. This knowledge, that there was a common cause in Great Britain and America, has taken away all bitterness between the two nations as to the American Revolution.

Symbolical of this common ground of freedom, on which stand the United States and Great Britain, is the statue of George Washington in one of the most impressive positions in London. At the time of the American Revolution, could any one have imagined that the British would ever honor the American Commander in Chief by giving his statue this distinguished place in their capital? But now all recognize that it is right and proper for the statue of George Washington to be there, as that of a leader in the struggle of the English-speaking race for liberty.

This is a bond that has strengthened kinship, and an-

STATUE OF WASHINGTON IN TRAFALGAR SQUARE, LONDON
A replica of the Houdon statue at Richmond

THE 'CROSSED SWORDS'
Now in the possession of the Massachusetts Historical Society
'ON the library wall of one of the most famous writers of America, there hang two crossed swords, which his relatives wore in the great War of Independence. The one sword was gallantly drawn in the service of the king, the other was the weapon of a brave and honoured republican soldier.'

The above is the beginning of the first chapter of Thackeray's 'The Virginians,' which was written when the two swords were in the house of Prescott, the historian.

other inspiring symbol of this kinship between the two English-speaking nations is reproduced with this chapter. In America, on a wall of the Massachusetts Historical Society, hang two crossed swords of the American Revolution, one of an American officer, the other of a British officer. As the inscription states, they are thus preserved 'in token of international friendship and family alliance.' These words give a true description of the unbreakable relation between the United States and Great Britain to-day.

Throughout all this period of remonstrance against the encroachments of the King's Ministers, Washington was unfaltering in his adherence to the right of representative government. As a member of the House of Burgesses, he had been in the midst of their debates at the various stages of the controversies. He had heard Patrick Henry's 'If this be treason, make the most of it.' And he had been present on the occasion of the misguided assertion of power by the Royal Governor, when Lord Dunmore arbitrarily dissolved the House of Burgesses in 1774. This act of folly in abolishing the legislative assembly of Virginia brought matters to a crisis in that Colony. The same measure that had taken away self-government from Massachusetts had been meted out to Virginia.

The immediate result showed the same spirit in Virginia. The ousted members of the House of Burgesses at once assembled in the long room of the Raleigh Tavern, and, after passing a resolution denouncing the Boston Port Bill, they made the first momentous recommendation for a General Congress of the American Colonies.

George Washington was sent as a delegate to this first Continental Congress, which met at Philadelphia in Carpenter's Hall on September 5, 1774. This marked an epoch

35

in the history of America, which was best expressed in the words of Patrick Henry: 'All America is thrown into one mass. Where are your landmarks — your boundaries of Colonies? They are all thrown down. The distinctions between Virginians, Pennsylvanians, New Yorkers and New Englanders, are no more. I am not a Virginian, but an American.' [1]

The membership of this first Continental Congress was a remarkable body of men. They prepared and adopted a 'Declaration of Colonial Rights,' to be transmitted to Great Britain. In this, the main issue was the right of legislating in their own assemblies, and a protest against having this right superseded by the Royal Governors and their Councils. This Declaration put things at once on a sound basis, as it formally proclaimed representative government as the doctrine of the united Colonies.

Here George Washington was certainly again being thrown into the 'bustling world,' of which he had taken his leave in his twenties. And Irving has quoted a most significant proof of that strong personal influence which he always exerted upon those with whom he came in contact: 'Patrick Henry, being asked, on his return home, whom he considered the greatest man in Congress, replied, "If you speak of eloquence, Mr. Rutledge, of South Carolina, is by far the greatest orator; but if you speak of solid information and sound judgment, Colonel Washington is unquestionably the greatest man on the floor."'

[1] John Adams' diary.

Chapter VI

THE OUTBREAK OF THE REVOLUTION

AT THIS stage, all eyes in the American Colonies were fixed on Massachusetts and Boston. There was the storm center of the elements that made the outbreak inevitable — for there the Ministerial policies had been carried to an extreme. Every trace of representative self-government had been taken away from Massachusetts, and the arbitrary rule of the Royal Governor had been substituted. British troops had been sent to Boston to enforce his authority. These British troops were supposed by the King's Ministers to be a force strong enough to control all the Colonies. The port of Boston had been closed to commerce.

It was an unprecedented state of affairs, and, under these existing conditions, General Gage, the Royal Governor, could only be called a military governor. He was exercising an autocratic control that was like the military occupation of hostile territory. And, the fact was, this military occupation was transforming the whole Colony into hostile territory, instead of subduing it to the Royal rule. It was the culmination of the mistaken policies of the King's Ministers — and the final exemplification of their total failure to understand what was happening in America, with the great principle involved.

To their minds, the situation about Boston was merely a local matter. They saw only a contumacious and dis-

37

orderly town, which could be repressed by a military force. They had full faith in the efficacy of their military force to overawe the Colony. It should be stated again that they had no intention of tyrannical acts. The error was of their times, and of their system, not of the individual men. For this reason, they could not foresee that their armed intervention would stir up armed resistance. They never realized that they had thrown a torch into a powder magazine — until after the disastrous explosion!

For, the truth was, the only effect of this Ministerial policy of military coercion had been to arouse the Americans to a united policy of military resistance. And this was creating an adverse military situation, of which the danger was never estimated by the British Ministers. But its seriousness must be set forth in this book, because it actually was bringing into being the one most important military condition that was present throughout the course of the American Revolution. It meant that, wherever the British troops moved in the ensuing war, they were always operating in a hostile territory, of which the inhabitants had been trained for armed resistance.

In Massachusetts, after the Royal Governor had forbidden its Assembly to meet, the members had organized a Provincial Congress of their own, with John Hancock as president, and with a strong Committee of Safety, of which Dr. Joseph Warren was chairman. Under their energetic control, a complete organization was effected of the militia of the different towns. Officers were appointed, military stores collected, and the town companies were drilled. These were the 'minute men,' who pledged themselves to be ready for immediate service at the summons of the Committee of Safety.

Similar military preparations were also being made in

the other Colonies. That they were united had been shown at the first meeting of the Continental Congress, and the situation at Boston was rousing them everywhere to the same military resistance. At this time Washington declared, 'If need be, I will raise one thousand men, subsist them at my own expense, and march myself at their head for the relief of Boston.' The second meeting of the Continental Congress had been called for May 10, 1775, but the outbreak of the American Revolution came before that date.

The warning signs of this increasing menace had not opened the eyes of the King's Ministers at the beginning of 1775. On the contrary, they were more blindly resolved than ever to coerce the Americans. In Parliament, which was absolutely under their control, they rejected the conciliatory measures of Pitt and Burke, and had a vote passed to increase the British troops in Boston to ten thousand. Upon this, Benjamin Franklin, who had been in England to lay the case of the American Colonies before the British Government, saw that it was hopeless for him to make any more efforts, and he returned to America (March, 1775).

Under these conditions, it was a certainty that the clash at arms would come. It came with its first shedding of blood on April 19, 1775 — and, in the broadest sense of the word, that day was decisive of the whole American Revolution.

On the part of the British Royal Governor, the expedition sent to Concord to destroy stores was an act of overconfident folly that would be incredible, if we did not take into account the European military doctrines of the day. At that time, all European wars were fought by the regular armies, in formal battles and with formal tactics. The idea that the people of any country would be able to resist a regular force was so contrary to all European military formulas that it was held to be out of the question. For this reason, the eight hundred British Regulars, sent to Concord under Lieutenant Colonel Smith and Major Pitcairn, were considered strong enough to march anywhere in the countryside, and no other thought entered their minds.

Major Pitcairn, who commanded the advance guard that fired on the small company of Americans at Lexington, was a humane man. And he declared, to the day of his death at Bunker Hill, that he did not give the order to fire, but that it was a mistake. We should believe this. But, on the other hand, it was woefully apparent that the British leaders had no conception of the serious thing they were doing, and had not considered in advance what action they should take in such a contingency. It was also evident that they had no idea, at the time, of the fearful consequences of their act, and they did not imagine that allowing the British troops to form on Lexington Green and give three cheers for victory was chanting the requiem of British rule over the American Colonies.

On their march to Lexington, it had become evident to the British that the news of their undertaking was being spread through the towns, and Smith had sent back to Boston for reinforcements. But, even then, the British had not perceived the real dangers of the impending storm, and they marched stolidly on to Concord. They did not realize that this meant marching into a circle of enemies, for the surrounding country had been aroused by Revere and Dawes, the messengers of the Committee of Safety to summon the militia. The swift response showed the efficiency of this organization of the town companies. At the call, these New England militia at once proved that they were indeed minute men! The rapidity with which they gathered about Concord was astonishing.

On the arrival of the British troops at Concord, Smith had

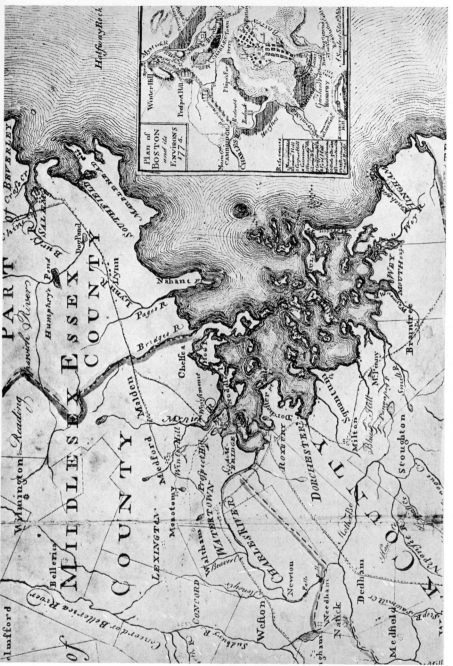

SCENE OF THE OUTBREAK OF THE AMERICAN REVOLUTION

placed a strong guard of two hundred Regulars at the North Bridge. These were attacked by double their strength of the town companies, which fired upon the Regulars,[1] rushed the bridge, and drove off the British. By noon Smith's command in Concord was beset by such overwhelming numbers that he ordered a retreat. Under the continued attacks of the Americans, this retreat became a disorganized flight, and the harassed British were in a desperate condition when they were rescued in Lexington by a reinforcement of twelve hundred Regulars under Lord Percy, which had been sent out from Boston.

But, as the companies from the towns continued to pour in to attack the retreating British, even this large force of Regulars became demoralized. And they were a stricken mass of fugitives when they barely gained the shelter of the fleet in Charlestown, leaving their wounded scattered along the line of their flight. The great numbers of companies from the different towns that arrived on the scene can only be called another astonishing feature of the day's events. Many of them had come from long distances. The list of killed and wounded Americans comprised men from twenty-three towns. This definite proof, that companies from so many towns actually were able to take part in the fighting, was the measure of the extraordinary thing that had happened — an uprising of the whole countryside to arms against the British troops.

To the minds of the British, the impossible had happened. But even this unexpected rout was not the end of the disaster for the Royal Governor. Other companies of the militia continued to arrive, until there was an improvised American army gathered about Boston — and the siege of Boston had begun.

[1] Emerson: 'Fired the shot heard round the world.'

The events of the siege, and in fact the events of the whole American Revolution, have been too often told in the usual terms of the European military operations of the times. These terms could not give an adequate description, as things happened which were far ahead of the times, and the formulas of contemporary European military doctrines could not be applied to the unconventional warfare of the Americans. Consequently, the many careful accounts of the details of April 19, 1775, have never given a full estimate at its true value of the sudden and complete decisiveness of the Lexington and Concord Fight.

It is most impressive to sum up this abrupt change of the whole military situation. On April 18, General Gage had been a Royal Governor, with naval and military forces considered ample to enforce his authority. In twenty-four hours this had been ended forever, and General Gage had been reduced to the position of being merely the commander of a British army hemmed into Boston. Outside of Boston he had no more authority, and no more hope of assistance, than if there had not been a Loyalist in the Colony.

This was an amazing overturn, and yet it had not been brought about by a destructive defeat that inflicted crippling losses upon his army. On the contrary, the Americans had not killed or wounded any great proportion of British troops. On the part of the Americans, it was a hurried rush of the different companies to attack the British anywhere in their line of retreat. There was no opportunity to coördinate in large numbers. The result was, it was each for himself, as they arrived in detached groups. Consequently, of the many companies that gathered from the various towns, there never at any one time was a large force imposed upon the British. It was not the proportion of actual losses, but it was the way the whole thing was done that demoralized the British Regulars. They had met something so utterly outside their knowledge that they were dazed.

The true explanation was, the irregular warfare, which the British encountered on April 19, could only be called a forecast of modern open-order fighting. For this reason, the running fight on the line of the British retreat became a test which at once proved that the British Regulars, drilled in the formal battle tactics of Frederick the Great, were pathetically helpless in the countryside against the tactics of the Americans. The Regulars were utterly unable to cope with what was actually a modern line of battle in extended order, taking advantage of every natural shelter, never giving a set battle, but attacking here, there, and everywhere.

This helplessness of the puzzled British Regulars is now no longer a matter of wonder, as it was to them in 1775. For the battle tactics instinctively adopted by the Americans were destined to supersede the artificial tactics of Frederick the Great. The Regulars had found their one disconcerting experience so convincing that no other test was ever attempted. Never again did the Regulars venture out into the open country around Boston.

But even this fact does not tell how absolutely the British had accepted this one object lesson as final. The motley forces of Americans, which had gathered about Boston so soon after the British defeat, were at first not only ill organized, but also lacking in supplies, ammunition, and artillery. Yet no efforts were made by the British to push back the Americans from the positions they had occupied so close to Boston, many of which were only thinly manned. Thus General Gage not only conceded that he was to be cut off from the surrounding country, but he also permitted him-

43

self to be hemmed in closely. Gage's quick and complete acquiescence in this shut-in situation was strikingly shown by the fact that, as early as April 22, he was negotiating with a Town Meeting in Boston as to passing people in and out of Boston. Consequently, we must regard the events of April 19, 1775, as decisive in the modern sense of the word, and as changing the whole military situation in New England.

Chapter VII

THE UPRISING
WASHINGTON MADE COMMANDER IN CHIEF

THE news of this first bloodshed was the electric shock that stirred the long-smouldering embers into living flame. The immediate response to the 'Lexington alarm' was general throughout New England. From all sides the town companies continued to throng to the vicinity of Boston, where the aroused and angered pursuers of April 19 remained, as they had no intention of going away without a reckoning. As has been stated, there had been hardly any coördinated military control in the hurried rush of the eventful first day of the American Revolution. What command there was had been exercised by General Heath. He was in general charge of affairs until General Artemas Ward assumed command of the rapidly growing numbers of Americans on the afternoon of April 20. The first council of officers was held on that day, as was the first placing of guards, which was carried out under Colonel William Prescott. It was an uncanny transformation that had been effected in so short a time. The dragon's teeth had quickly sprung forth from a peaceful soil.

On April 20, also, the Committee of Safety sent circulars to the Massachusetts towns calling out all the militia. Soon afterward there followed an appeal to the other New England Colonies. But before this last, there already had been

45

many accessions from the rest of New England. New Hampshire troops were in Medford under Colonel John Stark, and Connecticut troops, with General Israel Putnam, were in Cambridge. The Rhode Island troops under General Nathanael Greene lay at Jamaica Plain.

In this unusual 'army' each Colony maintained its own establishment, provided its own supplies and issues of ammunition — such as they were — and exercised command and control over its own troops. The command of General Ward was almost nominal, and there was great confusion as to rank and commissions. This gathering from New England grew to a force of about 16,000, of which the proportions were: Massachusetts, 11,500; Connecticut, 2300; New Hampshire, 1200; Rhode Island, 1000. As might have been expected, the personnel was constantly changing, with men drifting back and forth between home and the camp, and with enlistments and commissions on no regular basis.

The mere fact that this heterogeneous 'army' was able to keep up any existence at all, was a successful test of the value of the recent training of the militia in the different Colonies. It showed this training had given the Americans an unsuspected foundation of military strength, that had gone beyond the uprising of a day of excitement, even to the extent of providing the spectacle of the Royal Governor and his supposedly coercive force of Regular troops shut up in a state of siege in Boston.

In this regard, General Gage, when trying to explain the overturn of the whole military situation, put himself unmistakably on record. He was compelled to acknowledge that the troubles, which so unexpectedly beset him, were the product of what he called, in his report, 'a military spirit encouraged among them for a few years past, joined with an uncommon degree of zeal and enthusiasm.' These words are well worth studying, for this band of zealots were enforcing a siege that was perhaps unique in history.

It was the strange paradox of a siege maintained by enemies who actually were not able to bombard the besieged. For the Americans possessed no artillery that bore any resemblance to a siege train. Not only this, but they were so scantily supplied with powder for their muskets that they could have offered only the feeblest of defense, if the British had attacked to oust them from their positions so near Boston. But this the British did not attempt. It is a true description to write that the only real strength of the American besiegers lay in the stunning effect of the object lesson of April 19. Yet this prestige was sufficient to establish and maintain a close blockade of Boston.

Throughout the rest of the Colonies the 'Lexington alarm' was the same firebrand to arouse the flame of revolt. Any idea that the situation about Boston was merely local ended then and there. It was evident at once that the cause of New England was the cause of all. The inhabitants of the other Colonies had realized that the Ministers' adoption of their policy of increased coercion had only produced an increased danger of revolt. Affairs had come to the pass where all expected war. The best expression of this tense feeling was Patrick Henry's speech at Richmond (March 23, 1775): 'It is too late to retire from the contest. There is no retreat but in submission and slavery. The war is inevitable, and let it come. The next gale that sweeps from the north will bring to our ears the clash of resounding arms! I know not what course others may take, but as for me, give me liberty or give me death.' This has been familiar to all of us from childhood, as a burst of patriotic eloquence. But, in reality, it summed up accurately the military situation. And the fateful news, that was the fulfillment of his prophecy, spread

47

through the Colonies just before the assembling of the second Continental Congress.

The news of the outbreak of armed revolt had also a widespread effect in Great Britain. In this matter, the Americans had been farseeing in taking precautions that the truth as to the situation should be known to the British people. The Massachusetts Provincial Congress had met in Concord April 22, and had promptly appointed a special committee to take depositions as to the events of April 19 in Lexington and Concord. These affidavits were collected, with a letter 'To the Inhabitants of Great Britain' (composed by Dr. Warren, Mr. Freeman, Mr. Gardner, and Colonel Stone), and these papers were given to Captain Derby of Salem on April 27, with instructions to transmit them to London as soon as possible. Captain Derby made such a good passage in the fast-sailing *Quero* of Salem, that he arrived in London May 29, eleven days ahead of the British ship which brought General Gage's account of the Lexington and Concord Fight, although this British ship had sailed four days before the *Quero*. Upon the first printing and circulation of this news in England, the British Government published a card in the Gazette stating that 'no advices have as yet been received in the American department of any such event.'

To this Arthur Lee, the agent of the Massachusetts Provincial Congress replied, 'As a doubt of the authenticity of the account from Salem, touching an engagement between the King's troops and the provincials in the Massachusetts Bay, may arise from a paragraph in the Gazette of this evening (May 30, 1775), I desire to inform all those who wish to see the original affidavits which contain that account, that they are deposited at the Mansion House with the right honorable the Lord Mayor for their inspection.'

After this exchange, as can easily be imagined, there was much excitement in Great Britain concerning the expected dispatches from General Gage. Upon their arrival, the truth of the American account was so obviously confirmed, in spite of the careful euphemisms of General Gage's report, that there was a profound sensation in Great Britain. It was clear that there had been a serious British defeat — and all previous ideas as to the situation in America had to be revised.

The consequences of this act of straightforward common-sense on the part of the Americans, in sending these statements of facts to Great Britain, have not been appreciated. From that time on, the whole case rested on a different basis. Faith in the policies of the King's Ministers had received a rude shock — and, added to this, there was created a lasting distrust of statements of the Ministers concerning the events in America. The opponents of the Ministerial policies, as to the American Colonies, were thus given just grounds for their opposition. And their influence became more and more important as the war went on. This condition, that there were increasing numbers in Great Britain who made common cause with the Americans, must be taken into consideration as a determining factor in the American Revolution — the war fought not against Great Britain but against the King's Ministers.

When the second Continental Congress assembled (May 10, 1775) at Philadelphia, the first action of its members was most significant. As Peyton Randolph was obliged to return to Virginia, to preside over its Assembly, and Thomas Jefferson was sent as a delegate in his stead, it became necessary to choose a new president. Their choice was John Hancock of Massachusetts, proscribed by the King's Ministers as the arch rebel — and his election served an un-

49

mistakable notice that this Congress was aligned with Massachusetts.

Again there was adopted a petition to the King, stating the case of the Colonies. But this Congress defined itself as the representative body of a federal union of the Colonies, and exercised the functions of such a body. At the same time the right of self-government for each Colony in its own affairs was affirmed. Thus quickly was established the beginning of a system of government with the essentials of our government of to-day. Georgia, which hitherto had not sent delegates, soon joined the federation, which thus became a union of all the Colonies. The Continental Congress actually went to the length of authorizing an issue of notes of 'The United Colonies.'

This Congress of the United Colonies adopted the force blockading Boston as its own, designating it the Continental Army, in contrast to the Ministerial Army. For there was not yet any definite aim at separation from Great Britain. The question as to who should be Commander in Chief of the Continental Army found only one answer from the first. George Washington had been so generally recognized as the ablest man in the Colonies in military matters, that he had been chosen chairman of all the committees that had to do with military affairs. His ability and judgment made so great an impression upon his fellow members, that he stood out as the man best qualified to be the commander of the new American army.

Only one thing was in the way. There was some feeling that, as the force at the scene of contest was a New England army, it might be unwise to appoint a Southern commander. But this prejudice disappeared in consultation among the delegates, and, on June 15, 1775, George Washington was unanimously elected the Commander in Chief of

GEORGE WASHINGTON'S COMMISSION AS GENERAL AND COMMANDER IN CHIEF, 1775

the Continental Army. It was John Adams, delegate from Massachusetts, who had most strongly urged the choice of Washington. Adams has written in his diary: 'I had no hesitation to declare that I had but one gentleman in my mind for that important command, and that was a gentleman from Virginia, who was among us and very well known to all of us; a gentleman, whose skill and experience as an officer, whose independent fortune, great talents, and excellent universal character would command the approbation of all America, and unite the cordial exertions of all the colonies better than any other person in the Union.' These earnest words of John Adams were to be justified in the event.[1]

The vote in the Continental Congress, electing Washington Commander in Chief, was on June 15, 1775. On the next day, from his place in the Assembly, he formally accepted the appointment in an earnest speech to the members, in which he said: 'I beg they will accept my cordial thanks for this distinguished testimony of their approbation. But lest some unlucky event should happen, unfavorable to my reputation, I beg it may be remembered by every gentleman in the room that I this day declare with the utmost sincerity I do not think myself equal to the command I am honored with. As to pay, Sir, I beg leave to assure the Congress that as no pecuniary consideration could have tempted me to accept this arduous employment at the expense of my domestic ease and happiness, I do not wish to make any profit from it. I will keep an exact account of my expenses. Those I doubt not they will discharge, and that is all I desire.'

Of this John Adams wrote: 'There is something charming

[1] 'The only man, as events were to prove, who could possibly have carried the war to a successful issue.' (Fortescue: *History of the British Army*.)

to me in the conduct of Washington, a gentleman of one of the first fortunes upon the continent, leaving his delicious retirement, his family and friends, sacrificing his ease and hazarding all, in the cause of his country. His views are noble and disinterested. He declared, when he accepted the mighty trust, that he would lay before us an exact account of his expenses, and not accept a shilling of pay.'

Washington's commission as 'General and Commander in Chief of the Army of the United Colonies' (reproduced herewith) was dated June 19, 1775. Four major generals were commissioned: Artemas Ward, Charles Lee, Philip Schuyler, Israel Putnam. Eight brigadier generals were also commissioned: Seth Pomeroy, Richard Montgomery, David Wooster, William Heath, Joseph Spencer, John Thomas, John Sullivan, Nathanael Greene. At Washington's request, Horatio Gates was appointed Adjutant General, with the rank of Brigadier.

Washington received his commission on June 20, and without any delay, left Philadelphia for Boston on the following day.

1) D: The United States in ac

	Penj^a	Lawful
		i.e. Dollar a 6/

1775
June
N° 1 To the purchase of five
Horses (two of which
were had on credit
from M. James Mease)
to equip me for my
Journey to the Army
at Cambridge — & for
the Service I was then
going upon — having
sent my Chariot and
Horses back to Vir-
ginia .... £239 —

22 To a light Phaeton bo⁴
N° 2 of Doct. Renaudet .. - 55 —

. 3 To double Harness for d°
bought from M. Todd . 7-15 —

. 4 To Cash paid for Sadlery
a Letter Case, Maps,
Glasses, &c. &c. &c. for
the use of my Command - 29-13-6

. 5 To M. Benj. Flemmens
for keeping the above
Horses .... - 5-6-2

July To the acc⁴ of Thomas
N° 6 Mifflin Esq. for money
expended by him in
the Journey from Phi-
ladelphia to Cambridge
in which the expen-
ces of General Lee,
Col. Reed &c. were
included .... - 129-8-2

Am⁴ carr⁴ forw⁴ - £466-2-10

FIRST PAGE OF GENERAL WASHINGTON'S ACCOUNT OF
EXPENSES

Chapter VIII

THE BATTLE OF BUNKER HILL

AT BOSTON there was almost no fighting until the middle of June. The only clashes between the two opposing forces were on the harbor islands, and these were skirmishes over live stock. In May the Americans made a beginning of fortifying their positions about Boston, which are shown on the map with this chapter. As has been explained, their total lack of siege artillery prevented the Americans from undertaking any serious attacks upon General Gage's army. On the part of the British, Gage's army had remained passive in the limits of the peninsula of the town of Boston. They never took advantage of the weakness of the Americans to extend the British lines of defense, and Boston Neck remained the limit of British control.

The only offensive of either party was in an entirely different direction. Benedict Arnold had suggested to Dr. Warren the idea of an expedition to capture Ticonderoga and Crown Point. This plan at once found approval. Arnold was given a Massachusetts Commission as Colonel, and was instructed to raise a force in the western part of Massachusetts for this project. But another plan for the capture of these forts had originated in Connecticut, and was being carried out under the command of Ethan Allen, the eccentric leader of the 'Green Mountain Boys,' an asso-

54

ciation of the settlers of Vermont who upheld the New Hampshire Grants against the jurisdiction of New York.

Arnold attempted to take command of this force also. But, as the Vermont men stood out for their own leader, and as Arnold had few men with him, it ended that Arnold went with Ethan Allen's expedition as a volunteer, of doubtful authority so far as exercising any command. The little force only numbered about one hundred and fifty, and on the night of May 9, 1775, could find only boats enough to ferry eighty-three of the Americans across Lake Champlain to attack Ticonderoga. But this small band of Allen and Arnold was sufficient for their purpose. They found the British commander had never imagined that his post could be in any danger, and all discipline was relaxed. Under these circumstances, in the early morning of May 10, the Americans found no difficulty in rushing the fort and capturing its garrison of about fifty, without any fighting. In the same way, Seth Warner with another detachment of the Vermont men captured Crown Point, where there was a guard of only twelve soldiers.

This double exploit was very important for the Americans. The forts themselves were not of much value, as was proved by the subsequent history of the war. But the capture of two hundred British guns, with ammunition and military stores, made these posts, most fortunately, arsenals for the Americans at the very time of their greatest need.

At Boston, it was the same story of General Gage's continued apathy in failing to seize any of the surrounding positions, but at the last of May he received his expected reinforcement from England. Generals Howe, Clinton, and Burgoyne had arrived with them, and General Gage would be able to concentrate ten thousand Regulars. But nothing happened until June 12, 1775, when the Royal

Governor showed his increased confidence in the security of his position by putting forth a truculent proclamation, denouncing the rebellion, offering pardon to all who would lay down their arms, 'excepting only from the benefit of such pardon Samuel Adams and John Hancock' as offenders beyond forgiveness, and threatening with the gallows all who might be taken in arms.

It was natural that, after this, the Americans should look for military activity on the part of General Gage. Therefore, when information was received by the Americans that he might take possession of some of the heights about Boston, the Provincial Congress decided to forestall him. On June 15, the Committee of Safety passed a resolution 'that possession of the hill called Bunker's Hill, in Charlestown, be securely kept and defended.' Possession of Dorchester Neck was also mentioned in this resolve, but this was left indefinite.

The official account of the Committe of Safety (July 25, 1775), after stating that this movement was in anticipation of an attempt by General Gage to occupy Bunker Hill, stated: 'Accordingly, on the 16th ult., orders were issued, that a detachment of 1000 men should that evening march to Charlestown, and intrench upon the hill. Just before nine they left Cambridge, and proceeded to Breed's Hill situated on the farther part of the peninsula next to Boston, for, by some mistake, this hill was marked out for the intrenchment instead of the other.'

In the confusion among the unorganized groups of troops from the various Colonies, which made up the besieging army, there were no plans whatever for the support of this detachment, which was sent to Charlestown under the command of Colonel William Prescott. In a military sense, therefore, it must be regarded as an isolated force, and this

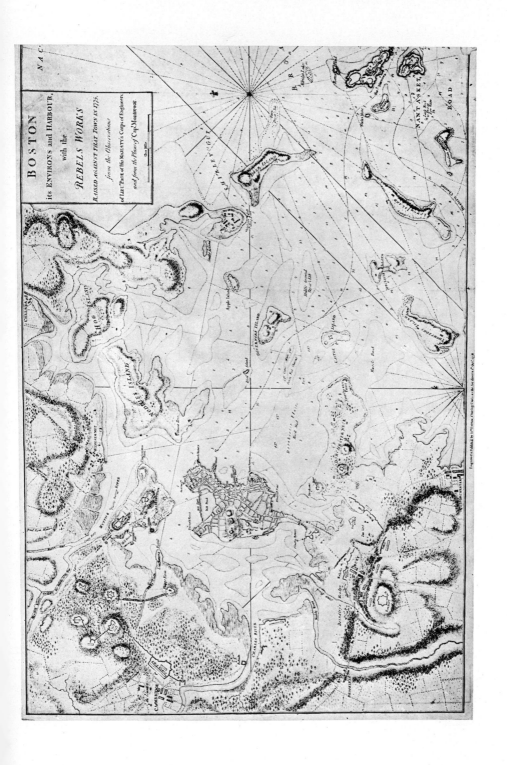

isolated American force was wretchedly equipped for the task it was ordered to perform. It had no heavy artillery, only six small field pieces which proved to be of little use. It was ill supplied in every way, and especially short of ammunition. To send such a weak detachment to the exposed position on the Charlestown peninsula was to court disaster.

A study of the map of the environs of Boston will show at once the dangers of the situation. There was a flood tide in the morning of June 17, and if the British had taken advantage of this to move the heavy guns in their shipping into the Mystic River, the position of the Americans would have become impossible. Instead of adopting this plan, General Gage decided to make a frontal attack upon the intrenched Americans. This decision transformed a situation precarious for the Americans into a scene of disaster for the British.

The reason for this costly error on the part of the British is to be found in what has been stated as to the effects of the Lexington and Concord Fight upon the British Regulars. They had been exasperated at being driven to shelter by tactics which did not offer a set battle. But a different situation was at once created by the surprising apparition of the American troops on Breed's Hill, which met their eyes on the morning of June 17, 1775. It was true that the Americans had been able to throw up their intrenchments without being discovered, but their presence meant that this time the Americans were in a fixed position, and were not the elusive enemies of April 19. To the minds of the British this situation implied, in itself, a set battle that must be fought in their own way. They welcomed this opportunity of crossing off the score against them, by driving the Americans from the field where they stood and offered battle. They had no idea that they were destined to encounter at

Charlestown another situation as novel and disconcerting as that of April 19.

It was true that, on any European battlefield of the times, this frontal attack of the British Regulars, with their superiority in numbers, would have been an easy charge — and the British had no suspicion of any other result. But there were two novel elements in the situation which made the Americans unexpectedly formidable. In the first place, although they were not at all marksmen of the Leatherstocking type, these American Colonists were used to handling firearms and aiming to kill. In addition, they were commanded by a remarkable group of officers, who had gained experience in the 'French wars,' and knew how to control their men to get the best results against the tactics used by the British Regulars. Consequently, the British were about to attack what was actually, in the modern military sense of the term, an intrenchment defended by instruments of precision.

At that time, no such thing had ever been encountered on a European battlefield. Precision in drilling and executing all movements had been rigidly taught — but precision in shooting had received no attention. The strict game laws of Europe had kept firearms out of the hands of the common people. It followed that the recruit was given a strange instrument, to handle in the series of movements of a manual that actually did not include aiming at any particular object.[1] As a result, musketry fire had not been

[1] British 'Manual Exercise of the Foot':
'V. . Present 1 motion: In presenting take away your thumb from the cock, and move your right Foot a little back, the toe turned a little to the right, the body to the front, and place the Butt-end in the Hollow between your Breast and Shoulder, keeping your forefinger before the Tricker (but without touching it) and the other three behind the Guard, the Elbow, in an equal Line (which is called Square) the Head upright, the Body strait, only pressing a little forward against the Butt-end of the firelock, the right knee stiff, and the left a little bend-

deadly, in a modern sense, on European battlefields. With 'the head upright,' and aim only secured by holding the firelock with 'the muzzle a little lower than the butt,' it is evident that any real sighting along the barrel to ensure accuracy was precluded for the British Regulars.

When we take into account the contrasts between the two sides engaged — and unquestionably these were the controlling factors in the Battle of Bunker Hill — we cannot help seeing that again something was happening altogether outside the military formulas of the times.

The Americans were well used to work with spade and shovel, and were able to accomplish in the night what seemed a miracle to the British. The intrenchment marked out by the engineer, Colonel Gridley, was described in the account of the Committee of Safety as 'a small redoubt about eight rods square.' There was also a breastwork beginning a short distance from the redoubt, on a line with its eastern side and extending about one hundred yards north. These earthworks were sufficiently completed on June 17 to be a good protection for the defenders. As it soon became evident to the Americans that this intrenched position could easily be outflanked by the British, the American line was extended to the Mystic River by making use of a fence about six hundred feet in the rear of the redoubt. This was the 'rail fence,' so called because it consisted of two wooden rails on top of a low stone wall. Parallel to this another fence of rails was built, and the space between was filled with newly cut hay, which was lying in the fields. This improvised defense was only a flimsy protection at the

ing: The muzzle should be a little lower than the Butt, in order to take Aim at the Center of the Body. VI. Fire: As soon as the Word of Command is given, draw the Tricker briskly with the fore-finger which was placed on it before: and though the lock should not go down with that Pull, you are not to attempt it a second Time, being only to draw the Tricker but once at exercise.'

59

best. It was described in Stedman's contemporary British account as 'nothing more than a breastwork of rails and hay easy to be scrambled over.'¹

The leisurely preparations of the British delayed their assault against the Charlestown heights until afternoon. For the Americans this was a period of actual suffering, after their exertions of the night, as the day was hot and they received very little to eat and drink. The British had bombarded the redoubt from Copp's Hill battery and from their shipping in the Charles, as shown on the map. Fortunately for the Americans the British shipping still neglected to go into the Mystic, and the vulnerable positions on that side of the peninsula were not subjected to bombardment. It was while the redoubt was under fire by artillery that Colonel Prescott walked around the top of the parapet, to encourage his men.

Prescott had sent to General Ward for reinforcements, and Putnam had also urged that more troops should be sent to Charlestown. But, in addition to the utter lack of organization of the Americans, General Ward was reluctant to weaken his main body, as he feared British attacks against Cambridge. It was only after a consultation with the Committee of Safety that he sent the New Hampshire troops of Colonels Stark and Reed to reinforce the Americans in Charlestown.

Dr. Warren and Seth Pomeroy had come to the redoubt to serve as volunteers in the coming action. The case of Joseph Warren was an eloquent act of patriotic devotion. He had recently been commissioned a Major General by the Provincial Congress, but he refused to take any command and declared that he only desired to share the dangers of his countrymen. This heroic example of their be-

¹ Stedman: *History of the American War.*

loved Dr. Warren had an inspiring effect upon the Americans, and did much to counteract the feeling in their ranks that they were being abandoned by their countrymen to the dangers of their exposed position. He remained at the redoubt throughout the assaults.

In the American dispositions to resist the British, Colonel Prescott was in personal command at the redoubt and breastwork. At the rail fence were the New Hampshire troops of Stark and Reed, with the Connecticut troops of Knowlton. These last had been in Prescott's original force. The troops in the earthworks and those at the rail fence were respectively the right and left of the American line of defense, and the circumstances of the action made each of these practically an independent force. Putnam was with the left, and on horseback he was zealous and tireless in bringing troops into the battle and directing the fighting on that part of the field. Straggling reinforcements arrived at different times during the action, but there was also a proportion of men drifting away from the field. A true estimate of the American strength in the battle can be given by stating that there never were more than fifteen hundred muskets available for the defense.

The British troops had been ferried across from Boston and landed on the present site of the Boston Navy Yard. Their main body formed at Moulton's Point and waited for reinforcements. These last were landed on the left of the main body. The British dispositions took a great deal of time, and it was nearly three o'clock when the whole British force was assembled. By that time about twenty-five hundred British troops had been landed in Charlestown. Thereupon, a heavy bombardment of the American intrenchments began from the British batteries in Boston and from the British shipping. This was to cover the advance of the British. There was also a cannonade directed against Roxbury from the British lines — and this was the only other demonstration against the Americans, instead of the British attacks anticipated by General Ward.

General Howe was in command of the British forces sent to Charlestown. Howe disposed his troops in two divisions. He himself commanded the attack against the American left in position at the rail fence. General Pigott commanded the division which attacked the American right in the earthworks. The British artillery was in position to move forward with the assaulting troops. Its fire practically put out of action in short order the light American field pieces, which had been placed in the gap between the breastworks and the rail fence. But the advance of the British artillery was stopped by the miry ground at the base of the hill.

The attacks of both divisions of the British were typical of the artificial tactics of the day. Following the usual prescribed forms, the Regulars were fully equipped for field service — and this meant that they were actually burdened with knapsacks and provisions for three days. This foolish addition to the stiff and cumbersome uniforms of the times was an unnecessary handicap through rough fields and long grass under the burning sun of the hot June day, with painful efforts to keep the stiff alignment of their ranks as they clambered over fences. The British troops were formed in close order, widely extended against the whole length of the American positions. And they thus offered the best possible target for their enemies, instead of moving forward in column with less exposure. As they advanced, they fired formal volleys, ineffective because their 'balls passed over the heads of the Americans.' All this would be almost unbelievable in these days, but it is a true description of the British array. In fact, when these wide ranks of

British Regulars moved forward, firing unaimed volleys as they advanced, it was the old order arrayed against the new order which was destined to supersede it.

On the part of the Americans, their officers were able to restrain them until the British were within sure range, and thus their fire was delivered in the way that would do the most harm. These causes produced their inevitable effect. The sudden well-aimed volume of fire from the Americans was so surprisingly deadly that the disciplined Regulars could not endure it. Both divisions of British broke and re-treated.

They were soon rallied by their officers and for a second time advanced, but in the same ill-judged order, against the American front. As was only natural, the result was the same. Again, at the prescribed distance, the British met such a destructive fire that they gave way and retreated out of range.

After the British had again been rallied, and had received another strong reinforcement from Boston, General Howe resolved upon a third attack in a different manner. He ordered his troops to discard the cumbersome knapsacks and to move forward in column to attack the redoubt alone. This was a more dangerous method of assault, but the Americans were no longer able to withstand any attacks. Their powder was exhausted, and, as hardly any of them were equipped with bayonets, the British found little diffi-culty in driving the Americans from the redoubt, against which the British assault in column had been concentrated.

Most of the American casualties were incurred at this stage. But these losses (441) were not so severe as might have been expected, because the retreating Americans were favored by the concealing cloud of dense dust which rose from trampling the newly dug-up earth of the intrenchments. The exhausted British did not pursue beyond Bunker Hill. Prescott's troops from the redoubt were also protected in their retreat by the men from the rail fence, who had not been attacked by the British in this last assault. The retreat was also covered by the arrival of tardy reinforcements which General Ward had at last been induced to send — too late to have any influence on the battle itself, but of help in the retreat. Under these conditions, the whole force of Americans escaped from their exposed position with comparatively little damage.

On the other hand, the outstanding feature of the battle was the awful loss of the British Regulars from musket fire. In the British dispatches, and in the letters sent home by British officers, the repulses of the Regulars were glossed over. As in the case of General Gage's report of the Lexington and Concord Fight, the British commander's report of the Battle of Bunker Hill was again a curiosity of war literature. His version, adopted in common for official dispatches and for letters, merely told of a repulse followed by a rally which carried the works impetuously by the bayonet.

This was also the tenor of the narrative of the battle in Stedman's contemporary British 'History of the American War.' From the first account in his text, no one would have imagined that the British had met disastrous reverses before the lack of powder ended the American resistance. But there was a complete change of tone a few pages later in this book. For the author, a British officer who served in America through the Revolution, in his eagerness to praise the gallantry of the British troops at Bunker Hill, broke away from the conventionalized version to which he had adhered at first. In summing up the course of the battle, he forgot its measured phrases, and wrote a spontaneous description of the difficulties encountered, so vivid that it stands to-day as the best picture of the British attacks:

'If anything had been wanting to show the bravery and discipline of the British troops, the action at Bunker Hill furnished an ample proof of both. Twice they were stopped, and twice returned to the charge.[1] In the midst of a hot summer day, incumbered with three days' provisions, their knapsacks on their backs, which together with cartouche-box, ammunition, and firelock, may be estimated one hundred and twenty-five pounds weight, with a steep hill to ascend, covered with grass reaching to their knees, and in the face of a hot and well-directed fire, they gained a complete victory over three times their own number [for such was the British general's estimate] of provincials strongly posted behind a breast-work, and defended by a redoubt.'

This exaggerated estimate of the numbers of the Americans, taken from the official report of the British commander, was a most notable tribute to the strength of the American resistance. It was equally striking as evidence of the effect of the unexpected losses on the minds of the British. It reflected the first impression of the British leaders, that there must have been the enormous superiority of 'over three times their own number' of Americans to inflict such great British losses. That was their only way of accounting for the disaster. Just after the battle, they had no inkling of the truth — that these devastating losses came from the increased efficiency of each aimed musket, not from an increased number of muskets. But, before long, the inferior numbers of the Americans became a matter of public knowledge, even in Great Britain. The account in the British 'Annual

---

[1] The modern British *History of the British Army* gives the same version: 'In truth the return of the British infantry to the third attack after two such bloody repulses is one of the greatest feats ever recorded of them.'

Register' for 1775 stated that the number of the Americans 'was not probably so large as it was made in the Gazette account.'

The British official return of losses was 1054. But it is known that this return did not tell the tale, which was softened as much as possible. The 'History of the British Army' has explained that the wounded of one regiment 'were accidentally omitted from the official list,' and that 'these probably numbered at least 100.' Taken altogether, it was very nearly a case of each American musket putting an enemy out of action. Such a loss by musketry was unprecedented. The same British authority has stated: 'The combat produced a remarkable effect on the future operations of the war. It shook the nerve of Howe, and showed the British that subjugation of the Colonies would be no child's play.' General Gage's dispatch expressed this change of mind in no uncertain terms: 'The trials we have had show the rebels are not the despicable rabble too many have supposed.' There is no mistaking this strong impression made upon the British by the Battle of Bunker Hill, the moral effect of which lasted throughout the Revolution and was a helpful influence for the campaigns of Washington.

But, at the time, the Americans did not appreciate this main result of the Battle of Bunker Hill. The 'History of the British Army' stated that the battle 'elated the Americans, as was but natural and just.' However, this must be considered as reading into the minds of the Americans the strong impression made upon the minds of the British. It did not portray the actual state of mind among the Americans, which, on the contrary, reflected general dissatisfaction. They censured the lack of leadership and support, which left the detachment in Charlestown exposed to the full strength of the British.

Yet the whole effect of the battle on the Americans was to unite them in the conviction that this was war, and that it must be fought out. Nothing could have been more dramatic than the action and its surroundings. It was an arena with thousands of spectators, and a scene that imprinted itself on the minds of those who heard its story. The burning of the town of Charlestown by the British aroused the people, although it was a retaliation justified by the usages of war.[1]

Another event which strongly moved the public imagination was the sacrifice of the life of Joseph Warren. He was killed in the retreat from the redoubt. He had been a leader among his countrymen in devotion to the cause of their liberties. He was President of the Provincial Congress, and he was esteemed and loved by all. The comments at the time made it evident that his noble death had an influence which kept him a leader in the path of liberty, as he had always been when alive.

[1] In the first attack, the British had been annoyed by small parties of Americans firing from the shelter of the houses. General Howe had sent word of this to Boston, with a request that the town should be destroyed. It was set on fire by burning carcases and parties from the shipping.

Chapter IX

THE SITUATION AT BOSTON

WHEN Washington left Philadelphia (June 21, 1775) to take command of the army besieging Boston, the news of the Battle of Bunker Hill had not been received. On his way, he soon met the tidings of this action. When he heard, in answer to his inquiries, that the New England militia had stood their ground and fought back the British Regulars, he exclaimed, 'The liberties of the country are safe!' As Irving has well written, 'It seemed as if a weight of doubt had been lifted from his heart.'

His progress through the country excited greater interest because the people had been stirred by the accounts of Bunker Hill. At New York the strange thing happened, that honors were paid to George Washington, as the newly commissioned American General, on the very day the returning Royal Governor Tryon was in the harbor and about to land.

On June 26, 1775, Washington received an address from the New York Provincial Congress, of which this was the first paragraph: 'At a time when the most loyal of his Majesty's subjects, from a regard to the laws and constitution by which he sits on the throne, feel themselves reduced to the unhappy necessity of taking up arms to defend their dearest rights and privileges, while we deplore the calamities of this divided Empire, we rejoice in the appointment of

68

a gentleman from whose abilities and virtue we are taught to expect both security and peace.'

The following was the tenor of Washington's reply: 'At the same time that with you I deplore the unhappy necessity of such an appointment, as that with which I am now honored, I cannot but feel sentiments of the highest gratitude for this affecting instance of distinction and regard. May your warmest wishes be realized in the success of America at this important and interesting period; and be assured that every exertion of my worthy colleagues and myself will be equally extended to the reëstablishment of peace and harmony between the mother country and these colonies, as to the fatal but necessary operations of war. When we assumed the soldier, we did not lay aside the citizen; and we shall most sincerely rejoice with you in that happy hour, when the establishment of American liberty, on the most firm and solid foundations, shall enable us to return to our private stations in the bosom of a free, peaceful, and happy country.'

This exchange is of interest, as showing the terms of thought in the minds of the American leaders at the time of Washington's becoming Commander in Chief. When he set out from Philadelphia, he had with him two of the newly commissioned major generals, Charles Lee and Philip Schuyler. Washington's first official act, in the authority of his command, was to appoint Schuyler to 'the command of all the troops destined for the New York department.' [1] His letter of instructions to Schuyler is extant, directing him to 'keep a watchful eye upon Governor Tryon,' and 'in a like manner, watch the movements of the Indian Agent [Colonel Guy Johnson].' Schuyler was also directed to have the captured forts on Lake Champlain 'properly sup-

[1] General Washington to Major General Schuyler, June 25, 1775.

69

plied with provisions and ammunition; and this I am persuaded you will aim at doing on the best terms to prevent our good cause from sinking under a heavy load of expense.'

His letters to the Continental Congress, on his journey, at once began to lay stress upon the need for powder. As soon as he came into personal touch with the situation, he feared that the lack of powder would be the most serious drawback — and the event justified this fear.

Washington was met at Springfield, on his way to Boston, by a committee of the Massachusetts Provincial Congress, who escorted him first to Watertown, where this Congress was in session, and then to Cambridge on July 2. The Provincial Congress presented to General Washington a congratulatory address, assuring him of their welcome. They had embodied in a resolution 'that General Ward be notified of the appointment of General Washington, as Commander in Chief of the American forces.' And there was nothing but the heartiest concurrence in giving over the troops of the Colony to his command. An address was also presented to Major General Charles Lee, who had accompanied General Washington. On July 3, 1775, Washington formally took command of the army.

His general order of July 4, 1775, at once explicitly put everything on a new basis, and this ended all divided command among the Americans: 'The Continental Congress, having now taken all the troops of the several colonies which have been raised, or which may hereafter be raised, for the support and defense of the liberties of America, into their pay and service, they are now troops of the United Provinces of North America; and it is to be hoped that all distinction of colonies will be laid aside, so that one and the same spirit may animate the whole, and the only contest be, who shall render, on this great and trying occasion, the most essential service to the common cause in which we are all engaged.' These high ideals remained the guiding influence of George Washington from the beginning to the end of his command of the American Army.

The new Commander in Chief left a written record of the military situation he found at Boston.[1] The British had retained possession of the Charlestown peninsula, and had built a strong intrenchment on Bunker Hill, 'with their sentries extended about one hundred and fifty yards on this side of the narrowest part of the Neck.' They had three floating batteries in the Mystic and a warship in the Charles upstream from the battery on Copp's Hill. 'Upon Roxbury Neck, they are also deeply intrenched and strongly fortified. . . . The bulk of their army, commanded by General Howe, lies on Bunker's Hill and the remainder on Roxbury Neck, except the light horse, and a few men in the town of Boston.'

As to the Americans, he reported as follows: 'On our side we have thrown up intrenchments on Winter and Prospect Hills, the Enemies' Camp in full view at the distance of little more than a mile. Such intermediate points, as would permit a Landing, I have since my arrival taken care to strengthen, down to Sewell's Farm, where a strong entrenchment has been thrown up. At Roxbury General Thomas has thrown up a strong work on the Hill, about 200 yards above the Meeting House which with the broken-ness of the ground and great numbers of rocks has made that Pass very secure. The troops raised in New Hampshire, with a Regiment from Rhode Island occupy Winter Hill. A part of those from Connecticut under General Putnam are on Prospect Hill. The troops in this town (Cambridge) are intirely of the Massachusetts: The remainder of the Rhode Island Men are at

[1] To the President of Congress, July 10, 1775.

71

Sewell's Farm: Two Regiments of Connecticut and 9 of the Massachusetts are at Roxbury. The Residue of the Army, to the number of about 700, are posted in several small Towns along the Coast, to prevent the Depredations of the Enemy.' [1]

Washington was evidently surprised at finding the American positions so well fortified, for he added: 'Upon the whole, I think myself authorized to say, that considering the great Extent of Line, and the nature of the Ground we are as well secured as we could be expected in so short a Time and under the disadvantages we labour.' But here ended any satisfaction for him in the general situation.

For it was also evident that he was horrified at the condition of the army. In the address of the Massachusetts Provincial Congress to him, it was stated, of the New England troops, 'that the greatest part of them have not seen service; and although naturally brave and of good understanding, yet, for want of experience in military life, have but little knowledge of divers things most essential to the preservation of health and even life.'

To this part of the Address Washington had replied: 'The course of human affairs forbids an expectation that troops formed under such circumstances should at once possess the order, regularity, and discipline of veterans. Whatever

---

[1] A private letter, also of July 10, gave a more particular account of the American works: 'About two hundred rods below the college we have a redoubt, which begins the line; then about sixty rods from that another redoubt, and the lines continued near an hundred rods; then, at Charlestown road, at the foot of Prospect Hill another redoubt and strong fortification; then on Prospect Hill is Putnam's Post, a very strong fortification; then between that and Winter Hill a strong citadel and lines over Charlestown road to Mystic; then in Mr. Temple's pasture (Ten Hill Farm) a strong redoubt that commands to Mystic River; so that we have a complete line of circumvallation from Charles River to Mystic River. On Roxbury side the enemy have dug across the Neck and let the water through; and our people in turn have intrenched across the outer end of the Neck, and are strongly fortified there, and on the hill by the Meeting House.'

deficiencies there may be, will, I doubt not, soon be made up by the activity and zeal of the officers, and the docility and obedience of the men.'

But this optimism had quickly faded from Washington's mind, and soon afterwards [1] he wrote: 'The abuses in this army, I fear, are considerable, and the new modelling of it, in the face of an enemy from whom we every hour expect an attack, is exceedingly difficult and dangerous.' In July he wrote to his brother: 'I found a mixed multitude of people here, under very little discipline, order, or government.' In a letter to Schuyler he was even more frank: 'Confusion and disorder reigned in every department, which, in a little time must have ended either in the separation of the army, or fatal contests with one another.'

Washington at once proceeded to organize the army besieging Boston into three grand divisions. Major General Ward commanded the right wing at Roxbury and its vicinity. The left wing was under the command of Major General Lee, of which the main positions were Prospect Hill, held by Brigadier General Greene, and Winter Hill under Brigadier General Sullivan. The center at Cambridge was commanded by Major General Putnam. General Washington's headquarters remained at Cambridge. He occupied the Vassall house, which was the property of a refugee Loyalist.[2]

By this organization of his army, Washington did away with the separate groups of Colonists, although the sensible policy was followed of keeping the troops of each Colony together, as much as possible. But the new Continental commissions made havoc among officers who held the

[1] To Richard Henry Lee in Congress, July 10, 1775.

[2] This beautiful house, afterwards known as the 'Craigie house,' was the residence of the poet Longfellow, and is still preserved in Cambridge.

73

higher grades of commissions from the different Colonies, and there was a great deal of trouble at first. In orders of July 4, Washington had announced the Continental appointments of Major Generals Ward, Lee, Schuyler, and Putnam.[1]

These Continental commissions conflicted with Colonial commissions, and several general officers withdrew from the army. There was danger of losing the services of General Thomas, one of the ablest officers in the camp. Washington fully appreciated the value of General Thomas and made his case an object of special intercession, both with the Continental Congress and with General Thomas himself. Congress responded by making General Thomas the ranking Brigadier General,[2] and Washington prevailed upon General Thomas to accept this rank and remain in the service. The letter written by Washington to General Thomas is given in full at the end of this chapter. Nothing could be more eloquent of the spirit of the times, and it is an example of the extraordinary ability of Washington in writing, when stirred by strong emotion.

Consequently, Washington was able to add, in his letter to General Schuyler: 'The better genius of America has prevailed, and most happily the ministerial troops have not availed themselves of their advantages, till I trust the opportunity is in a great measure passed over. The arrangement of the general officers in Massachusetts and Connecticut has been very unpopular, indeed I may say injudicious. It is returned to Congress for further consideration, and has

[1] At the same time Thomas Mifflin was appointed Aide-de-Camp, and Joseph Reed to be Secretary of the General.

[2] '*Resolved*, That General Thomas be appointed first brigadier general in the army of the United Colonies, in the room of General Pomeroy, who never acted under the commission sent to him, and that General Thomas's commission bear the same date as General Pomeroy's did.' (Journal, July 19, 1775.)

74

much retarded my plan of discipline. However we mend every day, and I flatter myself that in a little time we shall work up these raw materials into a good manufacture. I must recommend to you, what I endeavor to practice myself, patience and perseverance.'

The reason for this failure of the British to 'avail themselves of their advantages' was not far to seek. Their disastrous experiences in the Lexington and Concord Fight and the Battle of Bunker Hill had continued to be the best defense for the Americans. As a result of these reverses, Gage had no desire to attack the American positions. More than that, the Royal Governor had been so discouraged by these object lessons, that he was writing to the British Government [1] a description of the situation, in which he called Boston 'the most disadvantageous place for all operations, particularly when there is no diversion of the rebel forces, but all are collected in one point. Was this army in New York, that Province might, to all appearance be more easily reduced, and the friends of Government be able to raise forces to join the troops.'

This statement was a most significant admission of the general uprising against the King's Ministers throughout New England, and of the utter lack of support for the Royal Governor, except from the Loyalists in Boston. And this existing situation, described by General Gage, in itself, was enough to dispose of the nonsensical theory that the Revolution was brought about by a restless minority. It also should be emphasized, in this regard, that, when it came to the military test, the same thing was proved true of the other Colonies. Even in New York, in spite of the advantages of the best base for an army sustained by sea, that expectation of Loyalist 'forces to join the troops' was the ignis fatuus

[1] General Gage to Earl of Dartmouth, July 24, 1775.

which lured Burgoyne to his doom. There can be no question of the fact that the revolt was general throughout all the Colonies.

But this idea of transferring the British troops to New York did not come anywhere near being carried out. Gage's army remained passive, blockaded in Boston. The pessimism of the Royal Governor, as to the situation, thus insured for Washington immunity from attacks, although he did not realize his enemy's state of mind. On the other hand, the Americans were utterly lacking in the means for offensive operations against the British. As a result, there was one of the strangest cases in history, a balance struck by unprecedented conditions.

This was the astonishing situation at Boston. The force well equipped for fighting was so disconcerted and bewildered that fighting was considered out of the question. The opposing force was so poorly equipped that fighting was out of the question anyway. One would not — the other could not. That was the whole thing in a nutshell.

As was most natural, many of the inhabitants had left Boston. In Boston, the last week of July, the inhabitants were stated to be 6753; the British troops, with their dependents, women, and children, 13,000.

WASHINGTON'S LETTER TO GENERAL THOMAS

23 July, 1775

SIR:

The retirement of a General Officer possessing the confidence of his country and the army at so critical a period, appears to me to be big with fatal consequences both to the public cause and his own reputation. While it is unexecuted I think it my duty to use this last effort to prevent it, and your own virtue and good sense must decide upon it. In the usual contests of empire and ambition, the conscience of a soldier has so little share, that he may very properly insist upon his claims of rank, and extend his pretensions even to punctilio; — but in such a cause as this, when the object is neither glory nor extent of territory, but a defence of all that is dear and valuable in private and public life, surely every post ought to be deemed honorable in which a man can serve his country. What matter of triumph will it afford our enemies, that in less than one month, a spirit of discord should show itself in the highest ranks of the army, not to be extinguished by anything less than a total desertion of duty. How little reason shall we have to boast of American union and patriotism, if at such a time and in such a cause smaller and partial considerations cannot give way to the great and general interest. These remarks not only affect you as a member of the great American body, but as an inhabitant of Massachusetts Bay. Your own Province and the other Colonies have a peculiar and unquestionable claim to your services, and in my opinion you cannot refuse without relinquishing in some degree that character of public virtue and honor which you have hitherto supported. If our cause is just, it ought to be supported; but when shall it find support if gentlemen of merit and experience, unable to conquer the prejudices of a competition, withdraw themselves in the hour of danger? I admit, Sir, that your just claims and services have not had due respect, — it is by no means a singular case, — worthy men of all nations and countries have had reasons to make the same complaint, but they did not for this abandon the public cause, — they nobly stifled the dictates of resentment, and made their enemies ashamed of their injustice. And can America afford no such instances of magnanimity? For the sake of your bleeding country, — your devoted Province, — your charter rights, — and by the memories of those brave men who have already fallen in this great cause, I conjure you to banish from your mind every suggestion of anger and disappointment; your country will do ample justice to your merits, — they already do it by the regret and sorrow expressed on this occasion; and the sacrifice you are called to make, will in the judgment of every good man and lover of his country, do you more real honor than the most distinguished victory. You possess the confidence and affection of the troops of this Province particularly; — many of them are not capable of judging the propriety and reasons of your conduct, — should they esteem themselves authorized by your example to leave the service, the consequences may be fatal and irretrievable. There is reason to fear it from the personal attachment of the officers and men, and the obligations that are supposed to arise from these attachments.

But, sir, the other Colonies have also their claims upon you, not only as a native of America, but an inhabitant of this Province. They have made common cause with it, they have sacrificed their trade, loaded themselves with taxes, and are ready to spill their blood, in vindication of the rights of Massachusetts Bay, while all the security and profit of a neutrality have been offered them. But no acts or temptations could seduce them from your side, and leave you a prey to a cruel and perfidious ministry. Sure these reflections must have some weight with a mind as generous and considerate as yours. How will you be able to answer it to your country and to your own conscience, if such a step should lead to a division of the army or the loss and ruin of America be ascribed to measures which your counsels and conduct would have prevented! Before it is too late, I entreat, sir, you would weigh well the greatness of the stake, and upon how much smaller circumstances the fate of empires has depended. Of your own honor and reputation you are the best and only judge; but allow me to say, that a people contending for life and liberty, are seldom disposed to look with a favorable eye upon either men or measures, whose passions, interests or consequences will clash with those inestimable objects. As to myself, Sir, be assured, that I shall with pleasure do all in my power to make your situation both easy and honorable, and that the sentiments I have here expressed flow from a clear opinion that your duty to your country, your posterity, and yourself, most explicitly require your continuance in the service. The order and rank of the commissions is under the consideration of the Continental Congress, whose determination will be received in a few days. It may argue a want of respect to that august body not to wait that decision. But at all events, I shall flatter myself, that these reasons with others which your own good judgment will suggest, will strengthen your mind against those impressions which are incident to humanity, and laudable to a certain degree, and that the result will be your resolution to assist your country and friends in this day of distress. That you may reap the full reward of honor and public esteem which conduct deserves, is the sincere wish of, Sir, Yours, &c ——

Chapter x

THE SIEGE OF BOSTON

THIS situation at Boston was only the beginning of Washington's never-ending task of attempting to create an American army from what he had described as 'a mixed multitude.' In the letter to Schuyler, which has been quoted in the preceding chapter,[1] Washington wrote, in answer to Schuyler's complaints as to his difficulties in organizing the troops in his district: 'From my own experience I can easily judge of your difficulties to introduce order and discipline in troops, who have from their infancy imbibed ideas of the most contrary kind. It would be far beyond the compass of a letter for me to describe the situation of things here upon my arrival. Perhaps you will only be able to judge of it from my assuring you, that mine must be a portrait at full length of what you have a miniature.'

This apt comparison remained true throughout the Revolution. For each one of the other American leaders, there was the smaller scale of individual responsibility. But for George Washington there was always the 'full length,' which must be his work alone. His early recognition that this was destined to be his onerous rôle, his straightforward acceptance of its burdens, and his unfaltering devotion to the performance of this public duty, marked the greatness of his character. And at Boston were exemplified all the mani-

[1] To Major General Schuyler, July 28, 1775.

fold difficulties, which were to accumulate upon the shoulders of George Washington until he became the Atlas supporting the whole structure of the Revolution.

From the beginning to the end, it was a constant struggle for Washington to overcome the obstacles put in his way by Congress. It has always been exasperating to read of the failure of Congress to give adequate support to Washington. This remained an adverse factor throughout the war. But, on the other hand, when we realize the uncertain authority of that body of venturers into uncharted seas, the wonder was that they ever arrived anywhere at all. It is only common-sense to acknowledge that an efficient administration could not have been expected from Congress. It was beyond human possibilities to look for a Minerva of full wisdom at birth.

As to the other side of Washington's problem, the difficulties of organizing a disciplined American army, we must also acknowledge it was inconceivable that the desired order could be evoked quickly from the existing chaos. The militia had proved themselves unexpectedly efficient in rising to organized resistance. They had also proved unexpectedly formidable as a fighting force. But, when it came to the test of the discipline of an army in encampment, it was altogether a different matter. And it was no wonder that Washington was shocked at the conditions he found in his new command.

The main trouble was, these American volunteers could not be brought to see any reason why they should not return to their homes at will to look after their affairs, whenever there was inactivity for the army. Officers and men shared this opinion, and the habit of the army can only be described as an ebb and flow. The very fact that the British were intimidated, as has been explained, and had abandoned all intentions of attacking the Americans, caused a lull in hostilities which gave an excuse for these casual absences from the army. But, as Washington could not know that he was thus immune from British attacks, it was not surprising that his first weeks with the army comprised a period of the gravest anxiety. The question of powder for the army was desperate. Early in August, Washington was obliged to write to Congress, 'Our situation, in the article of powder, is much more alarming than I had the most distant idea of.' In spite of every effort to gather a supply from the neighboring Colonies, there remained such a shortage that the Americans were still left unable to offer a strong resistance against any resolute assault.

Confronted with this desperate situation, Washington devoted all his energies to strengthening the American positions. He was everywhere in the encampment, and the influence of his personality was felt — and shown in the results. As can be imagined, Washington was angered by the frequent absences from the army of officers and men. His comments on these absences were very severe, and he imposed strict disciplinary measures, with the harsh punishments of the times. But it was an almost impossible task to contend against the general laxity of a people unused to being ruled, or controlled in the military sense. In addition, Washington had to contend with jealousies, quarrels, and avarice for private gain. All these — and more — were obstacles which he alone must overcome. It would be difficult to find in history a leader placed in a more harassing situation.

Washington's letters at this stage were unsparing in their bitter criticisms of the unruly elements in the militia which composed his command. But nothing of this appeared in his conduct of affairs, and his unbroken serenity, with his

EQUESTRIAN STATUE OF WASHINGTON, BY THOMAS BALL,
ON THE PUBLIC GARDEN IN BOSTON

strength of purpose in his arduous duties, won the respect of all. There was a gradual improvement, due entirely to Washington's unremitting efforts — but it was not until December that Washington was able to write that 'things wear a better complexion here.'

In July, Congress had sent to the army a reinforcement of three thousand from Pennsylvania, Maryland, and Virginia, and from this time the besieging force began the change from New England militia into a Continental Army. Continental commissions were sent on to Washington in blocks, but the transfer was a work of many complications and difficulties.

With the first reinforcement, there had arrived the famous corps of rifle men under Daniel Morgan. The wonder expressed in the American Army at the skill of these riflemen should be enough to dispose of any idea that thousands of riflemen were available for the Americans. The fact was, Morgan's men came from the border, and skill with the rifle was confined to this comparatively small proportion of the population of the Colonies. It was true that a large part of the inhabitants throughout the Colonies were accustomed to firearms, as has been explained. But this was a general use of the smoothbore muskets of the time for shooting game, with ball or as shotguns. This was a very different thing from practice with rifles, which were an unknown quantity to most of the Colonists. For this reason, in studying the military history of the Revolution, it is necessary to put aside the false impression of hordes of American riflemen. There never was a possibility that there could be any such military factor at any time in the Revolution.

At Boston the situation was held in balance by the conditions which have been described. On the part of the British, General Gage was recalled in October, and General Howe succeeded him in command. Howe was as pessimistic as Gage, so far as concerned accomplishing anything in Massachusetts. He also did not delay in advising the King's Ministers to abandon Boston. In this half-hearted spirit the British continued to occupy Boston, and this main British force in America remained idle. But, although Howe thus committed his army to an inactive rôle, he had not the slightest idea that the Americans could ever be able to drive him from Boston, and he gave assurance that the town 'would be in no danger from the enemy during the winter.' However, the British commander's self-confidence ended at that. He settled down in submission to a close siege without even making a test of the weaknesses of the enemy. This remained the attitude of the British in Boston.

On the part of the Americans, there was also inactivity — but it was an enforced inactivity due to the utter lack of means for attacking the British. All Washington could do was to maintain as bold a front as possible, and make every effort to strengthen his army and its positions. In this he was unremitting, and, although he always knew that the weaknesses of his own army invited attack, yet he kept his enemy in constant fear of American attacks.

After this strange fashion, the unique siege went on through the ensuing winter. The besiegers never had the necessary artillery strength to bombard the besieged. They could only cut them off from the surrounding country. This did not even constitute a blockade, for the British were being supplied by sea. But it was characteristic of the resourcefulness of Washington that he found means to harass this British service of supplies, in spite of the fact that the British held absolute command of the seas.

At the end of the summer of 1775, Congress was still undecided as to the expediency of fitting out ships against the

British. But Washington took the matter into his own hands. He resolved to create a force of armed ships of his own, and it must be acknowledged that he accomplished this in a novel and ingenious way. He actually gave army commissions to the commanders of the ships he fitted out, and put on board detachments from his army as crews. This extraordinary process for procuring a naval personnel would have been impossible in any other army. But Washington had found in his own army a regiment which was made up of trained sailors. This was the Essex County regiment of Colonel John Glover, of Marblehead, which was well called 'amphibious.' With this element to draw upon, Washington fitted out his armed ships, manned, as he himself wrote, by 'soldiers who have been bred to the sea.'

The first of this fleet was the schooner *Hannah*, commanded by Captain Nicholson Broughton of Marblehead and manned by a detachment from Colonel Glover's regiment. The status of this vessel was fixed beyond any question, by Washington's orders to Captain Broughton (September 2, 1775) as 'fitted out and equipped with arms, ammunition, and provisions, at the Continental expense.'

Here was something altogether different from anything that had hitherto happened in the Revolution. The Americans had already begun to arm ships, with various authorizations from the Colonies. But this became the first warship regularly commissioned by authority derived from the United Colonies of North America, and given a definite mission against the enemy. Washington's letter of instructions [1] to Captain Broughton established this status of the

[1] General Washington to Captain Broughton (September 2, 1775): 'To Captain Nicholson Broughton:

'1. You being appointed a captain in the army of the United Colonies of North America, are hereby directed to take command of a detachment of said army, and proceed on board the schooner Hannah, at Beverly, lately fitted out

Hannah beyond any question. Moreover, the sequence of events made this act of Washington unquestionably the beginning of the United States Navy. Washington kept on and commissioned other armed ships in the same way, with the result that Congress was aroused, and on October 5, 1775, instructed Washington to fit out armed vessels. In addition, a committee of Congress called the 'Naval Committee,' consisting of John Adams, John Langdon, and Silas Deane, was appointed. So rapid was the course of events, that it was a matter of record, in February, 1776, that Congress provided an increase of 'the pay of Joseph Reed Esq., Secretary to General Washington, on account of the extraordinary services attending the office by reason of the direction of the Navy Department.'

The report of Colonel Reed, Washington's Secretary, gave a list of the other armed vessels, as follows: *Lynch*, schooner; *Lee*, schooner; *Warren*, schooner; *Washington*, 'a fine vessel'; *Harrison*, schooner. This little fleet was of real value in the siege of Boston. It captured over thirty prizes. The first of these was the ship *Unity* taken by the *Hannah*, September 6, 1775, the day after Captain Broughton had sailed on his first cruise.

The schooner *Lee*, commanded by Captain John Manley of Marblehead, was the most successful of these vessels. His ability won the approval of Washington, who made him Commodore of his fleet on January 1, 1776. The British showed little energy in protecting their supply ships by

and equipped with arms, ammunition, and provisions, at the Continental expense.

'2. You are to proceed as commander of said schooner, immediately on a cruise against such vessels as may be found on the high seas or elsewhere, bound inwards and outwards, to or from Boston, in the service of the Ministerial Army, and to take and sieze all such vessels laden with soldiers, arms, ammunition or provisions, for or from such army, or which you shall have good reason to suspect are in such service.'

means of their naval forces, against the depredations of these weak enemies. In November, 1775, the *Lee* actually was allowed to capture the *Nancy*, a large brigantine loaded with ordnance supplies for the British Army in Boston. This was the most important prize of the siege, and the capture was hailed with rejoicings throughout the camp.

Chapter XI

THE COURSE OF EVENTS IN THE WINTER OF
1775–1776

WHILE the main forces of the British and Americans remained in deadlock at Boston, the Americans had made the mistake of plunging into an offensive against Canada. This invasion of Canada was a false move from every point of view. There was no trace of a common cause that would unite Canada and the United Colonies in rebellion against Great Britain. Even if this ill-judged invasion had won success, it would have been only a source of weakness for the Americans.

But this idea was a legacy from the 'French Wars' when Lake Champlain had been the entry for forays of both sides. Information had been received that Sir Guy Carleton, Governor of Canada, was planning to recapture Ticonderoga. With the intention of forestalling him, Congress authorized an expedition to invade Canada. Schuyler, who commanded in the North, had ordered to Ticonderoga Richard Montgomery, one of the newly commissioned brigadier generals. Schuyler had not been well, and his health broke down entirely at the beginning of the campaign. Therefore the command of the invading force devolved upon Montgomery, an officer of great ability and of a high chivalrous spirit. He had served under Wolfe in Canada, and his own zeal was an inspiration for his men.

On September 12, 1775, after the withdrawal of Schuyler, Montgomery besieged the fortress of St. John's, which defended Montreal. In spite of the shortcomings of his equipment, his success was assured. The Royal Governor Carleton was wretchedly provided with troops, and could gather only nine hundred to attempt the relief of St. John's. These were easily beaten off by the American besieging force of two thousand, and St. John's surrendered on November 3, 1775. This left Montreal an easy prey, and Montgomery took possession of the city on November 12.

In the mean time, another American expedition had been sent forth against Canada. This was the mad enterprise of Arnold, to invade Canada by the way of the Kennebec and capture Quebec. It was the type of desperate adventure that would appeal to Arnold, and he was sanguine of success. He knew the country, for as a trader he had been in Quebec, and he confidently urged this project for its capture. Washington gave him a force of ten companies of New England troops, two of Pennsylvania, and one of Virginia — about eleven hundred in all. These included Morgan and his riflemen.

Washington's instructions to Arnold have been preserved,[1] and they reflected the erroneous idea of the times, that the Canadians would rise to join the Americans in revolt against Great Britain. As Bancroft has stated, these directions to Arnold 'enjoined respect for the rights of property and the freedom of opinion, and aimed at conciliating the affectionate coöperation of the Canadians.' A manifesto had also been drawn up, 'To the Inhabitants of Canada,' of which the last sentence was, 'Come, then, ye generous citizens, range yourselves under the standard of general liberty, against which all the force and artifices of

[1] Dated at Cambridge, September 14, 1775.

tyranny will never be able to prevail.' This was for circulation in Canada, but met with no general response.

Arnold's force sailed from Newburyport, September 19, 1775, and entered the Kennebec. Up this river the expedition laboriously made its way, with fearful hardships which exhausted their strength and diminished their numbers. Three companies gave up altogether and returned to Cambridge. The rest kept doggedly on, but they were reduced to seven hundred when Arnold reached Point Levis, on the St. Lawrence opposite Quebec (November 10, 1775). Moreover, the men of the expedition were ragged and worn from privations — and, not only were they without artillery, but they were also woefully lacking in ammunition and supplies of every kind.

Arnold's messages, sent in advance by friendly Indians to be circulated among the Canadians, instead of gaining him any aid, merely served notice to the British of his design against Quebec. Profiting by these warnings, the British leaders were also able to put the fortifications into so strong a condition that Arnold was obliged to admit, 'The enemy being apprised of our coming, we found it unpracticable to attack them without too great a risk.'

In the night of November 13, Arnold had ferried his troops over to the Plains of Abraham, and on the next day he summoned the city to surrender. But, as there was no rising of the Canadians in his favor, he was obliged to withdraw his feeble force, to encamp on the St. Lawrence above Quebec, and to wait for the coöperation of Montgomery.

After the Americans captured Montreal, the Royal Governor Carleton escaped down the St. Lawrence, and disguised as a peasant arrived at Quebec November 19. The news of the fall of Montreal had caused consternation in Quebec. Some of the inhabitants thought that Quebec also

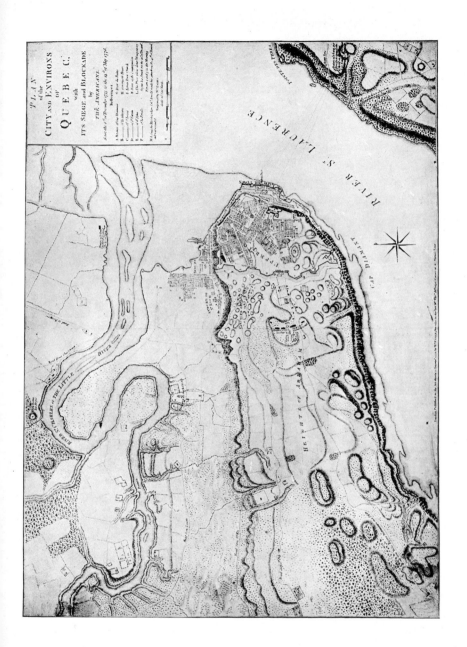

PLAN
of the
CITY and ENVIRONS
of
QUEBEC,
with
ITS SIEGE and BLOCKADE
by
THE AMERICANS
from the 8th December 1775 to the 13th May 1776.

References.
A. Redoute of four Demi-curtains
B. .... of St. Rocque
C. .... of ......
D. .... of St. Johns
E. .... of St. Lewis
F. .... of St. Foix

would be obliged to capitulate to Montgomery. But Sir
Guy Carleton at once put an end to any idea of surrender
by ordering all who would not join in the defense of the
town to leave Quebec. Without the help of the Canadian
inhabitants, there was no hope for the Americans of winning the Canadian stronghold, because, in contrast to the
situation at Montreal, Sir Guy Carleton had sufficient troops
to defend Quebec. Of Regulars, Canadians, armed sailors,
and marines, Carleton had more than fifteen hundred.
And this gave him a superiority in numbers over the depleted American forces available for an attack on the town.

Although Montgomery's numbers had not been cut down
by privations, as had been the case with Arnold's expedition, yet his command had shrunk away rapidly. It was too
late in the season; winter was approaching; the irregular
enlistments were about to expire; the men were homesick
and were leaving for home anyway; Congress was doing
nothing to fill the gaps in his ranks — still less was there any
hope that Congress would send reinforcements. Under
these circumstances, when Montgomery joined Arnold in
the first week of December, he found that he had less than a
thousand Americans, of both commands, that could be used
for operations against Quebec.

Consequently, there was no possibility of a successful
siege. But Montgomery would not admit failure, and resolved to take the desperate chance of an assault.[1] This was
attempted by a double attack in the early morning of
December 31, 1775, with a heavy snowstorm to help the
surprise in the dark hours. The very audacity of the assault
was the only thing in favor of this attempt, which was decisively defeated. In his share of the attack, Montgomery
was at once killed, gallantly leading his men. On the op-

[1] In his own words, 'To the storming we must come at last.'

posite side of the town, Arnold was severely wounded early in the attack and carried from the field. The van of his men under Morgan forced their way in, only to be overpowered by numbers and captured.

This defeat practically put an end to any chance of winning Canada from the British. Yet Arnold lingered in Canada through the winter, and an account will be given of the persistence of Congress in adhering to this plan in the spring. But the actual effects of this invasion, so far as it affected the course of the Revolution, can be summed up at this stage. For the Americans, it was a tragedy that the gallant Montgomery was lost to the service, and that other valuable lives were sacrificed. In every other respect, it was fortunate that the invasion of Canada was so decisively beaten. Success would only have done harm, and would have committed the Americans to a military situation that would have been a drag upon them in the Revolution.

As to the effect upon the British, it was one of the strange facts of this most unusual war, that the futile campaign against Canada actually accomplished the unexpected result of doing incalculable harm to the whole British conduct of the war. This harm was twofold, and has never been emphasized sufficiently in accounts of the Revolution. In the first place, the news of Montgomery's early successes made so great an impression on the King's Ministers, that it caused them to divert great numbers of troops to reinforce Canada — far greater numbers than were needed for its defense.

The second result was even more serious, as an adverse factor for the British. Not only were these heavy reinforcements diverted from their logical field of action in the Colonies, but there followed in sequence the development of the unsound idea of piling troops into Canada, to be used

for invading the Colonies from Canada. This was transferring from the Americans to the British the valueless
legacy of the 'French Wars,' that Lake Champlain was an
entrance for invasion. The ensuing narrative will show the
fatal damage wrought by the Ministers' adoption of this
policy, instead of concentrating their efforts on pouring
British troops into the Colonies by the assured and efficient
route over the sea.

These increased forces for service in America were being
collected at the last of 1775. The petition to the King from
Congress had been taken to London by Richard Penn, who
arrived there August 14, 1775. The King not only refused
to receive this petition, but regarded it as an act of rebellion.
The only result was to call forth a Royal Proclamation,[1] denouncing in severest terms the 'open and avowed Rebellion,'
and threatening 'to bring to condign punishment' all persons 'found carrying on Correspondence with, or in any
Manner or Degree aiding or abetting' those in revolt. Very
naturally the effect of this, both in America and in Great
Britain, amounted to closing the door in the faces of those
who still hoped for a solution of the questions at issue. This
unfavorable impression was increased by the measures
adopted by the King's Ministers for raising troops in Ger-
many to put down the revolt in America.

They first attempted to secure troops from Russia, but
they met refusal from the Empress Catherine. Next they
tried the German States, and secured contracts for some
twenty thousand troops from Brunswick, Hesse-Cassel, Wal-
deck, Anhalt-Zerbst, Ansbach-Bayreuth, and Hesse-Hanau.
These were to be the 'Hessians' of the American Revolution.
Hiring these foreign troops was in accordance with the prevailing European customs of the day, and, therefore, must

[1] August 23, 1775.

not be considered an act of atrocity or tyranny. But, in the unusual situation which existed, the news of this measure had an especially bad effect in arousing increased resentment in America, and it alienated many Americans from Great Britain. In Great Britain, also, it stirred up much opposition, but all complaints in Parliament fell on deaf ears, as that body remained under the control of the King's Ministers.

In America, as the year 1775 passed and the new year of 1776 began its course, there was another disturbing factor that was breeding aversion to British rule. It almost might be said that the deposed Royal Governors vied with one another to make the Royal cause unpopular. To Lord Dunmore must be awarded the palm, for he seemed inspired to do the wrong thing at every turn. The Colony of Virginia had never been inclined to independence. This conservative attitude was misunderstood by Lord Dunmore, although he had been driven to take refuge in British shipping, and he put himself on record by stating [1] that with three hundred men he could win back the Colony. He was to receive a consignment of arms for Loyalist troops, if he could raise them, and he issued a proclamation (November, 1775), calling upon the Negro slaves to enlist for the purpose of 'reducing the colony to a proper sense of its duty.' This foolish proclamation did not bring out recruits to aid Dunmore, but it united the Virginians against him.

In the next month Dunmore tried to get military control of Norfolk, and in his disappointment at failure, he set the town on fire by bombardment from his ships (January, 1776). These acts of the Royal Governor so exasperated the Virginians that the spring of 1776 found the Colony of Virginia ready to declare for independence.

[1] Secretary of State to Howe, October 22, 1775.

In North Carolina, the Royal Governor Martin was in the same predicament of having been driven on board ship. Yet he had confidence in an uprising of the Loyalists of the Colony — and this proved to be an early test of the comparative weakness of the Loyalists, which was confirmed by the subsequent history of the Revolution. In this Colony was a settlement of Highland Scots, who were all ardent Loyalists. They formed a military organization, and Martin asked for British troops to coöperate with them. General Clinton was sent from Boston (January, 1776) to command a British force for this purpose. But, long before Clinton could arrive on the scene, the overconfident Highlanders took the field, and were promptly overwhelmed by an uprising of the Colonists (Moore's Creek, February 27, 1776).[1]

At this call, such great numbers of North Carolina militia had assembled (ten thousand), that Clinton's force did not attempt to land. So aroused were the Colonists that North Carolina was the first Colony to put itself on record 'in declaring for independency.' [2] South Carolina and Georgia also aligned themselves to concur in the action of the other Colonies.

The unexpected had thus come to pass in the Southern Colonies, which were supposed to be the stronghold of the Royal cause. For it was in the South that the lead had been taken in advocating independence. This situation was a measure of how strongly the currents were running in the new year of 1776.

[1] It is interesting to note that the leaders of this failure were Macdonalds. One of these was the husband of Flora Macdonald, who had saved the Stuart Prince Charles Edward in 1745. Her husband was lodged in jail, with the other leaders, and this defeat ended all hopes for the Loyalists' cause in North Carolina.

[2] Instructions of North Carolina Provincial Congress to delegates in Continental Congress.

Chapter XII

EXPULSION OF THE BRITISH FROM BOSTON

AS TO the military situation at Boston, a paragraph of
a letter written by Washington [1] described the conditions he was obliged to face, in preparing to go through
the winter of 1775–1776: 'Since finishing our own lines of
defence, we, as well as the enemy, have been busily employed in putting our men under proper cover for the winter. Our advanced works, and theirs, are within musket-
shot of each other. We are obliged to submit to an almost
daily cannonade without returning a shot, from our scarcity
of powder, which we are necessitated to keep for closer work
than cannon-distance, whenever the red-coat gentry please
to come out of their intrenchments.'

That winter was a continuation of the discouragements
and difficulties for Washington, in his struggles to keep the
army together, and to maintain a bold front against the well-
equipped enemy. As he lacked all means of pushing a siege,
he was forced to submit to these limitations. The moral
effect of Lexington and Concord, and of Bunker Hill, still
kept the British in leash, but there was no chance for the
Americans to strike a blow at them.

Congress had grown impatient for action, and a delega-
tion was sent to Washington's camp. However, it was soon
evident to them that the American Commander in Chief

[1] To John Augustine Washington, October 13, 1775.

96

was anxious to fight, and only deterred from fighting because he was not equipped for attacking the British. They saw that, without powder and without any siege train, Washington could not make even a pretense of bombardment.

But Washington never allowed himself to be daunted by difficulties, and, in the face of what seemed unsurmountable obstacles, he was all the time persisting in a plan for securing a siege train which would enable him to force a decision. It appeared an impossibility. Neither friends nor foes had any idea that such a plan was feasible. Howe was reiterating to Lord Dartmouth his confidence in his position: 'We are not under the least apprehension of an attack upon this place from the rebels, by surprise or otherwise.' Yet Washington was preparing a 'surprise' that was to oust Howe from Boston.

His first step had been to make Henry Knox his Chief of Artillery in November, 1775.[1] This act not only insured the success of Washington's plan for acquiring a siege train, but it also gave him an executive officer whose services continued to be invaluable to the end of the Revolution. Knox was one of the men who were miracles of the war, if we think only in terms of the military formulas of the times. His friend General Greene was another miracle, if we consider him from the same point of view. But, the fact was, there was nothing miraculous in the career of either. Both were products of the Colonies, and of the electric currents that were stimulating into life a new order of men. Both were self-taught, in military knowledge as in other things, and each was an example of the effects of ardent self-tuition. Neither a bookshop nor a forge would appear a likely place

---

[1] To the President of Congress, November 8, 1775: 'I have taken the liberty of recommending Henry Knox to the consideration of Congress.'

of origin for a general. Yet Knox came from one, and Greene from the other.

Henry Knox was but twenty-five, when he gained the approval of Washington in 1775, but he was ripe for great undertakings. It was characteristic of Washington's energy in carrying out his plans, that the American Commander in Chief did not wait for Congress to issue the commission to Knox, but he at once sent the young man on an important mission to gather ordnance.[1] The crucial part of this mission was the execution of the scheme for bringing down siege artillery from the Lake Champlain forts.[2] This plan had been submitted to Washington by Henry Knox, and Washington had promptly adopted it as the only possible means of acquiring a siege train.

The energy and resource shown by Knox, in carrying out this mission, were beyond all praise. After only a short stay in New York, he was in Albany December 1, and at Ticonderoga December 5. He lost no time in getting the pieces of ordnance on board small craft and bringing them down the lakes to Fort George. From this point he wrote to Washington (December 17, 1775): 'I returned to this place on the 15th, and brought with me the cannon, it being nearly the time I had computed it would take us to transport them here. It is not easy to conceive the difficulties we have had in getting them over the lake, owing to the advanced season of the year and contrary winds; but this

[1] Knox's commission from the Continental Congress was dated November 17, 1775, but Knox did not receive it until his return from the Ticonderoga expedition.

[2] Washington's instructions to Knox, Cambridge, November 16, 1775: 'After you have procured as many of these necessaries as you can there (New York), you must go to Major General Schuyler, and get the remainder from Ticonderoga, Crown Point, or St. John's; if it should be necessary, from Quebec, if in our hands. The want of them is so great, that no trouble or expense must be spared to obtain them.'

MEDAL AWARDED TO WASHINGTON BY CONGRESS

danger is now past. Three days ago it was very uncertain whether we should have gotten them until next spring; but now, please God, they must go. I have had made 42 exceeding strong sleds, and have provided 80 yokes of oxen to draw them as far as Springfield, where I shall get fresh cattle to carry them to camp. The route will be from here to Kinderhook, from thence to Great Barrington, and down to Springfield. I have sent for sleds and teams to come here and expect to begin to move them to Saratoga, on Wednesday or Thursday next, trusting that between this and then we shall have a fine fall of snow, which will enable us to proceed further, and make the carriage easy. If that shall be the case, I hope in sixteen or seventeen days' time to present your excellency a noble train of artillery.'

This letter showed Knox's confidence in being able to overcome the difficulties of transporting this heavy ordnance through what was considered an impassable wilderness of snow and ice. The weather played him false and increased the natural obstacles to his progress. Yet the indomitable Knox pressed on and won through with his 'noble train of artillery.' [1] He thus accomplished the impossible, in making the captured British forts on far distant Lake Champlain the arsenals for the siege of Boston.

Consequently, in February, 1776, the whole situation was changed for Washington. At last he possessed the necessary strength to take the offensive against the British in Boston. There was no doubt in the mind of Washington as to the choice of the best move against the enemy. In fact, he had decided in advance that the occupation of Dorchester Heights would be undertaken as soon as the Americans received this artillery. Accordingly, on the night of March 4,

[1] Knox's inventory of this siege train (December 10, 1775) was: Mortars and Cohorns, brass 8, iron 6; Howitzers, 2; Cannon, brass 13, iron 30. Total 59.

there the Battle of Bunker Hill became a decisive American victory.

This is a true measure of the result, because the evacuation of Boston was decisive in every sense of the word. The phrase on Washington's medal, '*Hostibus primo fugatis,*' was most significant. For we cannot exaggerate the moral effect of this 'first putting the enemy to flight.' It was a fearful blow to British prestige throughout the Colonies, and it at once placed the war on a different basis. In Massachusetts it was a final blow. King Street was to become State Street, and Massachusetts a Commonwealth. Never again was there any danger of British rule in Massachusetts.

The negotiations and assurances of citizens of Boston brought the departure of the British forces without harm for either side. But, during the days when the British were preparing to leave the town, Washington did not cease to push his works nearer the town. The fortification by the Americans of Nook's Hill was a last military argument that emphasized to the British the necessity for withdrawal. On March 17, 1776, the British evacuated Boston.

The official British announcement was as follows: 'General Howe, commander-in-chief of his majesty's forces in North America, having taken a resolution on the seventh of March to remove from Boston to Halifax with the troops under his command, and such of the inhabitants, with their effects, as were desirous to continue under the protection of his majesty's forces; the embarkation was effected the 17th of the same month, with the greatest order and regularity, and without the least interference from the rebels.'

In this announcement was a reference to a pathetic phase of the evacuation. More than a thousand refugees left Boston with the British troops. These were Loyalists who had pinned their fortunes to the Royal cause. They had never imagined that it was possible for the Americans to drive the British from Boston. But, when they found that the Royal Governor had decided to evacuate the town, it was as if their world had fallen in ruins. Washington wrote, 'Not the last trump could have struck them with greater consternation.' For most of those who left with the British army it meant expatriation. The British army, upon which they had so confidently relied, never returned, and, when they went away with it, they were leaving their homes forever.

Chapter XIII

THE MILITARY SITUATION DEVELOPED

ALTHOUGH this has not been appreciated by military critics, yet it is undoubtedly true that the siege of Boston had already developed the military situation that was destined to control the American Revolution. The outstanding feature of this military situation was its demonstration of a state of affairs, differing from anything that could exist in the Europe of the times, which actually precluded the possibility of a war waged in the European meaning of the word. A European war in the eighteenth century implied, as a matter of course, campaigns and battles fought by regular armies, trained in the formal tactics of the day and equipped to conform to a high standard of requirements.

Even thus early in the Revolution, there had been tests which proved that conditions in America put out of the question this standardized warfare, fought by armies maneuvered according to European formulas and equipped according to European specifications. There could be no such war between the British and the Americans, because only one side could meet the demands of the game. The British were able to put well-equipped armies into the field. The Americans could not.

As has been stated, Washington's difficulties at Boston, in his attempts to organize an American army, were typical of his difficulties throughout the war. It is only necessary to

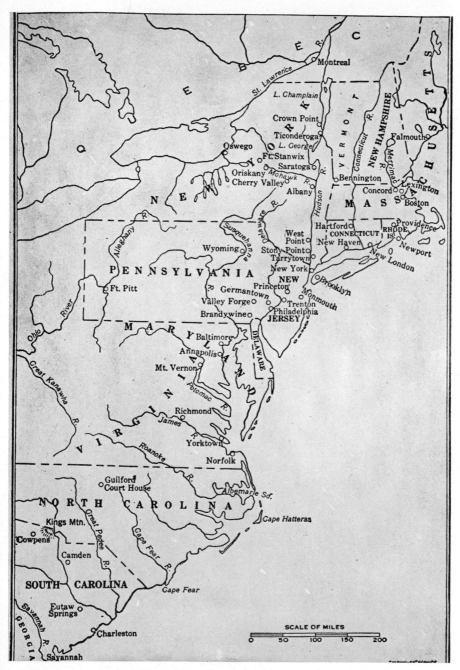

INDEX MAP OF THE AMERICAN REVOLUTION SHOWING ALL THE
ACTIONS OF THE WAR

face the facts, in order to realize that the American Colonies did not possess the resources to produce the equipment for American armies that would conform to European standards. If the British had been compelled to rely on the resources of America alone, they would have been in the same predicament. But the British were able to bring by sea all the necessary equipment for their armies. That was the reason for the inequality which prevented any chance of a formal war after the European fashion.

But this fixed condition, which was adverse to the Americans, was balanced by another already established condition that was adverse to the British. The Americans could resort to an irregular warfare, which was effective even to the point of being a forecast of modern warfare. As has been explained, the American Colonists were used to handling firearms, and had given themselves a militia training in the years of dissatisfaction against the King's Ministers. Consequently, the British Regulars were compelled to face a dangerous new element of warfare which was unknown to Europe.

The events which have been described had already proved that the British Regulars were not effective against this new element, a countryside that had risen to arms. The very perfection of their formal training was a disadvantage for them. Their errors were altogether the fault of this artificial school of training, and cast no reflection on their bravery. On the contrary, these troops showed great gallantry throughout the war. It was only when they were bewildered by novel tactics, incomprehensible to them, that they became demoralized. But we must recognize, as an existing condition of the Revolution, that the Regulars, officers and men, were unable to adapt themselves to irregular warfare — and this lasted to the end.

The explanation lay in the fact that all European warfare of that era was rigidly cast in the mould of artificial and formal tactics, of which Frederick the Great was the leading exponent. This has been cited in the preceding narratives, and never must be forgotten when studying the Revolution. For it is almost impossible to-day to have a conception of the state of mind of the trained European soldier of the last half of the eighteenth century. That was the most artificial and conventionalized epoch in military history, and all battles had been reduced to terms of parade-grounds tactics. The whole system soon was to be overthrown by the turbulent fighting armies of the French Revolution. But, while it lasted, it kept the professional European soldier tied to one trend of thought, and totally unable to admit the possibility of any defect in the perfected mechanism of his approved methods of making war.

For this reason the European soldiers, who came to subdue the revolting Americans, were so imbued with the formulas of their military training that they could not change to meet different conditions. Even the experiences of the French and Indian War had been buried under these doctrines. This seems strange, at first thought, but there was a double reason for it. In the first place, the prestige of the school of Frederick the Great had grown so strong that everything else was heresy. And, secondly, the reverses of the first years of that war had been overshadowed by the triumphs of the final years, when the British possessed so great a superiority and conquered Canada. Consequently, in the minds of the British, the whole impression of the French and Indian War was summed up in Wolfe's victory — a triumph for the Regulars.

As a result of all this, the British Regulars were not prepared for the Revolution. The British military leaders came to America with the utmost confidence that a people in arms would not be able to offer any effective resistance to their troops, and consequently they were unable to solve the problems of the unexpected situation which they encountered in America.[1]

This military situation, so different from anything that was possible in Europe, should be clearly understood. On the one hand, the well-equipped British armies possessed a superiority, throughout the ensuing war, that enabled them to win set battles, to take cities and occupy them, provided that these British armies were operating so near the coast that their supplies were assured by sea. The Americans never had the resources to overcome this superiority by equipping armies that could meet the British armies in set battles on equal terms.

But this assured British superiority was limited to the areas where the British armies could be supplied by sea. Inland the British were unable to maintain themselves, much less conquer the countryside. Whenever a British force marched out into the country, it met disaster, and, sooner or later, was either chased back or overwhelmed. Saratoga was only the Lexington and Concord Fight on a large scale. Burgoyne was a victim of the same conditions that had disconcerted the Regulars on the first day of the Revolution. This was also true of what Cornwallis called the 'hornets' nest' in the Carolinas.

These were the two great factors that balanced one another in the Revolution, and created one of the most extraordinary military situations in history. With the Americans never equipped to offer an equal battle in the European sense of the word, and with the British unable to do them-

[1] Lord Amherst, the one British general who best knew the Americans and the conditions in America, had refused to serve against the Americans.

selves justice in inland campaigns under American conditions, there was a strange *impasse*, indeed, which cannot be described in the terms of a European war. Not only must we keep this unusual situation in mind as influencing the course of the ensuing war, but we must also recognize it as imposing limitations on the military career of George Washington.

That Washington's path was beset with obstacles has been often stated. But, in not defining this actual military situation, the broad conditions which 'shaped his ends' have been missed. These two great balancing factors — the one unfavorable to the Americans, the other favorable — inexorably dictated the terms of his leadership. Fate had decreed that he must be a commander in chief who could not hope for an army that would be equal to the enemy's army in a set battle. But he could always count his enemy as being at a marked disadvantage in irregular warfare. This basis of restrictions must be taken into account, when we consider the question of what aims and objects were feasible for the American Commander in Chief in the American Revolution.

It was obvious that his best advantage would be in partisan warfare. But it was equally obvious that he could not induce his powerful enemy to fight the whole war in that way. Consequently, it was out of the question to rely solely on partisan bands to carry on the war. This last would have implied leaving the main British forces unopposed, and free to take possession at will of the important areas near the coast. Only in the outlying regions could partisan resistance be effective. We can dismiss, as impractical, all the fanciful ideas of fighting the war by means of large forces of American riflemen and mounted men. The truth as to the small numbers of riflemen in the American Colonies has been explained. It was the same story in regard to mounted forces. Mounted partisan bands did appear in favorable localities, but there was no possibility of raising large forces of mounted men in the Colonies.

Under these existing conditions, it is only common-sense to realize that the main task of Washington must be to produce the strongest organized army that he could gather. The reason for this was twofold. First of all, there must be an organized American Army, as the only means of neutralizing the British main forces. For it was necessary to restrict their operations as much as possible, even though the American Army would always be at a disadvantage. The second reason for an organized American Army was extremely important, as was shown by the event. Such a military organization was necessary, in order to provide a nucleus and framework for rallying the local militia into coördinated array, against any British force attempting to move into the countryside to subdue it.

In order to appreciate the great value of this special function of an organized American Army, it is only necessary to ask how it would have been possible to give order and direction to the uprising against Burgoyne's invasion, if there had not been an organized army to provide the framework of the structure. This made all the difference in the world. The zealous surge of the militia gathering against Burgoyne provided the numbers, but it was inconceivable that the result would have been attained if it had not been for the organized forces provided by Washington.

We cannot avoid these proofs that the creation of an American army organization was the necessary object of Washington, for the double purpose which has been described, of doing all that was possible to hold in check the superior main forces of the British, and of making the American forces efficient in other regions. In view of all this, the results of Washington's services cannot be estimated in terms of the results of battles, as in a European war. His own actions and campaigns, whether victories or defeats, did not represent the true measure of success or failure. This true measure can only be determined by counting the results over the whole broad field of the situation in America, which was an anomaly when considered from any European point of view.

In addition to this unusual situation in America, there was another unexpected factor which has never been assigned due importance in its influence on the Revolution. Strangely enough, it was on the sea that the Americans were able to score the greatest balance of harm against the British. Washington's little fleet at Boston, which preyed upon the British supplies, had led Congress to the beginning of naval activities. Naturally, the infant Navy was unable to accomplish much against the overwhelming power of the British Navy. But the kindred American privateers were already beginning their depredations, which were to do so much damage to British shipping that, for the first time, privateering became a determining factor in war. Before this, privateering had been a matter of give and take, with profits for each party. But, in the Revolution, there was no proportion of American shipping for the British privateers to prey on that would balance the enormous losses inflicted upon British shipping by the American privateers.[1]

The effect of these losses was constantly felt in Great Britain, even when the situation in America was an impasse. 'In all the memorials presented to Parliament the argument used to bring about peace was the unprecedented destruc-

---

[1] In the Revolution the American privateers captured or destroyed vessels of the value of $18,000,000. They were enormous losses for those days.

tion of British commerce.' [1] Consequently the unexpected was happening on the sea, as well as on land.

The foregoing chapter is not a brief in any controversy, but it is merely a statement of fact in regard to the extraordinary situation which must be taken into account when studying the military career of George Washington.

[1] Maclay: *History of the American Privateers.*

Chapter XIV

AFTER THE EVACUATION OF BOSTON

IT WAS so certain that the British would make a descent
in force upon New York in 1776, that it might almost be
called a matter of common knowledge. There had been
plenty of information of this intention, both from British
and Loyalist sources. Indeed, it was clearly the right move
for the superior main forces of the British, in the existing
military situation which has been described in the preceding
chapter.

New York, of all places in the American Colonies, was
best adapted to be the base of operations for a strong and
well-equipped army, that depended upon the sea for its
maintenance. As early as January, 1776, Washington had
sent Major General Lee to New York, with instructions 'to
put the City and fortifications in the best posture for defense the season and the circumstances will admit of.'[1]
As soon as it seemed definitely settled that the British would
evacuate Boston, Washington's first thought was for New
York — 'to frustrate the designs which the enemy have of
possessing it.'[2]

At this very time (March 7, 1776) Lee was ordered to
leave New York to take command of the newly organized
Southern Department, which comprised Virginia, the

[1] Washington to Governor Trumbull, January 7, 1776.
[2] Washington to the President of Congress, March 13, 1776.

112

Carolinas, and Georgia. Brigadier General Stirling was left in acting command. To Stirling, as commander at New York, Washington wrote a letter (March 14, 1776), in which he stated, 'I am of the opinion that New York is the place of their destination.' And he also pointed out the strategic value of New York and its river, by use of which the British might be able to 'stop the intercourse between the northern and southern colonies, upon which depends the safety of America.'

In thinking that the British general would follow this plan of operations, Washington was judging the intentions of the enemy by his own energetic intuition of what would be the best policy. He was undoubtedly right in this perception that the British ought to hasten to occupy New York, and he had good grounds for his apprehensions. But the British commander was cast in a different mould. Prompt seizure of New York was out of the question, because an energetic move was not at all in keeping with the deliberate methods and indolent nature of General Howe, who had no intention other than to proceed to Halifax. His one idea was to refit his army, and to move against New York at his leisure. And Howe's leisure always meant aimless procrastination. Even in departing for Halifax, he dallied, and kept his fleet off Boston from March 17 to March 27.

Washington could not understand this delay, and he wrote to General Stirling (March 19): 'The fleet is still in King's and Nantasket Roads, and where they intend to make a descent next is altogether unknown.' But, although Washington was much puzzled by this delay,[1] he was so convinced of the advantages for the British of an immediate descent upon New York, that he remained unchanged in

[1] 'What they are doing, the Lord knows. Various are the conjectures.' (Washington to Joseph Reed, March 25, 1776.)

113

'supposing New York to be an object of much importance and to be in their views.'

In this belief that New York would be the next theater of military operations Washington had planned, as soon as the British should leave Boston, to move his army at once from the vicinity of Boston to New York. But, while the enemy lingered near Boston, he could not offer the British an opening by leaving the city unguarded. He wrote to the President of Congress (March 19, 1776): 'But as they are still in the harbor, I thought it not prudent to march off with the main body of the army, until I should be fully satisfied they had quitted the coast.' Consequently he had remained, watching the enemy.

As soon as he was sure the British had actually sailed away from Boston Harbor, Washington carried out his intention of transferring the American Army to New York. He sent Major General Putnam to New York, in advance, with the following instructions: 'When you arrive there, you will assume the command, and immediately proceed in continuing to execute the plan proposed by Major General Lee for fortifying the city and the East and North River.' On April 1, 1776, Washington wrote to Joseph Reed that he was 'hurried in despatching one brigade after another to New York, and preparing for my own departure by pointing out the duties of those that remain behind me.'

The troops left behind were under the command of General Ward, who was instructed to fortify Boston against incursions of the enemy, although it was obvious that the British had abandoned serious military operations in Massachusetts. On April 4, Washington himself left Cambridge for New York.

Just after the British had sailed away from Boston, and when Washington could feel the first relief from his long strain of anxieties, he wrote an intimate letter to his brother,[1] in which, for the first time, he opened his heart as to the ordeal through which he had passed: 'I believe I may with great truth affirm, that no man perhaps since the first institution of armies ever commanded one under more difficult circumstances, than I have done. To enumerate the particulars would fill a volume. Many of my difficulties and distresses were of so peculiar a cast that, in order to conceal them from the enemy, I was obliged to conceal them from my friends, and indeed from my own army, subjecting my conduct to interpretations unfavorable to my character, especially by those at a distance who could not in the smallest degree be acquainted with the springs that govern it.' This was a moving revelation of the true Washington, alone and apart from all, contending through the long months with the manifold problems that he alone must solve.

In this letter, after explaining to his brother the constant shortage of ammunition, he summed up the events of the winter in one remarkable sentence, 'We have maintained our ground against the enemy, under this want of powder, and we have disbanded one army, and recruited another, within musket-shot of two and twenty regiments, the flower of the British Army.'

It was this knowledge, of having overawed the enemy with only so weak an army, that led Washington to censure the British for giving up Boston. And, it is interesting to read, this withdrawal reminded him of the demoralization after Braddock's defeat — a very sore memory for Washington. He wrote that the British 'embarked in as much hurry, precipitation, and confusion, as ever troops did, not taking time to fit their transports, but leaving the King's property in Boston to the amount, as is supposed, of thirty or forty

[1] George Washington to John Augustine Washington, March 31, 1776.

thousand pounds in provisions and stores. .... In short Dunbar's destruction of stores after General Braddock's defeat, which made so much noise, affords but a faint idea of what was to be met with here.'

While gathering the American Army to send to New York, Washington was handicapped by the expired enlistments, and these greatly reduced the numbers of troops available.[1] In this regard, Washington expressed himself forcibly: 'From former experience, we have found it as practicable to stop a torrent as these people when their time is up.' [2] This released some anger that had been held in check through the troubles of the siege.

The trusted Knox had been ordered to make a tour of the Rhode Island and Connecticut coast, on his way to New York, to gather supplies, and to devise protection against the enemy naval forces. Knox especially recommended New London and Newport, in conjunction, to 'afford a safe retreat to the American navy or their prizes in any wind that blows,' and he proposed plans for fortifying these ports. On March 6, Brigadier General Thomas had been promoted by Congress to the rank of Major General. He was assigned to command the American troops in Canada, and left to assume his duties on March 21, 1776.

As has been told, in the account of the mistaken American invasion of Canada, the project was already a failure. And this persistence to continue the invasion was only dooming it to worse disaster, upon the arrival of the great numbers of troops which the British Ministers were sending to Canada. The Americans had no idea of the strength of these forces, which had been so largely augmented by the soldiers secured from the German princes. Only when these Hessians began

[1] Return of Army, May 2, 1776, 8843.
[2] George Washington to Joseph Reed, March 25, 1776.

to arrive, did the Americans realize that the odds were hopelessly against them.

The depleted American troops, who had remained near Quebec through the winter, were left under the command of General Wooster. Arnold's wounded leg had been injured again, by his horse falling, and he had gone to Montreal, where he assumed command. Sir Guy Carleton had wisely remained in the fortress of Quebec. The Americans were too weak to threaten serious harm, and he could wait in security for his reinforcements. When General Thomas arrived to take command of the Americans, he had only time to make an abortive attempt with a fire ship (May 3, 1776). Then the arrival of the enemy reinforcements, both Regulars and Hessians, left him no alternative but to retreat before them.

The rest was only a story of sufferings and disaster. There was a frightful outbreak of smallpox among the Americans, and what reinforcements came to them merely shared their sufferings. General Thomas himself died of the smallpox (June 2, 1776), and Brigadier General Sullivan, who had arrived with the American reinforcements, assumed command.

At first Sullivan was optimistic over the situation, and reported that he would be able to continue the invasion. Upon this, Congress appointed Major General Gates to the command in Canada (June 18). But, just as this appointment was being made, the final curtain was falling for the American invasion. The new arrivals of Regulars and Hessians, which had not been estimated by the Americans, had increased the British forces in Canada to thirteen thousand.

Against the advance of these superior numbers, under General Burgoyne, Sullivan's twenty-five hundred Americans could offer no resistance. Sullivan's reluctance to give up all hold on Canada, and his attempt to make a stand on the Sorel, only led to increased losses. Arnold was driven from Montreal, and all that Sullivan could do was to bring the remnants of the American troops to the shelter of Crown Point. In a letter to Washington, at this stage, General Sullivan described 'this wretched army, now perhaps the most pitiful that ever was formed.'

In any account of this disaster, there always should be mention of the unvarying kindness and humanity shown by Sir Guy Carleton, in his treatment of the American prisoners. Many of these were sick and wounded, and all were in forlorn condition.

In the South, there was an opposite result, as the British met signal defeat in an attempt on South Carolina with strong forces. After the rising of the Loyalists had been suppressed so quickly and decisively in North Carolina, General Clinton had seen that it was useless to make any military effort in that Colony. He had kept his British force in its shipping off the Southern coast, waiting for the expected reinforcements from Great Britain. These troops consisted of six regiments and seven companies in transports, with accompanying warships, under Sir Peter Parker. His fleet had sailed from Cork on February 12, but it had a most unfavorable passage across the Atlantic. It was not until May 3 that the bulk of the convoy arrived at Cape Fear.

This put Clinton in command of a truly formidable force. He issued a proclamation to the 'inhabitants of the several colonies' and prepared to assert the Royal cause.[1] The deposed Royal Governor of South Carolina had persuaded

---

[1] 'The effect produced by this proclamation was trifling, and the cause of Great Britain acquired by it but a small addition of adherents.' (Stedman: *History of the American War.*)

118

him that there was a better field in South Carolina for arousing Loyalist support, and Clinton resolved to make a beginning by the capture of Charleston. It never entered his mind that there would be any difficulty in doing this — still less that the Americans would be able to devise a defense that would balk him.

In full confidence of success, Clinton's preparations were made with the dilatory slowness that came to be characteristic of the British operations in the Revolution. He waited to gather the last ships of his convoy, and did not arrive off Charleston until June 4. In the mean time, the Americans had built a fort on Sullivan's Island, in Charleston Harbor, which was garrisoned by twelve hundred men under Colonel William Moultrie, and General Lee had gathered five thousand militia near the city. Moultrie's fort was an innovation, as it had been built of green palmetto logs and sand, quite in the modern idea for resisting gunfire, and the event proved that it possessed this quality to an unexpected degree.[1]

The British commander, after delaying until June 28, made an attack upon this fort. But the British attack was so poorly devised that it had no chance of success. Clinton landed a strong force on an island, which was separated from Sullivan's Island by only a narrow stretch of water. This water Clinton, in a haphazard way, assumed would be fordable at low tide, and he planned to pass his troops across, under cover of a battery he built on shore. Sir Peter Parker's warships were to engage the fort at the same time.

The execution of this plan was a total failure. The water

[1] 'In his character of trained European officer, Lee laughed at Moultrie's palmetto stronghold, and would have ordered him to abandon it, but that he was positively overruled by John Rutledge, president of the Provincial Congress, who knew Moultrie and relied upon his sound judgment.' (John Fiske: *The American Revolution.*)

was too deep for the troops to wade through, and, consequently, the troops could not take part in the attack on the fort. It became merely an action between the fort and the British fleet. In this action Moultrie's fort had all the better of it. The gunfire of the fleet was unable to do any serious damage to the fort, but the fleet was so shattered by the gunfire of the fort that it was unfit for another action.

In fact, the attack was never renewed. For, after spending weeks in repairing the damages sustained by the warships of the fleet, Clinton's whole force sailed away, in the last week of July, to join Howe at New York. This reverse marked the cessation of serious British attempts to subdue the Southern Colonies for a period of two years.

Chapter xv

THE SHIFT OF THE SCENE TO NEW YORK

ON APRIL 15, 1776, Washington reported to the President of Congress, from New York: 'I am now to inform you, that on the 4th instant I set out from Cambridge and arrived here on Saturday last. I came through Providence, Norwich, and New London, in order to see and expedite the embarkation of the troops.' New York was inevitably to be the storm center of events, and Washington was moving into another field of harassing anxieties.

At New York, in addition to the certainty of the impending arrival of the British main forces, there was a situation similar to that in the Southern Colonies, which has been described. The deposed Royal Governor Tryon was on board British shipping in the lower bay, and was constantly making attempts to arouse the Loyalists to an outbreak. The strange condition existed that, by tacit consent, he had been allowed to maintain himself there by taking on board supplies from the shore,[1] and communication with the shore was not forbidden.

This state of affairs could not fail to do harm, and Washington at once put an end to it. In a strong letter to the Committee of Safety of New York,[2] he pointed out the evils

---

[1] '... and fresh provisions are to be delivered on the governor's Island for the *Asia.*' (Governor Tryon to Earl of Dartmouth, September 5, 1775.)

[2] April 17, 1776.

of 'the intercourse, which has hitherto subsisted between the inhabitants of this colony and the enemy on board their ships of war,' and asked the Committee to 'coöperate' in putting an end to such intercourse. The Committee of Safety at once acceded, and passed a resolution in accordance. This was followed by a Proclamation [1] from General Washington calling for 'utmost care and diligence for preventing the same, and apprehending and securing all persons who shall be guilty thereof.'

Washington's stand in this matter had a good effect on the situation in New York. From this time, there was little anxiety as to dangers within the Colony. Naturally, there were local plots in New York. In June one of Washington's guard was convicted of treachery and executed. But there was nothing that threatened a dangerous outbreak. The one real danger was the approaching arrival of the British troops.

Fortunately the long delays of the British, both in sailing from Halifax and in sending troops from Great Britain, were postponing their arrival at New York which was daily expected by Washington. The contemporary British historian of the Revolution was severe in his criticism of these delays: 'It may not be unnecessary to mention here, that it was the general opinion that Sir William Howe should have gone to Long Island instead of Halifax . . . and by that means have been enabled to have opened the campaign much earlier. . . . The late arrival of this reinforcement is to be particularly lamented, because, for some time before this period, General Washington's army did not amount to nine thousand men fit for duty; two thousand of whom were entirely destitute of arms. It must therefore be sufficiently apparent, that most important advantages would have accrued to the

[1] April 29, 1776.

British cause if the campaign had commenced two months earlier than it did. The American army must then have been inevitably overwhelmed by the superiority of numbers and of discipline opposed to it.' [1]

All this was a true picture of the situation. But any such early start of the campaign, on the part of the British, was out of the question. As has been stated, and as will be shown by the narratives of the events throughout the war, long delays invariably attended the British operations. These delays should not be counted as always the fault of the individual leaders, but rather as the result of the cumbersome methods of making war, which were then prevalent in Europe.

In the respite thus allowed to Washington, and in consequence of his own personal exertions, the American army in the vicinity of New York doubled its numbers. But the increase was of raw material, and he was again making a new army.

In May, Washington was commanded to Philadelphia, to confer with Congress on the military situation. This conference with Congress was of benefit. Washington persuaded Congress to authorize three-year enlistments, with the additional inducements of bounties.[2] A permanent Board of War and Ordnance was created.[3] Before this, military matters had been referred to committees of Congress appointed for the time being. It was also agreed that the American forces should be strengthened by a large increase of the militia in the neighboring Colonies, and Washington was given authority to summon these militia

[1] Stedman: *History of the American War.*

[2] Ten dollars for each recruit.

[3] First members, John Adams, Benjamin Harrison, Roger Sherman, James Wilson, Edward Rutledge, Richard Peters, Secretary.

at any emergency. At Washington's urgent request, his trusted confidant Joseph Reed was appointed Adjutant General of the army.

While Washington was at Philadelphia, he received the news of another instance of the efficiency of the little fleet of armed vessels he had commissioned during the siege of Boston. On May 17, Captain James Mugford, of Marblehead, brought into Boston the British ship *Hope* with fifteen hundred pounds of powder and other stores.[1] Two days later, Captain Mugford was killed in a desperate and successful defense of his vessel, the *Franklin*, against an attack by boats from a British warship off Nantasket.[2]

On Washington's return from Philadelphia, he wrote to the President of Congress (June 7, 1776), 'I found all in a state of peace and quiet.' This reflected the good results of the measures Washington had taken for the internal control of New York. These precautions had put an end to all worries concerning Governor Tryon and the Loyalists. And, it should be stated here, this remained a condition during the ensuing campaign. No bodies of Loyalists appeared that were strong enough to influence the military situation in the vicinity of New York. It became solely a question of coping with the British main forces.

In regard to the preparations to defend New York, Washington wrote in the same letter to the President of Congress, as to 'the works carrying on, and those ordered to be begun

[1] Washington to Putnam, Philadelphia, May 28, 1776:
'Sir: I received yours of the 24th inst with its several inclosures, and the Letters and Invoice from Genl Ward giving Intelligence of the fortunate capture made by our Armed Vessels, on which event you have my congratulations.'

[2] Although mortally wounded, Captain Mugford continued to animate his crew, exclaiming, 'Do not give up the ship—you will beat them off!' In a few minutes he died. His men beat off the enemy, and the body of Captain Mugford was carried to Marblehead for burial.

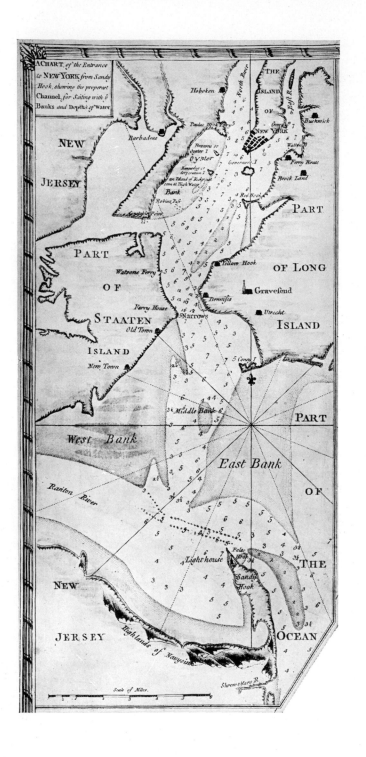

A CHART of the Entrance to NEW YORK from Sandy Hook, shewing the properest Channel, for Sailing with ye Banks and Depths of Water

NEW JERSEY

Barbadoes

Hoboken

THE ISLAND OF NEW YORK

Coney's

Bushwick

Paulus Hook Ferry

Branns or Oyster I.

Kennedys corporation I.

an Island of Rocks seen at High Water

Bank

Robins Rest

Sandy Point

Walton I.

Governors I.

Breck Land

Red Hook

PART

OF LONG

Yellow Hook

Watrons Ferry

Dennises

Gravesend

Ferry House

Narrows

Staaten

Island

Old Town

New Town

Utrecht

ISLAND

Coney I.

Middle Bank

West Bank

East Bank

PART

Rariton River

OF

Light house

Pale Hook

Sandy Hook

THE

NEW

JERSEY

Highlands of Navysin

OCEAN

Scale of Miles

Shrewsbury R.

when I went away'; 'I have reason to believe, from the report of such of the general and other officers I had the pleasure to see, that they had been prosecuted and forwarded with all possible diligence and despatch.'

These 'works' were the developments of the fortifications devised and begun by Lee, and continued after he had been sent to the Southern Department. That these fortifications were of very slight military value is now evident, beyond any question. Against incursions of the enemy in small force they might have been effective. But, against the strong British forces Howe was to have under his command at New York, they were utterly useless. There was no possibility of constructing a citadel that could stand a siege. And a study of the map will show also, that there was no possibility of devising a system of fortifications which would support one another, in order to provide a basis for defense against the superior British forces.

The locations of the adjacent islands, and the water courses of the Hudson River, made the American fortified positions merely isolated points against an enemy who possessed a strong fleet of warships. This was the condition in the ensuing operations. The British had a powerful naval force — the Americans had no naval force. The keen and able Knox, who met quick disillusion in the course of events, summed up this situation in words that expressed it all: 'The general features or outlines of what has already happened have, almost ever since I have been this way, been fully impressed on my mind. Islands separated from the main by navigable waters are not to be defended by a people without a navy against a nation who can send a powerful fleet to interrupt the communication.' [1]

With this existing situation, we must consider it estab-

[1] General Knox to his brother, September 23, 1776.

125

lished that the Americans did not possess the means to make a successful defense of New York against the overwhelming British forces that were to be brought into action. It is also true that the Americans, when they were making their preparations for defense, did not foresee this great strength of the British forces. The American leaders had been thinking too much in terms of the British army at Halifax. Washington's letters proved that it was not until May, 1776, that he had any intimation of the accession of German troops,[1] and he was at first inclined to the belief that the report was 'exaggerated.'[2]   All the preparations to defend New York were made with the idea that they would encounter British forces much less powerful than those destined to appear at New York.

In the mean time, the tide was running strongly for independence. The events in the South, which have been described, had given an impetus in this direction, and this made it inevitable Congress would declare the American Colonies independent States. When at last General Howe arrived off New York with his army from Halifax, the die was already cast, and the Declaration of Independence was about to be adopted.

Howe had sailed from Halifax on June 11, and his troop ships were in New York Bay on June 29. He landed his troops on Staten Island, where he encamped and waited for his expected reinforcements. Those from Great Britain, including the German troops, began to arrive in the next two weeks, convoyed by the fleet under General Howe's brother, Admiral Lord Howe. As these troops came into

[1] Letter to President of Congress, May 7, 1776, as to intelligence from Thomas Cushing.

[2] General Washington to Thomas Cushing, May 9, 1776: '...I hope is exaggerated; it appears inconsistent and impossible in part.'

the bay, they were also landed and encamped on Staten Island.

Lord Howe had made many friends in the American Colonies during the French and Indian War, and 'he sincerely designed to act the part of a mediator.' [1] Upon his arrival, he attempted to play this rôle with the American leaders, including Washington and Franklin. But it was then too late for any mediation. The Declaration of Independence had been adopted by Congress on July 4, 1776, and it had been approved by the Convention of New York at White Plains on July 9. The Colonies were thus aligned for independence.

Lord Howe's efforts to bring about a reconciliation were greatly to his credit. He showed a real feeling of friendship. But, aside from the fact that the rupture had already been effected, Lord Howe was handicapped by the wording of his instructions from the British Ministers. He and his brother were given only authority to treat with the revolting Colonists as individuals. When copies of his declaration were sent about in America, it became evident that the sole authority was to grant pardons and receive submissions. There was nothing as to the great questions at issue between America and Great Britain. Under these circumstances, Lord Howe's well-meant intercession only produced an effect unfavorable for Great Britain.

Among the negotiators had been the Adjutant General of Howe's army, and admitting him to an interview, at American Headquarters in New York, led to one result of great benefit, an arrangement for exchanges of prisoners. General Howe's instructions from the British Ministers had forbidden ' any treaty or agreement with the rebels for a regular cartel for exchange of prisoners.' However, this was modi-

[1] Bancroft: *History of the United States.*

fied by writing to him, 'But your own discretion will suggest to you the means of effecting such exchange without the King's dignity and honor being committed, or his majesty's name being used in any negotiations for that purpose.' With this discretionary permission, the British commander assented to a project adopted by Congress for giving each department commander the right to exchange prisoners of war. On this informal basis there was a practice of exchanging prisoners that lasted through the war.

The great fleet, bearing the British and German troops from Great Britain, had all arrived in New York Bay, and, in addition, the force of General Clinton from the South had joined General Howe. These accessions gave to the British commander early in August, 1776, an army of a strength beyond anything that had been expected by the Americans. The British account stated, 'The reinforcements brought from England amounted, with the troops already in America, to near thirty thousand men.' [1] Then and there the superiority of the British main forces was established. The British history has emphasized this numerical superiority: 'The British troops were, as usual, greatly superior in point of number to the Americans.' [2]

Needless to say, the odds against Washington for making a defense of New York were hopeless. Not only did Howe possess this greatly superior army, but Lord Howe's fleet of warships gave the British undisputed command of the waters about New York. The British commander could land his army at will for an attack on the American defenders.

In a letter to Governor Trumbull (August 7, 1776)

[1] Stedman: *History of the American War.*

[2] Stedman: *History of the American War.* On page 284, vol. 1, there is a table showing British superiority in 1776 and 1777.

Washington wrote of his first realization of the overwhelming strength of Howe's army: 'By two deserters this day, we have the following intelligence, namely, that General Clinton and Lord Cornwallis, with the whole southern army, have arrived and landed on Staten Island from South Carolina ... in the whole making about thirty thousand men.' At this, Washington recognized that the emergency existed for calling out the local militia, by using the authority given to him by Congress. In the same letter he wrote, 'I think it absolutely necessary that the neighboring militia should be immediately sent to our assistance.'

In a letter to the President of Congress (August 8, 1776) Washington wrote of 'information corroborating their accounts respecting the Hessian troops': 'Indeed his report makes the fleet and armament to be employed against us, greater than we have heard they would be. ... Persuaded of this, and knowing how much Inferior our Numbers are and will be to theirs, when the whole of the troops arrive — of the important consequences that may and will flow from the appeal that will soon be made, I have wrote to Connecticut and New Jersey for all the succor they could afford, and also to the Convention of this State.[1] What I may receive, and in what time the event must determine. But I would feign hope, the situation, the exigency of our affairs, will call forth the most strenuous efforts and early assistance of those, who are friends of the cause. I confess there is too much occasion for their exertions. I confidently trust they will not be withheld. ... Under every disadvantage my utmost exertions shall be employed to bring about the great end we have in view, and so far as I can judge from the professions and apparent disposition of my Troops, I shall have their

[1] It is interesting to note Washington's use of the term 'Convention of this State.' It was no longer a Colony.

support. The superiority of the Enemy and the expected attack, do not seem to have depressed their spirits. Those considerations lead me to think that tho' the appeal may not terminate so happily in our favor as I could wish, yet they will not succeed in their views without considerable loss. Any advantage they may get, I trust will cost them dear.'

Chapter XVI

THE BATTLE OF LONG ISLAND AND THE WITHDRAWAL OF THE AMERICANS

AFTER General Howe's army had reached its full strength at the first of August, 1776, his preparations to attack the Americans were made in the leisurely way that was characteristic of the British commander. He did not begin his campaign until the third week of the month. This gave time for Washington's emergency call upon the neighboring militia to add numbers to the American Army. On August 18, Washington was able to write to Governor Trumbull, 'Our situation was truly alarming a little while since; but, by the kind interposition and aid of our friends, it is now much better.'

In the same letter he wrote of an attempt with the fireships which had been prepared by the Americans. This attack on British ships (August 16) ended in failure. In fact, there was not any chance of fireships and obstructions in the river waters providing an effective defense against the strong British naval forces.

Reinforcements of militia had come in from New England, New York, and from the 'Flying Camp,' which had been established in New Jersey. But they were all new levies, with very little training, and although the American army was increased by these accessions to over eighteen thousand, they were not troops that could be relied upon in the test of hard service.

Washington wrote to the President of Congress (August 20, 1776) that, according to the general report among the British troops, 'they were to attack Long Island, and to secure our works there if possible, at the same time that another part of their army was to land above this city. This information is corroborated by many other accounts, and is probably true; nor will it be possible to prevent their landing on the Island, as its great extent affords a variety of places favorable for that purpose, and the whole of our works upon it are at the end opposite to the city. However we shall attempt to harass them as much as possible, which will be all that we can do.'

On August 22, Washington wrote to General Heath, who commanded the northern positions, as to the expected passage of the British above New York. On the next day he wrote to the New York Convention, urging the removal of the women and children from the city, and giving every assurance that there was no intention of burning New York, in case the Americans should be obliged to evacuate the place.

It was natural that the Americans should be apprehensive of a British expedition to push above the city,[1] but General Howe never had any such intention. His one plan was to land the main body of his troops on Long Island, and he had no idea of using his fleet for any other purpose. This meant an actual concentration of the British army against the American works on Long Island. There is no profit in considering the ensuing operations from any other point of

[1] Knox, in the letter to his brother after he had realized Howe's great strength, wrote: 'This would have left fifteen thousand men at least to have made a push up the North River, and landed in our rear and fortified. Had they taken this measure, which in good policy they ought to have done, they might at one stroke have reduced the whole army to the necessity of becoming prisoners without being able to fight in the least.'

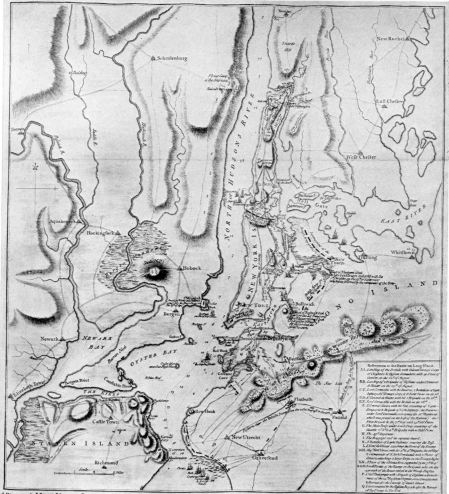

A PLAN of *NEW YORK ISLAND,* with part of *LONG ISLAND, STATEN ISLAND & EAST NEW JERSEY,* with a particular Description of the ENGAGEMENT on the Woody Heights of Long Island, between FLATBUSH and BROOKLYN, on the 27th of August 1776. between HIS MAJESTY'S FORCES Commanded by General HOWE and the AMERICANS under Major General PUTNAM. Shewing also the Landing of the BRITISH ARMY on New-York Island, and the Taking of the CITY of NEW YORK &c. on the 15th of September following, with the Subsequent Disposition of Both the Armies.

Engraved & Published according to Act of Parliament Oct.r 19.th 1776, by W.m Faden, successor to the late Mr.r Jefferys, Geographer to the King, Charing Cross LONDON.

view. In pursuance of this plan, General Howe landed twenty thousand men at Gravesend Bay on August 22.

The American works on Long Island were intrenchments to fortify Brooklyn Heights, and they shut off the point of land between the fringes of Wallabout Bay and the inlets of Gowanus Cove. Greene had been in command there after his arrival from Boston, and he had taken great pains to make the position as strong as possible. At the time of the British landing on Long Island, General Greene was very ill, and General Sullivan was in command in his place. At the news that the British were on Long Island, Washington reinforced the troops there to nine thousand men, and he had sent Putnam to take general command on the Island.

A study of the map will show at once that the Americans at Brooklyn Heights were at the disadvantage of being an isolated force. Moreover, they were so far separated by water from the rest of the army, that they not only were without hope of any support, but they were also in danger of being cut off by the naval superiority of the enemy. All that could be urged to justify this risk was contained in the words of Washington, which have been quoted — 'to harass them as much as possible, which will be all that we can do.' This cannot be held a sufficient excuse for exposing half the American army to so great a risk.

It was true that Washington's information led him at first to underestimate the number of troops Howe had landed on Long Island.[1] He had been told, 'The foreigners are yet upon Staten Island.' [2] This was an error, as a great part of the German troops, under General Heister and Colonel Dunop, had been also sent to Long Island. But the per-

---

[1] 'Eight or nine thousand.' (Letters of August 23 and 24, 1776.)
[2] Letter of August 24, 1776.

sistence in attempting to defend the American position at Brooklyn Heights, even after the full strength of the British had been developed, can only be considered unreasonable. This is a true description, because it was a military situation which was not founded on military reasons.

In this case, Washington was being dominated by public opinion. He was not yet asserting himself as a military Commander in Chief. It is not difficult to understand the pressure upon him. An exaggerated importance was attached to the possession of New York. Congress insisted upon its defense, and all local leaders joined in this demand. For many months fortifications had been prepared for this defense. Yet, if Brooklyn Heights were abandoned to the enemy, it would be another case of Dorchester Heights, and New York must be abandoned. Therefore Brooklyn Heights must be defended at all costs. This was the sequence to which Washington submitted.

But, granting all this, there was no excuse for the local dispositions of the defense, with an advance force pushed forward in a dangerously exposed position. It is self-evident that when an advance force has been sent out to harass an approaching superior enemy, this advance force must, above all else, be on the alert to avoid being enveloped by the superior enemy. Yet this precaution was utterly neglected by the Americans on Long Island, an inexcusable blunder of the officers on the field.

This American advance force occupied a wooded ridge two miles from the Brooklyn Heights intrenchments. On the right was a division under Stirling. In the center was a division under Sullivan. On the left, where the ridge was crossed by the Jamaica Road, there were not even guards or scouts. Against this faulty position of the American advance force, the British were allowed to operate at their leisure. It was not a matter of any quick surprise, but of over four days after the British landing.

What happened was best expressed in the words of the British contemporary historian: 'In the mean time Sir Henry Clinton and Sir William Erskine, having reconnoitred the position of the enemy, saw that it would not be a difficult matter to turn their left flank, which would either oblige them to risk an engagement, or to retire under manifest disadvantage. This intelligence being communicated to Sir William Howe, he consented to make the attempt.' [1]

In carrying out the flanking movement, it is almost incredible to relate, more than half of Howe's army was able to march, over the Jamaica Road to Bedford in the rear of the American advance force, without being observed by the Americans. This march began in the night of August 26, and, in the morning of the next day, Howe was in position to attack Sullivan and Stirling in the rear, while the rest of the British and German troops engaged their fronts.

Under these conditions, the two American divisions, of which the combined numbers were not much in excess of four thousand, were enveloped by over four times their strength, and, as a matter of course, they were totally defeated.[2] The Americans offered a stubborn resistance, especially the Maryland troops under Stirling. But it was only by scattering, and finding their way back to Brooklyn Heights, that the defeated Americans were able to escape. About four hundred were killed and wounded on each side, but Howe captured over one thousand of the Americans. Both Sullivan and Stirling were captured by the British. This was the battle of Long Island (August 27, 1776).

[1] Stedman: *History of the American War.*
[2] 'They in their first attack on Long Island, lost us by our own fault in not guarding the passes.' (Knox, letter of September 23, 1776.)

But the success of that day was not pressed by the British general. Again the caution, which had been instilled into Howe by his experiences at Boston, served as a protection for the Americans. Howe sent what Fiske justly called a 'somewhat highly colored' [1] dispatch to England, giving an exaggerated account of his victory, for effect in Great Britain. On the other hand, Howe resolved upon a continued policy of caution, and he made this a matter of record by writing, 'As it was apparent that the lines must become ours, at a very cheap rate, by regular approaches, I would not risk the loss that might have been sustained in the assault, and ordered them back to a hollow way out of reach of the musketry.' Consequently, as the British historian expressed it, 'On the evening of the twenty-seventh, our army encamped in front of the enemy's lines; and on the twenty-eighth broke ground about six hundred yards from one of the redoubts on the left.' [2]

General Putnam had been in command on Long Island throughout the operations that culminated in the action of August 27. On that day, at the news of the battle, Washington crossed over to Brooklyn Heights, and busied himself to reorganize the defense after the defeat. On the next day he brought over reinforcements, and prepared to resist a British assault. But, when he saw that Howe, instead of intending to make an attack, was beginning siege operations, Washington at once realized that the position at Brooklyn Heights was untenable. The only course was to remove the American troops from Brooklyn Heights before the British commander made this impossible by means of his naval forces.

At this crisis, for it cannot be described in any other

[1] Fiske: *The American Revolution.*
[2] Stedman: *History of the American War.*

136

terms, Washington suddenly became the American Commander in Chief, in every sense of the word. He called a council of war, and the decision was made to abandon Brooklyn Heights. Upon this decision, Washington at once acted, with the volcanic energy that was always latent under his self-controlled demeanor — and he accomplished a feat that seemed an impossibility.

In the next twenty-four hours he gathered enough of the local small craft, in addition to the boats already in use for transportation, to enable him to remove all the American troops, with their artillery and equipment to the New York side. And this was accomplished in the one night of August 29. It was truly an extraordinary achievement — and only made possible by the personal exertions of Washington. He again made use of Glover's Essex County regiment, from which he had drawn the crews of his little fleet of warships at Boston. And again this Massachusetts regiment proved its title to be called 'amphibious,' as it provided experienced boatmen to man the craft used for this difficult task of transportation. Probably no other regiment in the world would have been able to meet this demand.

In Washington's letter to the President of Congress, giving his report of the event (August 31, 1776), there is the following description of the tense hours of this withdrawal, 'Since Monday, scarce any of us have been out of the lines till our passage across the East River was effected yesterday morning; and, for forty-eight hours preceding that, I had hardly been off my horse, and had never closed my eyes; so that I was quite unfit to write or to dictate till this morning.'

The account of the British contemporary historian [1] showed vividly the impression made at the time upon the

[1] Stedman: *History of the American War.*

British, and it is also a good statement of the situation: 'The retreat was effected in thirteen hours, though nine thousand men had to pass over the river, besides field artillery, ammunition, provisions, cattle, horses, and carts. The circumstances of this retreat were particularly glorious to the Americans. They had been driven to the corner of an island where they were hemmed in within the narrow space of two square miles. In their front was an encampment of twenty thousand men; in their rear, an arm of the sea, a mile wide, which they could not cross, but in several embarkations. Notwithstanding these difficulties, they secured a retreat without the loss of a man.'

The foregoing has given a true account of the essentials of the Battle of Long Island and the withdrawal of the American army. The controversies over these events have dealt too much with details. There can be no question of the fact that half the American army was placed in a position that ran the risk of what would have been the greatest disaster of the war. For this Washington must bear the blame, as allowing other considerations to impose this false military position. But, on the other hand, Washington redeemed this dangerous situation by his own energetic conduct.

As to the withdrawal of the American troops to the New York side, this must be considered only as a very wonderful feat of transportation. All the discussions as to the possibilities of interference on the part of the British have been wasted words, because it never entered the mind of Howe, nor the minds of the other British leaders, that such a retreat was feasible. From their point of view, it was inconceivable that so many troops could be transported over the East River in one night, and therefore they never imagined that the withdrawal would be attempted. For this reason, the Americans were in no danger from the British. It was only a question of the Americans being able to accomplish this unprecedented task.

The achievement of this retreat was a complete surprise for the astonished British commander, who woke to find that what he had deemed his sure prey had disappeared like a phantom of the night.

Washington's statement for the Orderly Book (August 31, 1776) was as follows, 'In these circumstances it was thought unsafe to transport the whole of an Army on an Island, or to engage them with a part, and therefore unequal numbers; whereas now, one whole Army is collected together, without water intervening.' Washington thus gave a sound basis for strategy in the ensuing campaign, but again other influences were to prove harmful.

Chapter XVII

THE BRITISH OCCUPATION OF NEW YORK

THE English, being now in possession of Long Island, commanded New York; and Governor's Island, being of course no longer tenable by the enemy, was also evacuated on the night of the thirtieth of August...and thus was all communication with New York prevented by sea.' This was the statement of the British historian [1] as to the situation, after the American retreat from Long Island. The American detachment on Governor's Island, under the command of Colonel William Prescott,[2] had been also transported to New York by means of the same efficient service of boats, 'under the very eyes of the fleet.' [3]

The fact that Washington was able to bring away these American troops, without interruption the very night after the retreat of the main body from Brooklyn Heights, was proof positive, if any other evidence were needed, to show how far the British naval forces were from any idea of interfering with the withdrawal of the Americans from Long Island. This was explained in the preceding chapter, but it should be emphasized again.

It also was evident that General Howe and Lord Howe, instead of realizing the truth, that the British had missed a

---

[1] Stedman: *History of the American War.*
[2] Who commanded at Bunker Hill.
[3] John Fiske: *The American Revolution.*

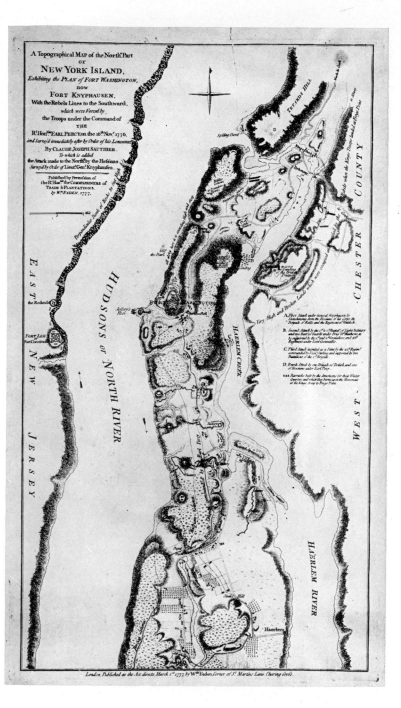

great opportunity,[1] cherished a hope that the reverse on Long Island might exert a demoralizing effect on the revolting Americans. Consequently, Lord Howe thought that it was a propitious time to renew his attempts at negotiations. In this belief, the captured American General Sullivan was sent to Congress by the Howes, to ask for another conference. But again it was made clear that Lord Howe had no authority except to treat with individuals, and could give no assurances beyond saying that the British Government would reconsider the measures which had given offense to the Americans. For this reason, Lord Howe's renewed attempt to negotiate was again without result. The same was true of a declaration he afterwards published, addressed 'to the people of America.' [2]

In the mean time Washington was facing a perplexing problem. It was only too clear to him that he could not hope to defend New York. Yet he was under constant pressure from Congress, and from many of his officers in consequence, urging him to hold the city. From the first, as has been explained, he never possessed forces sufficient to defend New York against the assembled British forces. But at this stage he was worse off, for even the troops he had been able to gather for the emergency were shrinking in numbers. It was the same tale of the militia, undoubtedly possessing fighting qualities at the call of action, but impossible to hold together for a long strain. As Washington wrote to the President of Congress:[3] 'The impulse for going home was so irresistible, that it answered no purpose to oppose it. Though I would not discharge them, I have been

[1] 'So rare a chance of ending the war at a blow was never again to be offered to the British commanders.' (John Fiske: *The American Revolution.*)

[2] 'This declaration however produced but little effect.' (Stedman: *History of the American War.*)

[3] September 8, 1776.

obliged to acquiesce; and it affords one more melancholy proof, how delusive such dependences are.'

Under these circumstances, with rapidly diminishing forces, Washington was still less able to attempt a defense. In his report to the President of Congress Washington gave a clear statement of the situation: [1] 'That the enemy mean to winter in New York, there can be no doubt; that with such an armament, they can drive us out is equally clear. The Congress having resolved, that it should not be destroyed, nothing seems to remain, but to determine the time of their taking possession. It is our interest and wish to prolong it as much as possible, provided the delay does not affect our future measures.'

In the above there is a reference to the veto of Congress against destroying the city, if it should be found necessary to abandon New York. As this has been a point very much misunderstood, the facts of the case, which were a matter of record, should be given. Washington had laid the matter before Congress in a letter of September 2, 1776: 'If we should be obliged to abandon the town, ought it to stand as winter-quarters for the enemy? They would derive great convenience from it on the one hand; and much property would be destroyed on the other. It is an important question, but will admit of but little time for deliberation. At present, I dare say the enemy mean to preserve it, if they can. If Congress, therefore, should resolve upon the destruction of it, the resolution should be a profound secret, as the knowledge of it will make a change in their plans.'

Congress promptly acted on this question, and it was resolved 'that General Washington be acquainted, that Congress would have special care taken, in case he should find it necessary to quit New York, that no damage be done to the

[1] September 8, 1776.

said city by his troops on their leaving it; the Congress having no doubt of their being able to recover the same, though the enemy should for a time obtain possession of it.' This settled any question of the Americans burning New York upon evacuating the city.

The matter of the evacuation itself was laid before 'the whole council of general officers,' and the following was Washington's report [1] of the result of their deliberations: 'All agreed that the town would not be tenable, if the enemy resolved to bombard and cannonade it; but the difficulty attending a removal operated so strongly, that a course was taken between abandoning it totally and concentrating our whole strength for its defence.... It was concluded to arrange the army under three divisions; five thousand to remain for the defence of the city; nine thousand at Kingsbridge and its dependences, as well to possess and secure those posts, as to be ready to attack the enemy, who are moving eastward on Long Island, if they should attempt to land on this side; the remainder to occupy the intermediate space, and support either; that the sick should be immediately removed to Orangetown, and barracks be prepared at Kingsbridge with all expedition to cover the troops.'

Washington's forces were disposed in accordance, and they thus awaited the movements of the British. Washington himself well expressed the disadvantage of these dispositions — 'the great danger of one part of the army being cut off, before the other can support it, the extremities being at least sixteen miles apart.' He cited the opinion of some of his best officers in favor of 'a total and immediate removal from the city.' Greene was strongly in favor of this. 'But they were overruled by a majority, who thought for the pre-

[1] September 8, 1776.

sent a part of our force might be kept here, and attempt to maintain the city a little longer.' [1]

In these dispositions of troops agreed upon, Putnam was placed in command of the useless five thousand men retained in lower New York, Heath in command of the forces in the Kingsbridge area, and Greene in command of the third division, in the vicinity of Turtle Bay and Kip's Bay. Most fortunately, upon indications of movements on the part of the enemy, Washington had reconvened his council of generals, to urge an immediate evacuation of New York. In this he brought about a change of heart, with the assistance of the special advocacy of Greene and other generals. This council agreed (September 12, 1776) that New York should be abandoned at once, in spite of the opposition of three generals who obstinately clung to the idea of holding the city.

Washington acted promptly upon this resolution to evacuate, and consequently, when General Howe at last decided to occupy New York, the American preparations for evacuation were well under way. Stores and artillery were being removed, and Washington was busy in arranging the retirement of the troops. This was a great benefit in correcting the bad military situation on Manhattan Island, and it was just in time. For the event showed that the British could land at will, and the danger of their cutting off American troops had not been exaggerated. [2]

The British warships found no difficulty in sailing up the North River and the East River and commanding both. After some delays, on September 15, five British warships

[1] Washington to the President of Congress, September 8, 1776.

[2] '...That was extremely perilous; and from every movement of the enemy, and the intelligence received, their plan of operations was to get in our rear.' (Washington to President of Congress, September 14, 1776.)

moved farther up the East River to cover the landing of Howe's first division under Clinton at Kip's Bay (near Thirty-Fourth Street). This was well above the New York of that time. The fire of the warships at once scattered the militia who were stationed at the point, to Washington's great disgust. He had ridden to the spot at the sound of the firing, and he was witness of their retreat in disorder. However, they could not have made a successful resistance to the landing of Clinton's overpowering numbers under the cover of the heavy fire from the warships.

All that remained for the American commander, was to hasten urgent orders to Putnam to get his troops to the north of this British incursion as soon as possible. And he made it his own task to organize the defensive position of the American army at Harlem. Putnam showed the greatest energy in directing the retreat of his troops in person, on horseback and everywhere at need.

Putnam's troops had the narrowest possible escape, in getting north of the British forces just before the British stretched their lines across the narrow island. Putnam's retreat was effected by using the road along the North River to the Bloomingdale Road. At this time the celebrated incident occurred, when Mrs. Murray detained Howe and his officers [1] by giving them a luncheon served with feminine delaying wiles. This actually happened, and the lady should receive all the credit that has been given to her. But, after all, she could not offer her delaying luncheon to the whole British army — and, if Howe had made any preparations to throw his troops promptly across Manhattan with the object of cutting off the Americans below, it would have needed more than this luncheon to avert the danger. But, the fact was, Howe was conducting his operation in char-

[1] On present site of Murray Hill.

145

acteristic leisurely fashion, and he had no plan for cutting off the Americans by a quick movement of the British troops.

Here again the British commander missed a rare opportunity. If the British had landed, with the definite plan of throwing a cordon as quickly as possible across the narrow island, the net would have gathered a goodly haul. Even as it was, Knox barely escaped capture. He had been in New York superintending the withdrawal of the artillery, and was one of the last to leave the city, after Colonel Aaron Burr, one of Putnam's aides, had shown the troops the river way to the Bloomingdale Road.[1]

As to the actual events, it only can be said that the Americans had a fortunate escape from a most faulty position. They had to abandon heavy cannon and quantities of stores, but their losses in men were negligible. On the other hand, the British had gained possession of New York, with practically no losses at all. 'The English encampment extended across the island, on each side of which were stationed ships of war, in order to secure the right and left flanks.'[2]

This description of the British historian not only emphasized a strong feature of the British dispositions, but it also indicated the outstanding weakness of the military position of Washington's army. Lord Howe's naval forces, which defended the flanks of the British, also gave the British the means of outflanking the Americans at will. The British historian has given a vivid picture of this danger, in a criticism of General Howe: 'Instead, therefore, of directing his attention to New York, Sir William Howe ought to have

---

[1] 'His arrival at Harlem, where great anxiety was felt for his safety, was greeted with a shout of welcome, and by an embrace from Washington.' (Drake: *Life and Correspondence of Henry Knox.*)

[2] Stedman: *History of the American War.*

thrown his army round King's Bridge, by which means he would have hemmed in the whole American army; and such a step was not at all impracticable, when we consider the extent of the military and naval resources subservient to his will.' This offensive value of the British naval forces has not been fully estimated in accounts of the campaign. It gave the British commander an advantage, which was the most threatening menace to Washington's army. However, as the British historian has stated, General Howe neglected to use these means against his enemy. After some sharp fighting of detachments on September 16, the British commander remained for an interval of inactivity, with his army disposed opposite the position of Washington's army at Harlem Heights.

As to the situation after the retreat of September 15, Washington reported to Congress on the next day: 'We are now encamped with the main body of the army on the Heights of Harlem, where I should hope the enemy would meet with a defeat in case of an attack, if the generality of our troops would behave with tolerable bravery. But experience, to my extreme affliction, has convinced me that this is rather to be wished for than expected. However I trust there are many who will act like men, and show themselves worthy of the blessings of freedom.'

The last sentences reflected the chagrin of Washington at the retreat of the militia on September 15, of which he had been a witness. But on September 16, the same day he wrote this pessimistic report, his troops redeemed themselves in his eyes by their spirited conduct in action against the British. Washington had this entry made in the Orderly Book (September 17, 1776): 'The behavior of yesterday was such a contrast to that of some troops the day before, as must show what may be done, where Officers and Soldiers will exert themselves — Once more therefore, the General calls upon Officers and men, to act up to the noble cause, in which they are engaged, and to support the Honor and Liberties of their Country.'

Washington's change of mind, and his renewed confidence in his troops can also be seen in his report to Congress,[1] 'This affair I am in hopes will be attended with many salutary consequences, as it seems to have greatly inspirited the whole of our troops.'

[1] To the President of Congress, September 18, 1776.

Chapter XVIII

THE ABANDONMENT OF ALL MANHATTAN ISLAND

AFTER the events of September 15–16, which resulted in the escape of Washington's army to the position on Harlem Heights and the disposition of the British army, facing this American position, there was another
interval of inactivity. For the British commander waited a
long time before he made his next move against Washington's army. On September 21 there was a devastating fire
in New York, which broke out in some wooden storehouses.
At the time, the British very naturally attributed this fire
to a plan of destruction on the part of the Americans. But
this theory had no foundation in fact. The American policy,
dictated by Congress for preserving the city, has been
described in the preceding chapter, and this prohibited the
Americans from burning New York. In a letter to Governor
Trumbull,[1] Washington wrote explicitly, 'By what means it
happened we do not know.'

For Washington, this interval was not occupied solely in
considering the future conduct of his army. Much more
serious was the question of the very existence of his army.
This was in most imminent danger. It was not merely the
matter of losing the militia which had been summoned for
the emergency, but the term of service of almost the whole
army was to expire by the end of 1776. In a report to Con-

[1] September 23, 1776.

gress,[1] Washington made a blunt statement of the case: 'We are now, as it were, upon the eve of another dissolution of our army.' And he wrote a very able and practical plea for 'establishing your army upon a permanent basis.'

Washington pointed out the futility of trusting to militia in extended campaigns, 'as this contest is not likely to be the work of a day, as the war must be carried on systematically.' He stated emphatically that, under these conditions, 'to place any dependence upon militia is assuredly resting upon a broken staff.' He described the disorder and lack of discipline that had attended the attempts to carry out operations for any extent of time with militia that were constantly coming and going, 'for of these we have only two sorts, the six-months men, and those sent in as temporary aid.'

He advocated, as the one means for carrying on the war, an army 'with enlistments for and during the war,' and he stated that the only way to obtain such an army was to offer liberal pay, with bounties of money and land. He gave warning that 'unless some speedy and effectual measures are adopted by Congress, our cause will be lost.'

This letter to Congress has been quoted, because it summed up the arguments which had been put forward by Washington, throughout the months of his command, to induce Congress to abandon its policy of relying upon the local militia.[2] But, when he was writing this message, Washington had already won his case. His arguments, reinforced by the object lessons of the events at New York, had at last brought about a complete change of mind in Congress.

[1] September 24, 1776.

[2] 'The policy of Congress has been the most absurd and ridiculous imaginable, pouring in militia-men who come and go every month. A military force established upon such principles defeats itself.' (General Greene, September 28, 1776.)

There had been bitter debates, as was natural where it was a question of the reversal of all the previous military policies of Congress. But Washington's victory was never in doubt. The bugbear of a 'standing army' [1] had been cast aside, and Congress had adopted the scheme of an American army, with enlistments 'to serve during the present war.' This army was to be of eighty-eight battalions, of which each State was to furnish a proportionate quota.

A bounty of twenty dollars was offered as an inducement to enlist, for each non-commissioned officer or private. There was also a promise of liberal grants of land to all officers and soldiers who should serve throughout the war, ranging from five hundred acres for a colonel to one hundred acres for a private. The appointments of all general officers were to be made by the State, but Congress was to issue the commissions. Each State was to furnish arms, clothing, and all equipment for its quota.

Crude and faulty as was this scheme, yet it was a definite beginning of the reforms so long advocated by Washington,[2] and this enactment by Congress at once put Washington's army on a new basis. Its importance, aside from all details, lay in the new principle established by Congress for military service. It meant that each State, instead of providing temporary forces, was to contribute line troops of long-term enlistments, with officers commissioned by Congress. This was a great stride forward, on the only path that would lead to an army organization upon which Washington could rely

[1] 'The jealousy of a standing army, and the evils to be apprehended from one, are remote, and, in my judgment, situated and circumstanced as we are, not at all to be dreaded; but the consequences of wanting one, according to my ideas formed from the present view of things, is certain and inevitable ruin.' (Washington to President of Congress, September 24, 1776.)

[2] 'In making them known to the States, Hancock used the arguments advanced by Washington in his letters urging the adoption of a better system, often in his own words.' (*The Writings of George Washington*, vol. IV, p. 451, note.)

for a long strain. As has been explained, Washington's own uphill task must be to neutralize the superior strength of the British main forces. This implied long periods of dogged opposition to the enemy, which would have been impossible if Washington had merely temporary troops at his disposal. The new policy of Congress was a move to remedy the mistake of relying upon temporary forces, and it gave Washington the first foundation for the organization of a real army.

But it was only a beginning—not, in any sense, a panacea that would cure the ills of the existing situation of Washington's army. It insured more reliable troops in the future, but it could not bring any help against the imminent attacks of the superior British forces at New York. In this regard, Washington could not found any hopes upon the new enactment of Congress so late in the season.[1] He must face the existing situation with the diminishing American forces at his command.

Washington's position at Harlem was strong only in the sense that Howe was daunted by the dangers of making frontal attacks upon the Americans. Again Bunker Hill was rendering its service to Washington's army. The British commander thus allowed himself to be delayed, before he made any attempt to use the river ways, which rendered both flanks of Washington's army unprotected.

The East River was free to Howe's naval forces at any time. On the North River there were two fortified posts opposite one another, Fort Washington on the New York side, and Fort Lee on the Jersey shore at the Palisades. In the bed of the river, between the two, obstructions had been placed to prevent the passage of British ships. But these

---

[1] 'True it is you have voted a larger one in lieu of it; but the season is late; and there is a material difference between voting of battalions and raising of men.' (Washington to President of Congress, October 4, 1776.)

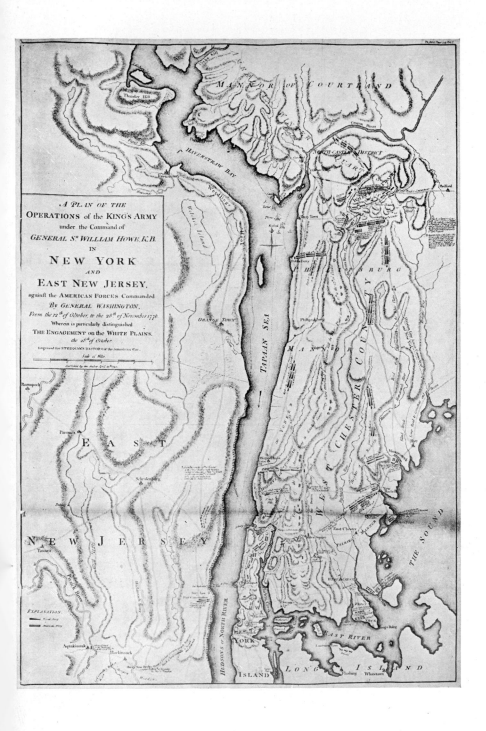

A PLAN OF THE
OPERATIONS of the KING'S ARMY
under the Command of
GENERAL Sʳ WILLIAM HOWE, K.B.
IN
NEW YORK
AND
EAST NEW JERSEY,
against the AMERICAN FORCES Commanded
By GENERAL WASHINGTON,
From the 12ᵗʰ of October, to the 28ᵗʰ of November 1776.
Wherein is particularly distinguished
THE ENGAGEMENT on the WHITE PLAINS.
the 28ᵗʰ of October.
Engraved for STEDMAN'S HISTORY of the American War.

already had been shown to be of no value, before Howe began operations anew. October 9, Washington wrote,[1] 'On yesterday morning three ships of war (two of forty four and the other of twenty guns), with two or three tenders, passed up the North River, without meeting any interruption from the chevaux-de-frise, or receiving any material damage from our batteries, though they kept a heavy fire at them from both sides of the river.' The Americans made efforts to increase the effectiveness of these obstructions,[2] but this test of their failure was sufficient for Washington, as will be evident in the ensuing narrative.

At length, on October 12, Howe resumed operations against the Americans, by making the expected attempt to take Washington in the rear,[3] after passing his flank by water. Howe put the greater part of his army on board his shipping, and moved nine miles up the East River to Throg's Neck (Frog's Neck) where he made a landing. But Washington had foreseen Howe's plan, and the British general found the bridge and causeway cut off, and the marshy approaches bristling with defenders. In this situation Howe was delayed for six days.

The delay ended any possibility of the British getting into the rear of the American army, for Washington thus gained ample time to move his army to White Plains where he concentrated all his forces from Manhattan Island, leaving only the garrison at Fort Washington. It was not until October 28 that Howe attacked Washington at White Plains. The British were able to effect a lodgement in one

[1] Washington to Governor Trumbull, October 9, 1776.

[2] 'He (General Putnam) will also attend to the works about Mount Washington, and to the obstructions in the River which should be increased as fast as possible.' Orderly Book, October 14, 1776.

[3] 'This was the plan which after long delay he at last adopted.' (Fortescue: *History of the British Army.*)

American position at Chatterton Hill. But, again, Howe delayed his general attack for three days — and again Washington was able to change position to his advantage. By moving his army to North Castle, Washington posted it so strongly behind the Croton, that Howe could not venture to attack the Americans.[1]

Howe, therefore, turned away from Washington's lines (November 5, 1776), and moved his army south, to the east bank of the North River at Dobb's Ferry. This was a double threat, not only a menace to the garrison left in Fort Washington, but also implying the invasion of New Jersey. Washington at once made a right estimate of the military situation: 'This sudden and unexpected movement is a matter of much speculation. Some suppose they are going into winter quarters, and will sit down in New York, without more than investing Fort Washington. I cannot subscribe wholly to this opinion myself. That they will invest Fort Washington is a matter of which there can be no doubt; and I think there is a strong probability, that General Howe will detach a part of his force to make an incursion into the Jerseys, providing he is going to New York. He must attempt something on account of his reputation; for what has he done as yet with his great army?' [2]

Under these circumstances, it was not enough for Washington to retain his army in its stronghold north of the Croton. He must do what he could to hold back the encroachments of the enemy. To meet this new situation, Washington made new dispositions of his army. He sent five thousand men, under General Putnam, to take post in

[1] 'Their position was now so advantageous, that any attack on them must have proved unsuccessful, for the river Croton stretched across their front, and their rear was defended by woods and heights.' (Stedman: *History of the American War*.)

[2] Letter to Governor Livingston, November 7, 1776.

New Jersey near Hackensack. He left seven thousand men under General Lee [1] at North Castle, and sent three thousand under Heath up the Hudson to Peekskill to defend the entrance to the Highlands. Washington himself went to Peekskill to inspect the sites for these new fortifications on the Hudson.

Before going north for this purpose, Washington left instructions for General Greene, who was in command of Fort Washington and Fort Lee, with headquarters at the latter post: [2] 'Sir, The last passage of three Vessels up the North River (which we have just recd. advice of), is so plain a proof of the inefficacy of all the obstructions we have thrown into it, that I cannot but think it will fully justify a change in the Disposition, which has been made. If we cannot prevent vessels from passing up, and the Enemy are possessed of the surrounding country, what valuable Purpose can it answer to attempt to hold a Post from which the expected Benefit cannot be had? I am therefore inclined to think that it will not be prudent to hazard the Men and Stores at Mount Washington; but, as you are on the spot, leave it to you to give such orders, as to evacuating Mount Washington, as you may judge best, and so far revoking the orders given to Colonel Magaw to defend it to the last.'

These instructions were clear enough, as to the uselessness of attempting to hold Fort Washington, but they undoubtedly 'left the matter somewhat within Greene's discretion.' [3] And there was the additional complication of special instructions from Congress, that the post should be defended to the last. This was another case of the interference of Con-

---

[1] Lee had rejoined the army from his Southern command, and Generals Sullivan and Stirling had been exchanged.

[2] Washington to Greene, November 8, 1776.

[3] John Fiske: *The American Revolution.*

gress, which had been so great a handicap to Washington throughout the New York campaign. And this time it was to bring actual disaster.

When Washington returned from Peekskill (November 14), he found that Greene, far from making any preparations to evacuate Fort Washington, had been influenced to make a defense of the post. Instead of taking away troops and stores, Greene had thrown useless reinforcements into the doomed fort. For that was all it could be called, after the British invested it. Washington went at once to Greene. In company with Greene, he inspected the position at Fort Washington. But it was too late to help matters, and he could only go over to Fort Lee [1] — to watch the loss of the isolated force across the river (November 6, 1776).

The works at Fort Washington had never been laid out with any scheme of defense against such superior numbers as the British brought against them.[2] Some of the British attacks were repulsed, but, as soon as one of their many assaults broke through, it was all over. The garrison was crowded into a narrow space where resistance was impossible, and the commander, Colonel Magaw, was obliged to surrender — a loss of two thousand men from Washington's fast-shrinking army.

The collapse of the defense of Fort Washington was a matter of great mortification to Greene. He wrote to Knox: 'I feel mad, vexed, sick, and sorry. Never did I need the consoling voice of a friend more than now.' It was Greene's

---

[1] 'We all urged his Excellency to come off. I offered to stay, General Putnam did the same, and so did General Mercer; but his Excellency thought it best for us all to come off together, which we did about half an hour before the enemy surrounded the fort.' (General Greene to Colonel Knox, November 17, 1776.)

[2] 'The redoubt you and I advised, too, was not done, or little or nothing done to it. Had that been completed, I think the garrison might have defended themselves a long while, or been brought off.' (Greene to Knox, November 17, 1776.)

one error in military judgment in the whole war. But there never was a trace of criticism from Washington. The American Commander in Chief recognized the fact that he had left Greene in a position of many complications, and that it would have been a grave injustice to impute any blame to him. There never was a break in the trusting relationship between the two, and Washington was to see his faith in Greene vindicated, as he proved to be Washington's ablest general.

Chapter XIX

RETREAT AND COUNTERATTACK IN NEW JERSEY

THE easy capture of Fort Washington was at once followed by the expected British invasion of New Jersey. On November 18, General Cornwallis, with five thousand men, crossed the Hudson, and made a 'march with great secrecy and despatch,'[1] to surprise the American garrison at Fort Lee. Greene, who remained in command at Fort Lee, received information of this advance of the enemy only just in time to withdraw his troops (two thousand) to safety. But, again, the unfortunate policy of persisting in holding the Hudson River forts brought losses of guns and stores, which had to be abandoned in the hurried retreat.

Greene, with the troops from Fort Lee, was able to cross the bridge over the Hackensack and join Washington's force in New Jersey. Washington's position behind the Hackensack became too exposed when Cornwallis was given increased numbers. Therefore Washington withdrew across the Passaic to Newark, where he remained, to wait for the arrival of the troops he had left east of the Hudson under the command of Lee. These he had ordered Lee to bring at once to join him.

Here came the culmination of the many difficulties and obstructions, against which Washington had been obliged to

[1] Stedman: *History of the American War.*

158

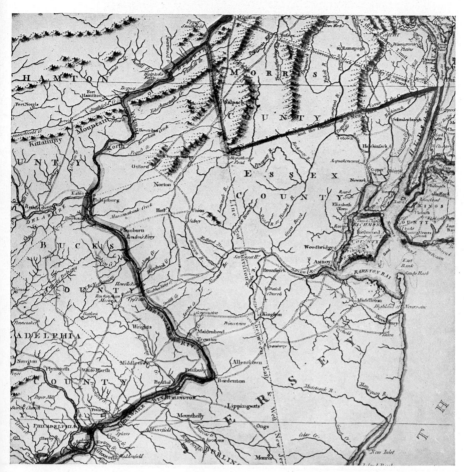

SCENE OF OPERATIONS IN NEW JERSEY

contend throughout this campaign of 1776. Instead of joining his chief, Lee was holding off, because he was treacher-
ously scheming to set up a separate command of his own,
and to supplant Washington. The man had been given an
exaggerated importance, on account of his experience as an
officer of the British Army, and his eccentricities had been
considered the oddities of genius. The fact was, these last
were indices of his real character. He was a charlatan and
only shallow-pated. He had returned from his Southern
command with the borrowed glory of Clinton's defeat at
Charleston — for Congress and the public did not know
that Moultrie's fort had won the victory, and Lee had
wanted to abandon it! He was second in command of the
American Army, and the idea had become an obsession
with him, that here was his opportunity to undermine
Washington and to be the great man of the situation.

That Lee was under the influence of this mania is now a
matter of common knowledge. It has been proved beyond
question by Lee's own letters, written to people of influence
to promote his sordid intrigue. His letters contained a
farrago of malicious nonsense, intended to injure Washington, and to set himself up in contrast. He claimed that
Washington's army and his own army 'must each rest on its
own bottom' [1] — 'Had I the powers, I could do you much
good, might I dictate one week. Did none of the congress
ever read the Roman history?' [2] To cover these treacherous
designs, Lee made to Washington the excuse for his delay,
that 'withdrawing our troops from hence would be attended
with some very serious consequences, which at present would
be tedious to enumerate.' [3] Lee even attempted the subter-
fuge of ordering Heath to march to the support of Washington, instead of moving his own command. For Heath, this

[1] Lee to Bowdoin. [2] Lee to Rush. [3] November 21, 1776.

would have meant abandoning the important post in the Highlands, assigned to him by Washington in person, and Heath very properly refused to obey any such order from Lee.

As was natural, the high-souled Washington did not have any idea of what was passing in the schemer's mind. Washington at first attributed Lee's delays to misunderstandings of orders and miscarriages of letters. But, on November 27, he wrote to Lee from Newark: 'My former Letters were so full and explicit, as to the necessity of your marching as early as possible, that it is unnecessary to add more on that Head. I confess I expected you would have been sooner in motion.' After communications from Washington, Congress passed the significant resolve: 'That General Washington be informed that he has the approbation of Congress to order the troops on the east side of Hudson's river over to the west side of that River, whenever he shall think it conductive to the public service so to do.' [1]

Consequently, Lee was at length obliged to move his troops across the Hudson, and they were ferried over December 2–3. But Lee still clung to his scheme of playing his own hand for his own benefit, and he had no intention of joining Washington. Instead, he moved by leisurely stages toward Morristown, 'to make an important diversion.'

In the mean time, Washington was retreating through New Jersey, pressed by the superior forces of Cornwallis. In the absence of Lee's troops, he could not even offer a delaying resistance. On November 28 Washington left Newark. On December 1 he retired over the Raritan and destroyed the bridge. There Cornwallis halted for five days at New Brunswick. He stated in Parliament that his troops were hungry and worn out with fatigue. On December 6

[1] Journals of Congress, December 1, 1776.

Howe joined Cornwallis, and the British continued the pursuit.

Washington had withdrawn to Princeton. His forces were at a low ebb from expired enlistments, and were reduced to three thousand men. His only recourse was to escape across the Delaware. This Washington accomplished by retreating to Trenton, and ferrying his army over the river from that place. Again, as at Long Island, he gathered every boat that could be found for miles, and again he was able to save all his guns and stores. This crossing was on December 8. The enemy had been slow in following the Americans from Princeton, and the British historian was very caustic in describing the delay: 'At Prince Town the British general waited seventeen hours, marched at nine o'clock in the morning of the eighth, and arrived at Trenton at four o'clock in the afternoon; just when the last boat of General Washington's embarkation crossed the river, as if he had calculated, it was observed, with great accuracy, the exact time necessary for his enemy to make his escape.' [1]

On the day Washington escaped across the Delaware, he wrote to the President of Congress, as to Lee, 'I cannot account for the slowness of his march.' In fact, Lee was still lingering near Morristown. Instead of making any effort to join Washington, Lee was actually on the point of diverting other reinforcements from the hard-pressed American commander. In accordance with a resolve of Congress, Washington had written to General Schuyler, directing him to send to the main army all troops not needed in the Northern Department, after Sir Guy Carleton had retreated from Crown Point. These had come down from Albany, seven regiments in all, of which three went to Peekskill, and the other four, under General Gates, were marching through

[1] Stedman: *History of the American War.*

northern New Jersey to join Washington. As Gates was in doubt as to where to find the retreating Washington, he sent forward an aide to ask instructions from Lee.

Gates' aide, Major Wilkinson, found Lee on the morning of December 13, at an outlying tavern, where Lee recklessly made his quarters, four miles from his troops and without even posting a guard. Lee welcomed this opportunity to enlist Gates in his intrigue against Washington. Accordingly Lee wrote a characteristic letter to Gates, in which was the phrase, 'a certain great man is damnably deficient.' Lee had just signed this treacherous letter, when a dramatic event abruptly ended his machinations. A party of British dragoons suddenly surrounded the tavern, and the vainglorious Lee was ignominiously bundled off, a disheveled prisoner in a flannel dressing-gown.

Never was an enemy act of so great benefit. Of course, there is no knowing how much harm might have been done by his presumptuous folly. But, already, Lee had carried matters to the point that made it certain the troops under his command never would have joined Washington in the critical month of December, 1776, if Lee himself had not been captured by the British. But, after the fortunate removal of Lee, Sullivan succeeded to the command of these much-needed American troops, and, with Gates' force also, made haste to join Washington's army on December 20. The value of this timely reinforcement can only be measured by the ensuing events, which changed the whole military situation.

For everything had seemed lost, when Washington was driven across the Delaware with only the remnant of his army. Friends and foes alike thought that the *coup de grâce* had been given. The despondency among the Americans was widespread. Congress withdrew from Philadelphia to

Baltimore on December 12, leaving to Washington 'full power to order and direct all things relative to the department and to the operations of war.'

The British leaders believed that the defeat of the Americans had been complete. So confident was General Howe that, on December 7, he had even diverted forces from the campaign by sending a strong expedition of six thousand men under Clinton to seize Newport. Embarked on transports, and convoyed by Sir Peter Parker's fleet, the British found no difficulty, as Rhode Island could offer no resistance. But this expedition was against the wishes of Clinton, who asked instead to be sent to the Delaware, where he might have done much harm. The British historian called this Newport expedition 'an unlucky measure, as it had no use but to keep a great body of troops unemployed during three years.' [1]

From the European point of view, the affair was ended, and, to the mind of Howe, it only remained to go into winter quarters as if in a conquered territory, without a suspicion that it was possible for the defeated Americans to attempt a move against his troops. But one enemy Howe had not conquered — and that was George Washington. Washington's indomitable soul had never acknowledged defeat, and, even in this 'almost desperate situation,' [2] Washington was resolutely planning a counter-stroke against the victorious British.

And here, aside from his unconquerable courage, a candid estimate of the facts of the case cannot fail to reach the conclusion that Washington showed high qualities of generalship. He did not plan merely a daring raid against the

---

[1] Stedman: *History of the American War.*

[2] 'The situation of the Americans was now almost desperate.' (Stedman: *History of the American War.*)

enemy. On the contrary, Washington found the right solution of a complicated military problem. He foresaw the effect of his Jersey operations on the mind of his enemy. He divined the dispositions of forces his enemy would make in consequence, and he devised the one plan of campaign that would be effective against these dispositions.

Not enough stress has been laid upon the actual results achieved by Washington, in prolonging and delaying Howe's campaign of 1776. The American commander had been hopelessly inferior in forces from the first. He had to contend with the many disadvantages which have been described. And yet it had taken Howe's powerful army six months to drive Washington across the Delaware, after Howe had waited until June 11 before leaving Halifax. This long lapse of time had consumed the year 1776 to the stage when the advanced season had become an important factor in the military situation. Winter operations were not in accordance with European military ideas, and Washington was right in assuming that Howe would return to New York, after leaving garrisons in New Jersey. European troops, in winter quarters in the American countryside, would be at a disadvantage. To attack and dislocate these, their supplies, and their communications, in detail, was Washington's sound plan of campaign.

Only Washington's courageous mind could conceive that this plan was feasible, in the forlorn plight of the American army. But Washington never faltered in his purpose. He was unremitting in his efforts to gather what troops he could, as the last days of the expirations of enlistments approached. He even used the authority of Congress, which has been quoted, to raise troops in person. On the arrival of Sullivan's and Gates' troops, Washington only had about six thousand men, including all scattered detachments, many of which were not available for his projected operation.

This left but a slender force for so momentous an expedition. But, as Washington himself expressed it, 'necessity, dire necessity will, nay must, justify an attack.' The night of Christmas, December 25, 1776, was chosen for crossing the Delaware. By that time the wearied troops of Sullivan and Gates would be ready for active duty.

In New Jersey the condition existed which Washington had anticipated, the very condition upon which he had predicated his plan. Howe had returned to New York, and had left scattered garrisons in New Jersey under the command of General Grant. The inexcusable isolation of these positions, in the eighty miles between the Delaware and the Hackensack, was the measure of the overconfidence of the British leaders. These separate posts could not be of use in controlling the inhabitants, and they could not offer an adequate defense against enemy attacks. But enemy attacks were held to be out of the question at the late season of the year. This false security was best summed up in a message from Grant to Colonel Donop, one of his subordinates: 'The story of Washington crossing the Delaware at this season of the year is not to be believed.' In this conviction, Cornwallis was about to sail for England, and New York was to celebrate the honors accorded to General Howe.

Washington's plan was to make a sudden attack upon the enemy's advance posts, which were held by Hessians, Trenton under the command of Colonel Rahl, and Burlington and Bordentown under Colonel Donop. The American army was to cross the Delaware in three divisions. The right wing of two thousand under Gates was to engage Donop, and keep his forces (about two thousand) occupied. The center division, under Ewing, was to move directly upon

Trenton, the real object of attack. But the mission of these two forces was to divert the attention of the enemy, while Washington himself was to deliver the main attack, by crossing above Trenton with twenty-four hundred men and falling upon its garrison (about twelve hundred) from the north. Before the operation began, Gates had gone to talk with Congress at Baltimore, as he also was inclined to intrigue.[1] His departure left Cadwallader in command of the right wing.

The night of December 25 was fearfully cold, with a bitter wind that brought a driving snowstorm. The surface of the Delaware River was a mass of floating cakes of ice. Although Cadwallader and Ewing were zealous for their tasks, both thought it would be impossible to cross the Delaware that night, and, as the conditions grew worse and worse, both gave up the attempt. They did not imagine that Washington would try to cross the river.

But their chief was in a mood that refused to be daunted by difficulties and dangers. Washington was so highly resolved to carry through his undertaking that nothing would stop him. Although he received word that the troops on the right could do nothing,[2] he persevered with his own command, and he succeeded in making the dangerous crossing. Again the 'amphibious' soldiers of Glover's Essex County regiment rendered invaluable service — for it was an extraordinary feat, to handle the laden boats under such adverse circumstances, and to get them across in spite of the floating ice and the driving storm.

It was not until four o'clock in the morning of December

---

[1] Washington had given Gates leave to go to Philadelphia, but Gates had stretched this leave as far as Baltimore — to the surprise of Washington.

[2] On receiving this news, Washington sent word to Cadwallader, 'If you can do nothing real, at least create as great a diversion as possible.'

26 that Washington's troops were across the Delaware and ready to begin their descent on Trenton. Their march south was of extreme hardship, over nine miles of snow and ice in the roads, and through a raging storm of sleet and snow. But this was an ususual body of men, all of whom shared the resolute spirit of their leader.[1] It was daylight before the Americans reached Trenton. Yet, in spite of the fact that Cadwallader and Ewing had not been able to make any diversion that would occupy the attention of the enemy, the approach of Washington's force was not discovered. The blinding storm was still raging, but the chief protection from discovery was the enemy's feeling of carefree security, which made them neglect any proper guard against attacks. Hitherto, what alarms there had been, were caused by small roving parties that could do no harm — and the enemy assumed that nothing more dangerous would be met in New Jersey.

As he approached Trenton, Washington detached a part of his force under Sullivan, and the two divisions attacked Trenton from opposite quarters. By this sudden double attack the Hessians were thrown into utter confusion, being unable to rally for any effective defense. When Washington's cannon began to sweep the streets, and after a disorderly attempt to break out had been blocked, the Hessians surrendered. A few had escaped from the outskirts of the town, before Sullivan secured the Assumpink bridge. With this exception, Rahl's whole force was taken, at the

[1] Bancroft's remarkable description should be quoted: 'But they were veterans and patriots, chiefly of New England, Pennsylvania, and Virginia. Among his general officers were Greene and Mercer and Stirling and Sullivan; of field officers and others, Stark of New Hampshire, Hand of Pennsylvania, Glover and Knox of Massachusetts, Webb of Connecticut, Scott and William Washington and James Monroe of Virginia, and Alexander Hamilton of New York.' It would be difficult to find a parallel to this list of distinguished names in the roster of any military expedition of equal force.

price of almost no loss for the Americans.[1] Rahl himself was mortally wounded, but the collapse of the Hessians had come so quickly that they surrendered before they had lost heavily. Only seventeen were killed, and less than eighty wounded.

Washington's victory was complete, because Donop, instead of making any move against him, on hearing the news from Trenton, hastily retreated to Princeton, 'abandoning his sick and his heavy baggage.'[2] On the next day Cadwallader succeeded in crossing the river, to make the diversion on the right ordered by Washington, but the retreat of Donop had ended any danger in that quarter. Consequently, Washington was enabled to recross the Delaware unmolested, with his prisoners[3] and spoils, and to give his exhausted troops the opportunity to recover from the effects of their long exposure to the rigors of the winter storm.[4]

[1] Two were frozen to death on the march but it is doubtful if there was a death in action. Washington reported to the President of Congress, 'Our loss is very trifling indeed, only two officers and one or two privates wounded.'

[2] Fortescue: *History of the British Army.*   [3] About one thousand.

[4] It has been stated that half of the officers and men of Washington's force were disabled by the extreme hardships of the Trenton expedition.

Chapter xx

THE SITUATION SAVED

THE effects of Washington's *coup* at Trenton were immediate and far reaching. For the British, it was a bolt from the blue that shattered their whole structure.[1] For it was not alone the loss of Rahl's force. It meant the dislocation of their whole system of posts to guard New Jersey. Donop had retreated to Princeton, and it was evident to the British leaders that their hold upon the western part of New Jersey had been broken.

For the Americans, the sudden transition from depression to exultation was equally marked. And the prestige of his victory placed Washington in a position to use the powers granted to him by Congress, and to save his army from disappearing, when the enlistments expired at the last of the year. Congress had yielded to his insistence, which was well seconded by Greene, and had extended the powers given to him at the time of the withdrawal to Baltimore, when Congress left Washington with the whole responsibility for the conduct of military affairs.

The new powers granted to Washington by Congress,[2]

[1] 'All our hopes were blasted by the unhappy affair at Trenton.' (Lord George Germaine.)

[2] 'That Congress, having maturely considered the present crisis; and having perfect reliance in the wisdom, vigor, and uprightness of General Washington, do hereby

'RESOLVE, that General Washington shall be, and he is hereby, vested with full, ample, and complete powers to raise and collect together, in the most

which are here given in full, were so extraordinary that Lord George Germaine, in the House of Commons, declared they made Washington a 'dictator of America.' But this was not at all a true description. There was nothing political in the measure. It meant only that Congress had at last recognized the wisdom of Washington's military counsels. This grant of plenary powers to Washington, instead of the grudging support hitherto doled out to him, was a tribute to Washington, the significance of which can be seen at once. It was a formal acknowledgment, at this crisis, that the only hope rested in Washington.

This confidence of Congress was soon justified by the acts of Washington. With all the energy that burned beneath his self-controlled demeanor, he was intent on pursuing his plan against the enemy in New Jersey. On December 29, with what troops he could collect, he again crossed the Delaware to occupy Trenton.

Here it must be reiterated that these incursions of Washington were not merely raids, but parts of a far-reaching plan for ousting the forces of the enemy, and driving them

speedy and effective manner, from any or all of the United States, sixteen battalions of infantry, in addition to those already voted by Congress; to appoint officers for the said battalions of infantry; to raise, officer, and equip three thousand light-horse, three regiments of artillery, a corps of engineers, and to establish their pay; to apply to any of the States for such aid of the militia as he shall judge necessary; to form such magazines of provisions, and in such places as he shall think proper; to dispose and appoint all officers under the rank of brigadier-general, and to fill all vacancies in every other department of the American army; to take, wherever he may be, whatever he may want for the use of the army, if the inhabitants will not sell it, allowing a reasonable price for the same; to arrest and confine persons who refuse to take the Continental currency, or are otherwise disaffected to the American cause; and return to the States, of which they are citizens, the names and the nature of their offenses, together with the witnesses to prove them.

'That the foregoing powers be vested in General Washington, for and during the term of six months from the date hereof, unless sooner determined by Congress.' December 27, 1776. Copies sent to each State December 30, 1776.

back from New Jersey. That this was a carefully thought-out plan of campaign was established by the fact that Washington gave instructions in advance [1] for all other available troops to move toward Morristown to coöperate with his own forces. This early selection of Morristown as his future base of operations showed rare judgment, as was proved by the event.

Washington's own force was only kept in existence by his own efforts, at the time when the enlistments expired. He made full use of the powers given him by Congress, but it was difficult to induce the soldiers to stay on. 'The paymaster was out of money, and the public credit was exhausted by frequent vain promises.' [2] At this emergency, Washington pledged his own private fortune. In this he was joined by other officers. Washington also made an earnest appeal to Robert Morris, [3] who responded by going from house to house, and sending Washington on January 1 fifty thousand dollars which he had borrowed on his own credit.

By these means, soldiers were induced to remain in the army, and new recruits were secured by Washington. [4] Consequently, on January 2, 1777, Washington was able to concentrate in the vicinity of Trenton nearly five thousand men. These included Cadwallader's force of eighteen hundred, and an additional eighteen hundred recruits that Mifflin had brought to Bordentown. With this force at his command, Washington reported to Congress, 'We are now

[1] Letters to Heath, Macdougal, Maxwell, Stirling, etc.   [2] Bancroft.

[3] 'Borrow money while it can be done; we are doing it upon our private credit. Every man of interest, every lover of his country, must strain his credit upon such an occasion.'

[4] 'Since their arrival, we have been parading the regiments whose term of service is now expired, in order to know what force we should have to depend on.' (Washington to President of Congress, January 1, 1777.)

making our arrangements, and concerting a plan of operations, which I shall attempt to execute as soon as possible, and which I hope will be attended with some success.'

At this time, Cornwallis was moving against Washington with eight thousand troops. Upon the surprising news from Trenton, Cornwallis had given up all idea of sailing to England, and had hastened to resume command of the troops in New Jersey. His march against Washington had been harassed by skirmishers, which hung about his flanks. This annoyance increased as Cornwallis drew near Trenton, and it made his advance difficult. In addition, there had been a thaw, and the roads were deep in mud.

Washington could not hope to give battle at Trenton with any chance of success. Consequently, on the approach of Cornwallis, in the afternoon of January 2, he withdrew the American troops across the Assumpink River, behind which he posted them in a strong defensive position. The opposition of the skirmishers, with the skillful handling of a small covering force (six hundred) under Greene, held up the advance of Cornwallis, and it was late in the afternoon when he reached the Assumpink.

Cornwallis made attempts to cross the Assumpink, but these were repulsed, as Washington's artillery was well placed to protect the fords. The British commander made up his mind that Washington's position was too strong to attempt a general assault that afternoon, as darkness was approaching and the troops of his army were weary. Accordingly, Cornwallis decided to put off his attack until the next day, and sent messages to summon the troops he had left behind at Princeton and Maidenhead, to reinforce his army for the battle which Cornwallis believed would destroy Washington's force.[1]

[1] Cornwallis accordingly went to bed in high spirits, 'At last we have run down

But this battle was never to take place, for the essential of Washington's plan was to strike quick blows at the British supplies and outlying positions — but to avoid battle with their main forces. Adhering to this purpose, Washington had made sure in advance of a route by which he could withdraw to the left of Cornwallis' army, and make a sudden descent upon Princeton.

This secret design Washington executed with great skill. All through the night small parties of Americans kept the camp fires burning along the Assumpink, and made a noisy pretense of throwing up intrenchments, while the whole American army was marching off on the way to Princeton. The success of Washington's daring maneuver was complete. Not a suspicion entered the minds of the British officers that Washington's army had not remained all night on the Assumpink and actually the puzzled Cornwallis gained his first knowledge of the whereabouts of Washington from the noise of cannon at Princeton.

In the early morning of January 3, the advance of Washington's army, on its march to Princeton, encountered the British troops which had been left there by Cornwallis. These were three British regiments under Colonel Marwood, and they were hastening, at the summons of Cornwallis, to join his army at Trenton. When the British saw the Americans on the road, Mawhood thought Washington's army had been defeated by Cornwallis, and that these were retreating fugitives.

With this mistaken idea, which was natural under the circumstances, Mawhood attacked the supposedly fleeing Americans. In the first British charge of this encounter, General Mercer, in command of the American advance,

the old fox,' said he, 'and we will bag him in the morning.' (John Fiske: *The American Revolution.*)

was unhorsed and fatally wounded by bayonets. Consequently, at first there was some confusion among the Americans. But Washington himself 'came galloping up to rally Mercer's men,' [1] and he quickly brought into action superior numbers, which overwhelmed the British and put them to flight. The loss of the Americans was less than one hundred. The British lost in killed, wounded, and prisoners about five hundred. But this did not tell the whole story, as the British force was broken and disorganized, part of their troops fleeing toward Cornwallis and part toward Brunswick.

From the fugitives Cornwallis learned the news of the defeat at Princeton, after a wearying march over bad roads in vain search for Washington. But the American commander, having delivered his successful blow at Princeton, again eluded the main force of the enemy. And the other American troops, which he had summoned to that region as a part of his plan, began to take part in the campaign. Heath's troops became his left wing, and the other forces were soon harassing the enemy in New Jersey. All this happened so quickly that Cornwallis was in a quandary. His army was superior, but it was now in an enemy's country — and, in addition, the enemy was actively engaged in cutting off his supplies and threatening his communications.

The difficulties of this military situation were too great for Cornwallis to face. He withdrew entirely from western New Jersey. Putnam crossed from Philadelphia and occupied Princeton. Disconcerted and harassed, Cornwallis continued his retreat, 'leaving Howe with no more of New Jersey than the slip of land enclosed within a line drawn from Paulus Hook southward to New Brunswick and thence to Amboy.' [2]

[1] Fortescue: *History of the British Army.*   [2] *Ibid.*

This was an extraordinary overturn, in a military situation that had been considered by the British a total loss for the Americans. Its results, and its effects upon the enemy, were vividly described by the contemporary British historian: 'General Washington overran both East and West Jersey, spreading his army over the Rariton, and penetrating into Essex County, where he made himself master of the coast opposite to Staten Island, by seizing Newark, Elizabeth Town, and Woodbridge. His head-quarters he fixed at Morris-Town. This place is situated amongst hills which are difficult of access. A fine country was in his rear, whence he could draw supplies, and through which he could at any time secure an easy passage over the Delaware. By such judicious movements did General Washington not only save Philadelphia and Pennsylvania, but recover the greatest part of the Jerseys, in defiance of an army infinitely superior to his, in discipline, resources, and numbers.' [1]

The result of this short campaign of only three weeks has been expressed in still stronger terms by a modern British military historian: [2] ... 'As things fell out, the whole cause of the revolution in America was saved by Washington's very bold and skilful action. The spirits of the revolutionary party revived; and an advance of 5000 militia upon Kingsbridge showed Howe that enemies were ready to swarm upon him from every side at the first sign of a British reverse. In a word, the moral effect of the past campaign was in a great measure cancelled, and the whole of the work, excepting the capture of New York, required to be done again.'

[1] Stedman: *History of the American War.*
[2] Fortescue: *History of the British Army.*

Chapter XXI

1777 — FRANKLIN AND BURGOYNE

THIS unexpected overturn of Howe's campaign of conquest had created a new and surprising military situation in America for the British at the beginning of 1777. Instead of subduing the revolt of the Americans, as had been confidently predicted, all Howe could show for gains, after his use of the great forces given to him in 1776, were the conquest of New York and the barren occupation of Rhode Island. In the other areas the British had accomplished nothing in 1776.

The repulse of Clinton's expedition in the South has been described. In the North, after the Americans had been driven back from their rash invasion of Canada, Sir Guy Carleton had stopped short of taking Ticonderoga, and had gone into winter quarters in Canada. The only other British offensive, the outbreak of the Cherokee Indians on the Southern border, incited by British agents, had been decisively put down.

These were most disappointing results for the British in the year 1776, and, in casting the balance for that year, another unfavorable factor must be taken into account as scoring against the British. The depredations of the American privateers were already exacting a heavy toll from British commerce. This has been lost to sight in the many discussions of details of the Revolution. But the fact must be

176

faced that the American raids upon British shipping had mounted to large totals, even so early as 1776. The contemporary British historian stated, 'The British nation, by these captures alone during the year 1776, lost property to the amount of above a million sterling.'[1] These were serious losses, and they had a serious effect upon the public, especially as these losses of shipping increased from year to year and caused insurance rates to go to high figures, which became a matter of distress and complaint for British merchants.

Upon the cessation for the winter of all British military efforts in America, Europe became the scene of two simultaneous activities, totally different in character, and yet destined to combine in an influence upon the war that cannot be stated too strongly. Franklin had been sent by Congress on his embassy to France, and Burgoyne had gone to England, to urge the adoption of his plan of an invasion from Canada for the main military operation of the British in 1777. Both arrived in Europe in December, 1776, and, although no one could foresee this outcome at the time, it was as if Franklin had been sent to France for the one special purpose of preparing the French to join the Americans on the occasion of the failure of the very plan that was then being adopted in London upon the representations of Burgoyne.

For, from the first, it was a foregone conclusion that Burgoyne would induce the British Ministers to carry out his unsound plan. Lord George Germaine, who was all-powerful in military affairs as Colonial Secretary,[2] at once was strongly in favor of Burgoyne's scheme. This question was soon settled beyond recall. The plan for an invasion

[1] Stedman: *History of the American War.*
[2] He had succeeded Lord Dartmouth in office.

from Canada was adopted, and Burgoyne was assigned the command of the invading force. This was superseding Sir Guy Carleton in military control of operations against the Americans.

The adoption of Burgoyne's plan was a matter of maps in England — and of imaginary conditions set down on paper in England — which utterly failed to express the actual problem in America. The futility of the plan has been masked by statements of the value of seizing the line of the Hudson. But, in order to get at the truth, it is only necessary to state the problem in its military essentials. Control of the Hudson implied gathering and maintaining superior British forces on the line of the Hudson River itself. Where was there any sense in sending part of these forces by the difficult route from Canada, instead of by water? By water, not only was transportation safe, but the troops would have been assured of maintenance and supplies on the Hudson. By the land route from Canada, not only was there the inherent defect of divided forces, but Burgoyne's army was to be put in the most disadvantageous situation for a British force in America, cut off from water communications and exposed to a hostile countryside in arms, against which European tactics were especially ineffective.

But in England the problem was never approached from this essential military point of view. On the maps in London, the invasion did not seem to present difficulties to the British. There were two reasons for this error. In the first place, it was the familiar scene of the operations of the French and Indian War, where the British forces had been before. Neither the British General nor the British Ministers had any conception of how totally conditions had changed in that region. The second reason for not seeing the dangers that were to beset Burgoyne was the delusion

178

then entertained by the King's Ministers, that military assistance would be given by the Loyalists. This had become an article of faith, in spite of previous disappointments.

Thus far in the course of the Revolution, all hopes of military aid from the Loyalists had proved vain. As has been shown in the preceding narrative, the assurances of the deposed royal governors had never been fulfilled when they were subjected to the test of military service.[1] But, in the case of the projected expedition of Burgoyne, the King's Ministers thought there were special reasons for confidence in the Loyalists. In the center of the State of New York were many avowed Tories, of whom the most prominent were Sir John Johnson and Guy Johnson, and these had informed the Ministers that the whole population would take the side of the King, if only a strong Royal army appeared in that region.

With this mistaken spirit of optimism,[2] the plan of Burgoyne's invasion was adopted in March, 1777,[3] and Burgoyne at once sailed for Canada to take command. In England it was confidently assumed that his task would involve nothing more than the difficulties of the movements of troops, as in the French and Indian War. In the minds of the Ministers, there was the fixed conviction that Burgoyne would command so strong an army that resistance would be out of the question, and, at the approach of his powerful army, the people would rise to his support. Seldom has an

---

[1] The modern *History of the British Army* made this comment as to the campaign of 1776, 'The operations had been based on the assistance of the loyalists; but the loyalists, as might have been anticipated, had not fulfilled the requirements expected of them.'

[2] First wager in the betting book in Brooks's Club, dated Christmas Day, 1776: Gen. George Burgoyne wagers Charles Fox one pony (fifty guineas) that he will be home victorious from America by Christmas Day, 1777. This is a significant record of Burgoyne's overconfidence.

[3] Germaine's instructions for Burgoyne's invasion were dated March 26, 1777.

expedition been begun with so much overconfidence. No one was able to imagine that the people, instead of rising to support Burgoyne, would rise to overwhelm and capture Burgoyne's army.

While the King's Ministers were casting their lot for this fatal plan of campaign, Franklin was making a profound impression in France. The commission, appointed by Congress in 1776 to negotiate with France, consisted of three members. Franklin was its head, and associated with him were Silas Deane and Arthur Lee. But the two others were not considered important by the French. In their eyes, Franklin was the one outstanding figure, and the immediate and continued success of the negotiations must be attributed wholly to Franklin himself. In fact, the effect produced by Franklin's magnetic personality was so extraordinary, and the results of his persuasive powers so far reaching, that he must be considered one of the great diplomatists of all time.

Franklin was then at the height of his powers. His versatility was notable — and he could be all things to all men. Not only was he popular with all classes in France, but it is no exaggeration to say that he became the rage, and in the minds of all France he was the personification of the American cause. He soon secured from the French financial aid, and all the privileges for American privateers that could be granted without an open break. Franklin was also instrumental in inducing Spain to take a favorable attitude toward the United States.

Of course at this time the assistance from France was covert. Vergennes, the French Foreign Minister, did not yet venture to commit the French Government to any official act that would mean war with Great Britain. But the intrigue was skillfully carried to all lengths that were possible, with only a thin concealing surface of neutrality. The departure of the young Lafayette, to serve as a volunteer with the Americans, was an indication of the French enthusiasm for the Americans, and it was also an influence which increased that feeling in 1777.

Lafayette sailed for America in April, 1777, with chosen companions, among whom was de Kalb. The King of France had forbidden Lafayette's going — and the circumstances of his romantic adventure made a great stir that was favorable to America. Altogether, it became evident, so great a sentiment for the Americans was being created in 1777 among the French, that it would require only an American military success to bring France into the war on the side of the United States.

For this reason it was an irony of fate, that, at the very time this strong feeling for America was being fostered in France, the British were concentrating their efforts upon the one means of providing the Americans with the military success necessary to bring France into the war. For it is difficult to see any other plan the British could have adopted that would have subjected a British army to so certain a defeat. Each in his own way, Burgoyne and Franklin were weaving a fatal web for the British in 1777.

Chapter XXII

THE MILITARY SITUATION IN AMERICA IN THE FIRST HALF OF 1777

IN AMERICA, it was again shown that the military situation in the Revolution was an anomaly, utterly unlike any that could exist in Europe. The beginning of 1776 had seen Washington, with no siege train whatever, enforcing a close siege of Howe's army in Boston. The beginning of 1777 found Washington, with only the shadow of an army, containing, in the full military sense of the word, Howe's army in the environs of New York. It was the same story in each case. Again the experience of warfare in the American countryside had proved baffling to the British Army. The rough handling the British had received in Washington's Trenton-Princeton campaign magnified the strength of Washington's forces in their eyes, and served to keep Howe's army confined to its narrow limits.

Washington himself had expressed his hope for this situation, 'if we can once put the enemy into winter quarters.' [1] And he reported to the President of Congress [2] that his rôle must be to 'keep up an appearance before an enemy.' Accordingly, with this deliberate purpose of giving his enemy the impression of stronger forces than he possessed, he began a series of raiding activities, by attacking the

[1] Letter to Governor Trumbull, January 10, 1777.
[2] January 19, 1777.

British whenever they ventured out into the surrounding country and 'preventing them from sending their foraging parties to any great distance.' [1]

This policy Washington pursued unremittingly,[2] and it not only cut off supplies from his enemy,[3] but also created the desired impression that the country was swarming with American troops prepared to fall upon any sorties of the British. An advance of Heath's troops to Kingsbridge, in January, 1777, helped to increase the effect of this fiction upon the British.[4]

At the time it was a matter of chagrin to Washington that Heath merely summoned Fort Independence to surrender, instead of carrying the fort by storm, which Washington thought possible. But this could only have been a temporary success, and Heath accomplished the main object by the impression made upon Howe. Washington kept up the show of activity in this region north of New York by detaching light troops from Heath's force, to operate in Westchester County.[5]

Thus, from his chosen base at Morristown, Washington dominated the country about Howe's positions. On the other hand, the American commander was struggling with the lowest ebb of his army. As has been told, Washington's own exertions had been the one means of preserving the

[1] Letter to General Schuyler, January 18, 1777.

[2] 'Throughout the spring also petty warfare never ceased before the cantonments in New Jersey...more injurious to the British than to the Americans.' (Fortescue: *History of the British Army*.)

[3] Washington's account of one of the first of these raids gave the following list of spoils: '...forty wagons and upwards of a hundred horses, most of them of the English draft breed, and a number of sheep and cattle, which they had collected.' (Report to President of Congress, January 22, 1777.)

[4] '...showed Howe that enemies were ready to swarm upon him from every side at the first sign of a British reverse.' (Fortescue: *History of the British Army*.)

[5] Washington to Heath, February 3, 1777.

army from total extinction. But the work of recruiting the new army authorized by Congress made only slow progress. In addition to the difficulty of securing recruits in the winter season, when the lull in operations did not provide the stimulus of a call to action, Washington was obliged to report to Congress: [1] 'The Treasury has been for some time empty, and the army has labored under the greatest inconvenience for want of money. The recruiting service is particularly injured by this.'

The outbreak of smallpox among the American troops was also a deterrent for the program of recruiting. The spread of this disease bid fair to become an epidemic that would paralyze the army, but Washington took prompt action that saved the situation. On February 5 he reported to Congress: 'The smallpox has made such head in every quarter, that I find it impossible to keep it from spreading through the whole army in the natural way. I have therefore determined, not only to inoculate all the troops now here that have not had it, but shall order Dr. Shippen to inoculate the recruits so fast as they come to Philadelphia. They lose no time, because they will go through the disorder while their clothing, arms, and accoutrements are getting ready.' The success of this wise measure was immediate, and on March 3 Washington was able to write, 'Inoculation at Philadelphia and in this neighborhood has been attended with amazing success.' [2]

But, although this danger was averted, the problem of recruiting the Continental Army was far from being solved. As everything devolved upon Washington, the tasks of the American Commander in Chief again became difficult beyond words. His correspondence at that period was a succession of urgent efforts to forward that object, and to stimu-

[1] January 22, 1777.   [2] Letter to Governor Trumbull.

late the flagging work of the different States in furnishing their respective quotas for the Continental Army. Washington's burdens were also increased by the constant necessity for reconciling the misunderstandings and jealousies occasioned by the readjustments of commissions, in the change from State to Continental service. It was a situation of almost hopeless chaos, with one man the only hope for bringing order out of it.

In spite of all Washington's exertions, there was very little increase of the army in the winter and following spring. On March 14, Washington reported: 'The whole of our numbers in Jersey, fit for duty at this time, is under three thousand....The troops under inoculation, including their attendants, amount to one thousand.' On April 12 Washington sent to Congress a report of the standings of the quotas of the several States, with the following unmistakable comment: 'I wish I could see any prospect of an Army fit to make proper opposition formed any where.[1] You will perhaps be surprised at this, after the public Reports of the great Success of recruiting in all the States, but to convince you that these have been but bare Reports, I will give you the best information I have been able to collect from actual Returns and other accounts.'

One instance will serve to show the difficulties of recruiting, and it should be cited also as the origin of a special corps that was of great value in the Revolution. In the fall of 1776 Congress had authorized the 'Rifle Regiment,' and Washington had nominated Morgan to be its commander. Morgan was accordingly given a commission as Colonel of this corps,[2] but he was debarred from going on duty until

[1] Congress had transmitted to Washington a 'Resolve for forming an army upon the West Side of the Delaware.'
[2] November 12, 1776.

the last of the year 1776, when his exchange released him from his status as a paroled prisoner of war. Upon his exchange, he attempted in Virginia to recruit his regiment. But in April he was only able to bring to Washington less than two hundred men. By gathering chosen men from the other units of the army, this corps was at last filled to its strength of five hundred, with selected officers. But it was not until June 13 that Colonel Morgan could assume command of the Rifle Regiment ready for active service.[1]

But, at the end of May, Washington's efforts began to bear fruit in the gathering of the Continental Army. This became the foundation and the framework, upon which was built the whole military structure of the Americans throughout the war. Instead of merely a fluctuating group of short-term militia, here was at last a permanent army organization. To this the zealous local militia could rally, at the summons of danger, and thus gain coördination by becoming affiliated with its organized force. The value of this organizing function of the Continental Army has been explained — and the events of the war proved that only by this means could there have been an efficient military resistance.

This creation of the Continental Army must be considered as entirely the work of Washington. Against every obstacle, he had won his way. He had not only put American military resistance on a new basis, but it was his own army in every sense of the word. A British historian has thus described it:[2] 'The military force which Washington brought into shape at Morristown — waxing or waning in numbers, but constantly improving in quality — followed

[1] '...to be considered as a body of light infantry, and are to act as such; for which reason they will be exempted from the common duties of the line.' (Letter of Instruction, General Washington to Colonel Morgan, June 13, 1777.)

[2] Trevelyan: *The American Revolution.*

him obediently, resolutely, and devotedly as long as their country had occasion for a general and an army.'

Bringing this army into being had been a long task for Washington. Yet, through all the months before there were any tangible results, Washington's policy of 'keeping up an appearance' had held his enemy inactive. Of course a winter campaign was something outside the minds of the British. But it was inexcusable for Howe to waste the whole spring. In this regard, it is enough to know that General Howe, in all this long period of British inactivity, never had less than twenty-seven thousand troops under his command. The truth was, the British commander's state of mind was a direct military result of Washington's New Jersey campaign and subsequent conduct of affairs.

Howe had never wavered in regarding Philadelphia as his next object of attack, but he shrank from another campaign in the Jerseys. With Washington's lack of real military strength, Howe could have marched to Philadelphia at will, as no opposition was possible. But, behind the screen of Washington's raiding activities, Howe imagined hordes of Americans ready to fall upon his army, if he advanced into the Jerseys.

These dangers loomed so large to Howe, that, to avoid them, he even went to the length of deciding, early in 1777, to conduct the expedition against Philadelphia by sea. This project Howe communicated to Germaine, and it received the assent of the King's Ministers.

In regard to the other alternative, of having Howe co-operate at once with Burgoyne in simultaneous movements of their armies against the line of the Hudson, the evidence is complete that the British plans were never on that basis. In fact, there never was any definite plan for combining the movements of the two armies. As late as May 18, 1777,

Germaine wrote to Howe, renewing consent to the embarkation for Philadelphia, and merely trusting that the project would be 'executed in time for you to coöperate with the army to proceed from Canada.' This easy-going attitude was far removed from the true point of view, that a supporting force from the south would be actually necessary for Burgoyne's safety. This need was missed entirely in the calculations of the British, and this omission was their fatal error. As a British authority has stated,[1] 'Never was there a finer example of the art of organizing disaster.'

Howe had assigned to Philadelphia an artificial importance, far beyond its value in a military sense. He thought that the capture of the 'rebel capital' would be a *coup* that would have a decisive effect upon the Americans. He also was led astray by the delusion that there would be assistance from the Loyalists. In this belief he was encouraged by General Charles Lee, 'who while a prisoner at New York had turned traitor and had represented that both Maryland and Pennsylvania were full of Loyalists, waiting only for the arrival of the King's army to rise against the party of revolution.'[2] This wretched schemer, although Washington was doing everything possible to protect him and secure his exchange, went over to the enemy to gain his ends. He first promised Howe to meet a committee of Congress to induce them to return to their allegiance. Congress rejected Lee's proposals for an interview.[3] Lee then wrote out for Howe a detailed plan for a British campaign that would include the capture of Philadelphia. This document remained a proof in Lee's own handwriting of his treach-

[1] Fortescue: *History of the British Army.*   [2] *Ibid.*

[3] As before, Washington's nature could not have any idea of Lee's treacherous intrigues. In his efforts to help Lee and arrange for his exchange, Washington even favored Lee's proposed interview with a committee of Congress, thinking it might bring good feeling.

ery.[1] Whatever influence the shallow marplot may have exerted was the reverse of helping the British, as diverting Howe's army to Philadelphia was a potent factor in 'organizing disaster.'

For a man of Howe's incurably sluggish temperament any military project implied long delays in its execution. In the case of his Philadelphia expedition, Howe's dread of a march by land, and the added element of preparing for the cumbersome embarkation of his army, to be transported by sea, lengthened these delays beyond all reason. It is merely a statement of fact, to record that the first six months of 1777 went to waste, before Howe's strong army made any move toward the expected reconquest of the Colonies. Six months, and not an effort to strike a blow!

Up to the last of April the total of Howe's offensives was summed up by a British account as follows: 'On the 22nd of March a small British detachment was sent to Peekskill, which, meeting with no resistance, destroyed such few stores as were found in that post. A month later [April 25] a far stronger force of two thousand men was sent up to Danbury, which met with better success so far as regarded the destruction of supplies, but was intercepted on its return and subjected to much the same treatment as the expedition to Concord in 1775. It was, in fact, compelled to fight for every yard of its retreat, and escaped only with the loss of three hundred and sixty men killed and wounded.' [2]

For bravery in the Danbury fight, Arnold, who had a horse killed under him, was voted by Congress 'a horse, caparisoned, as a token of their approbation of his gallant conduct.' Washington had kept Arnold in New England

[1] Found in archives of the Strachey family, endorsed by Howe's secretary as 'Mr. Lee's plan, March 29, 1777.'

[2] Fortescue: *History of the British Army.*

and had been advocating his promotion. Arnold's case was one of the many in which Washington met difficulties as to commissions. Congress had passed over Arnold, and it was not until May 2, 1777, that Washington could induce Congress to grant him the major general's commission which was his due. It was most fortunate for the Americans in the ensuing campaign against Burgoyne that Arnold had this rank.

Chapter XXIII

WASHINGTON WATCHING HOWE

ALTHOUGH Washington had taken every pains to 'keep up an appearance' and deceive General Howe as to his numbers, he did not believe that he would be able to maintain the deception through the spring of 1777. It seemed impossible that Howe could fail to discover the weakness of the Americans. In April Washington thus expressed his feeling as to the situation: 'To my great surprise we are still in a calm. How long it can remain is beyond my skill to determine. That it has continued much beyond my expectation already, is certain. But, to expect General Howe will not avail himself of our weak state is, I think, to say in so many words, that he does not know how to take advantage of circumstances, and of course is unfit for the trust imposed in him.' [1]

Washington had early divined that Howe would make Philadelphia his objective. In March Washington wrote, 'Confirmed by every piece of intelligence we obtain this spring, it scarce admits a doubt of Philadelphia being the object in view at the opening of this campaign.' [2] In the letter of April 12, from which quotation has been made, Washington reiterated the same conviction, 'That Philadelphia is the object I have not myself the smallest doubt.'

[1] To John Augustine Washington, April 12, 1777.
[2] To General Schuyler, March 12, 1777.

Throughout all his labors in pushing forward his program for the Continental Army, with the long delays before there was any tangible result, there was an ever-present anxiety in the mind of Washington. At any time Howe might wake to the realization that Washington's weakness made Philadelphia an easy prey.

But the intimidated Howe let his opportunity slip by, and Washington accomplished what he himself thought impossible. Throughout the first half of 1777 he had prevented his enemy from moving against Philadelphia. And this long delay of the British commander was destined to exert a most unfavorable effect upon the British operations. In the first half of 1777, Howe might have captured Philadelphia without difficulty, and in time to coöperate with Burgoyne's invasion. But, after it had been delayed until the last half of 1777, Howe's Philadelphia expedition made any coöperation with Burgoyne out of the question.

Throughout all this time Howe's strong forces were stolidly immovable, restricted in New Jersey to Brunswick and Amboy.[1] It actually remained for the American Commander in Chief to make the first move in force. At the last of May the accessions to Washington's army had increased its strength to eight thousand. Thereupon, Washington resolved to make a bold front against the daily expected march of the British upon Philadelphia. Accordingly, on May 28, he moved his army to Middlebrook, within ten miles of Brunswick. There he placed his army in a strong intrenched position on the heights, which threatened the expected line of march of Howe's army.

As has been stated, Howe had made up his mind to move his army by sea against Philadelphia. But, with his characteristic disregard of loss of time, he made a leisurely concen-

[1] There were some five thousand troops at each of these places.

tration of eighteen thousand troops at Brunswick and took the field, not to attack Washington, but to attempt to draw him into an engagement.

The contemporary British account of this episode is enlightening: [1] 'Until the beginning of June, the numbers of General Washington's army did not exceed 8000 men, militia included; a circumstance which naturally pointed to the expediency of an early campaign; but the British commander...did not take the field with the main army till the twelfth of June, when he assembled his troops at Brunswick. ...Sir William Howe was thoroughly sensible of the impracticality of making an attack on General Washington in his present situation. He therefore made use of every possible effort to induce him to quit his position, and to hazard an engagement. The American general, however, easily penetrated into the designs of the commander in chief, and eluded them by his cool, collected, and prudent conduct.'

On June 19, Howe withdrew toward Brunswick. Washington followed in hopes of cutting off the British rear guard, but warily determined not to be drawn into a general action. The Americans only succeeded in harassing the rear of the British, and Howe, in turn, attempted to cut off troops of Washington's army. There was sharp fighing on June 25 and June 26 but without heavy losses to the Americans. The contemporary British historian gave the following account of the result: 'General Washington immediately regained his station on the hills, and at the same time secured those passes, of which it was in the contemplation of Lord Cornwallis to have possessed himself. Sir William Howe, being now sensible that every scheme of bringing the Americans to an engagement would be unattended with success, resolved to retire from the Jerseys. Accordingly, on the

[1] Stedman: *History of the American War.*

twenty-eighth of June, he returned with the army to Amboy, and on the succeeding day crossed over to Staten Island. A short cessation of course occurred on each side.' [1]

This 'cessation' meant that Howe, in the first days of July, was putting his troops on board ship for the expedition against Philadelphia. But there were more delays. As the British account expressed it,[2] 'the British troops...on the fifth of July embarked in transports, where both foot and cavalry remained pent up, in the hottest season of the year, in the holds of the vessels, until the twenty-third, when they sailed from Sandy Hook; but meeting with contrary winds, did not arrive at the Capes of the Delaware till the thirtieth.'

For the American Commander in Chief, this was an interval of uncertainty as to the designs of the enemy. Burgoyne's invasion was impending. At the first news that the British were 'beginning to operate against Ticonderoga,' Washington wrote, 'If this proves to be anything more than a diversion, there is no doubt General Howe will proceed up Hudsons River; for if they have any rational end in view, it must be a junction of the two armies to intercept the communication between the Eastern and Southern States, and will make it necessary for Howe and Carleton to coöperate.' [3]

This was an example of Washington's sound military judgment, and a whole volume could not give a more just condemnation of the uncoördinated British plans than that implied in the short sentence, 'If they have any rational end in view, it must be a junction of the two armies.' It was the true measure of the enemy's 'organizing disaster,' that Washington did not think it possible the invasion from

[1] Stedman: *History of the American War.*　　[2] *Ibid.*
[3] Letter to Governor Rutledge, July 5, 1777.

Canada could take place except as 'a preconcerted plan with General Howe.' [1]

Earlier in the year, Washington had expressed the opinion [2] that 'the northern army dare not penetrate' if Howe's army stayed away. At the first of July, Washington only needed to know that the move of Burgoyne was not a feint, in order to feel sure Howe would go up the Hudson. But, fortunately, Washington kept an open mind, as he wrote: [3] 'From their [deserters'] information and a variety of circumstances, — such as, that berths are fitting up for the light-horse on board the transports, provender taken in and providing for three or four weeks, the embarkation of the officers' baggage, with their names and corps endorsed thereon, and the ships watering, — it would seem most probable, that General Howe has in contemplation some other object than the North River. Whether he has, or what it is, however, is unknown to us.'

In this perplexity as to Howe's movements,[4] Washington never strayed away from his sound conviction that the military objective of his army must be Howe's main British army, to curb it and neutralize it wherever it might move. This was the one right solution of his problem, to put himself in position to press upon Howe in either alternative. Washington very ably stated this purpose to Congress (July 10): 'In consequence of the advices from General St. Clair, and the strong probability there is that General Howe will push against the Highland passes to coöperate with Burgoyne, I shall, by the advice of my officers, move the army

[1] To the President of Congress, July 2, 1777, '... and that the latter is to coöperate with him, by pushing his whole force up the North River.'

[2] Letter to Schuyler, March 12, 1777.

[3] Washington to the Governors of the Eastern States, July 7, 1777.

[4] 'I am yet perplexed to find out the real intentions of the enemy.' (To Major General Armstrong, July 4, 1777.)

from hence to-morrow morning towards the North River. If such should be his intention, we shall not be too early, as a favorable wind and tide will carry him up in a few hours. On the other hand, if Philadelphia is his object, he cannot get round before we can arrive there; nor can he well debark his troops, and proceed across the land before we can oppose him.'

Affairs remained in this state of doubt as to Howe's movements. Washington had at once perceived that the Northern campaign offered an opportunity, 'with the assistance of the militia, to check Burgoyne in a country, which I am informed is very strong by nature.' [1] This must be the task of New England, and Washington drew up an eloquent appeal, which was sent to brigadier generals of militia.[2] He wrote: 'It cannot be supposed that the small number of Continental troops assembled at Fort Edward is alone sufficient to check the progress of the enemy. To the militia therefore we must look for support in the time of trial,' and he called upon them to 'rendezvous at Saratoga, unless directed to some other place by General Schuyler or General Arnold.'

In these circular letters Washington showed his knowledge of conditions in the militia, the result of his experience. He wrote: 'I would recommend it to you to engage your men to remain in service for a limited time, to be regularly relieved by others at the expiration of that time. We shall then know what force we have to depend upon, and it will be more convenient for the men, part of whom may be gathering their harvests while the others are bravely defending their country.'

Another paragraph had a widespread effect: 'General Arnold, who is so well known to you all, goes up at my request to take the command of the militia in particular, and I have no doubt but you will, under his conduct and direc-

[1] Letter to Governor Trumbull, July 17, 1777.   [2] July 18, 1777.

tion, repel an enemy from your borders, who, not content with hiring mercenaries to lay waste to your country, have now brought savages, with the avowed and express intent of adding murder to desolation.'

It was a wise move on the part of Washington to secure the appointment of Arnold to command the militia. Washington had held aloof from the vexed question as to whether Gates or Schuyler should command the Northern Department. But he knew the prejudices of New England, and by stating that its militia would serve under Arnold, Washington allayed antagonism. This good impression was increased by Washington's sending Major General Lincoln 'to take the command of the eastern militia, over whom I am informed you have influence, and who place confidence in you.' [1]

But the most effective part of his appeal was the summons for defense against the Indians. No one knew better than Washington what was meant by the advent of these savages with Burgoyne's army. But it was a just nemesis, that the presence of the Indians only served to arouse the whole surrounding country against Burgoyne, without being of the slightest military value to him.

Of all the blunders of this ill-starred invasion, the worst was taking the pack of hundreds of useless Indians with Burgoyne's army. Burgoyne was a humane man, and he undoubtedly thought he would be able to control his savages. But, in his initial proclamation (June 20, 1777), he made the incredibly stupid mistake of the following threat: 'I have but to give stretch to the Indian forces under my direction, and they amount to thousands, to overtake the hardened enemies of Great Britain and America (I consider them the same), wherever they may lurk.'

Utterly unconscious of the effect of this folly, and ignor-

[1] Letter of Instructions to General Lincoln, July 24, 1777.

ant of the flood that was rising to overwhelm him, Burgoyne never had a doubt of success at this time. The easy capture of Ticonderoga (July 5, 1777) had given a first appearance of success to the invasion. Burgoyne mistakenly reported to the British Government that St. Clair's garrison was 'disbanded and totally ruined.' The affair increased Burgoyne's overconfidence — and also the overconfidence of Howe. Before sailing for Philadelphia, Howe congratulated Burgoyne, as if the road to success had been made sure: 'My intention is for Pennsylvania, where I expect to meet Washington; but if he goes to the northward, contrary to my expectations, and you can keep him at bay, be assured I shall soon be after him to relieve you.' This last must be considered a curiosity of military sapiency. Howe added: 'Sir Henry Clinton remains in the command here, and will act as occurences may direct.' There was no trace of 'a preconcerted plan' in any of this.

The fall of Ticonderoga had depressed the Americans at the time. But, the truth was, it was the best thing that could have happened — abandoning the place at once without losses. The importance of this fort was altogether imaginary, a relic of the ideas of the French and Indian Wars. It could not be defended against Burgoyne's army, and attempting to hold it longer would have involved the risk of losing the garrison. These American troops under St. Clair were much needed to augment Schuyler's army. After St. Clair's troops had safely joined him at Fort Edward, Schuyler had under his command, all told, about twenty-eight hundred of the Continental Army and eighteen hundred militia. These provided an organized force, the necessary essential for receiving the militia that were to assemble against Burgoyne. Without this basis to build up an organization, the militia could not have rendered their decisive service.

Washington had shared the disappointment at the early fall of Ticonderoga. But he soon took a different view of the situation. He wrote to Schuyler (July 22, 1777): 'I trust General Burgoyne's army will meet sooner or later an effectual check, and, as I suggested before, that the success he has had will precipitate his ruin. From your account he appears to be pursuing that line of conduct, which of all others is most favorable to us; I mean acting in detachments.' And Washington pointed out that enterprises to cut off any British detachments 'would inspirit the people' and 'they would fly to arms and afford every aid in their power.'

The truth of this forecast was proved at Bennington. Washington also gave to Schuyler some sound military advice: 'Stopping the roads and ordering the cattle removed were certainly right and judicious. If they are well accomplished, the enemy must be greatly retarded and distressed. ...It will not be advisable to repose too much confidence in the works you are about to erect, and thence to collect a large quantity of stores. I begin to consider lines as a kind of trap, and as not answering the valuable purpose expected from them, unless they are on passes that cannot be avoided by an enemy.' This last showed an insight far ahead of his times — in fact the modern doctrine of to-day — and a revolt from the military doctrines of his times which was quite extraordinary.

In this spirit, Schuyler did not make any useless stand in his advanced position, but, before he retreated, he did everything possible to put obstructions in the way of Burgoyne's advance. Schuyler left behind him broken bridges, dammed-up streams, and a tangle of felled trees. The British account [1] reflected vividly the result: 'In this undertaking, the difficulties which the royal army had to encounter

[1] Stedman: *History of the American War.*

199

were infinite. Swamps and morasses were to be passed. Bridges were to be constructed, not only over creeks, but over ravines and gullies. The roads were to be cleared of the forest trees, which had been felled and disposed in such a manner as to intersect each other.'

Burgoyne's army was especially ill adapted to contend with these difficulties. Its make-up [1] and cumbersome organization implied delays from the beginning. When he was in touch with communications and supplies by water, Burgoyne's army was a formidable force. As soon as he broke away from these, and attempted to penetrate the country, his expedition only lumbered along, with interminable delays — and delays were fatal, as they were giving time for the militia to assemble.

The whole countryside was rising against Burgoyne, and a rapid movement would be his only salvation. But any quick advance was inherently out of the question for the formal organizations of the British Regulars and German troops. But, at this stage, Burgoyne had no suspicion of the true situation. His advance was already floundering, but he kept on, with blind confidence in the mere weight of his army to plunge through to victory.

In the mean time, Washington remained perplexed as to Howe's intentions. On July 24 he wrote: [2] 'His conduct is puzzling and embarrassing beyond measure; so are the informations which I get. At one time the ships are standing up towards the North River; in a little while they are going up the Sound; and in an hour they are going out of the Hook. I think in a day or two we must know something of his intentions.' But on the same day Washington was able

[1] British Regulars, 4135; German troops ('Hessians'), 3116; Canadian militia, 148; Indians, 503.
[2] To General Schuyler.

to write: 'I have just received information that the fleet left the Hook yesterday, and, as I think the Delaware the most probable place of their destination, I shall immediately move the army that way.' [1]

Upon this decision, Washington wrote a letter to Schuyler, in which he reaffirmed his confidence in the New England militia, 'as I cannot but think the eastern States, which are so intimately concerned in the matter, will exert themselves to throw in effectual succours to enable you to check the progress of the enemy, and repel a danger, with which they are so immediately threatened.' Of Lincoln Washington wrote: 'I have destined him more particularly to the command of them, and I promise myself it will have a powerful tendency to make them turn out with more cheerfulness, and to inspire them with perseverance to remain in the field and spirit to do their duty while in it.'

Washington also again assured Schuyler as to the situation: 'As they can never think of advancing, without securing their rear by leaving garrisons in the fortresses behind, the force with which they can come against you will be greatly reduced by the detachments necessary for the purpose. And as they have to cut out their road, and remove the impediments you have put in the way, this circumstance, with the encumbrance they must feel in their baggage, will inevitably retard their march a considerable time, and give you leisure and opportunity to prepare a good reception for them. If they continue to act in detachments, you will have it in your power to improve it to very great advantage.... You intimate the propriety of having a body of men stationed somewhere about the Grants (Vermont). The expediency of such a measure appears to me evident.... From the view I have of the matter, I should also think it neces-

[1] To Lincoln, July 24, 1777.

sary to send General Arnold, or some other sensible, spirited officer to Fort Schuyler.' The events showed that this was a most able analysis of the impending campaign.

Howe had taken great pains in an effort to delude Washington into the belief that his fleet had sailed for Boston. With this purpose he wrote out a letter in his own hand,[1] and contrived to have it intercepted and brought to Washington. But Washington was not to be deceived: 'To me a stronger proof could not be given that the former is not going to Eastward than this letter adduces. It was evidently intended to fall into our hands.' [2]

Even after he knew that Howe's army had put to sea, Washington kept his troops in position to move against Howe in either direction: 'As we are yet uncertain as to the real destination of the enemy, tho the Delaware seems most probable, I have thought it prudent to halt the army at this place (Coryell's Ferry), Howell's Ferry, and Trenton, at least till the Fleet actually enters the Bay, and put the matter beyond a doubt. From hence we can be upon the Grounds to oppose them, before they can possibly make their arrangements and dispositions for an attack.' [3]

Washington had 'ordered Sullivan's division to halt at Morris Town whence it will march southward, if there should be occasion, or northward upon the first advice that the enemy should be throwing any force up the North River. Gen¹ Howe's in a manner abandoning General Burgoyne is so unaccountable a matter, that, till I am fully satisfied it is so, I cannot help casting my Eyes continually behind me.' [4]

[1] Given in full in *The Writings of Washington*, vol. 5, p. 514.
[2] To Putnam, July 25, 1777.
[3] Letter of July 30, 1777, to Gates, who was in Philadelphia.
[4] To Gates, July 30, 1777.

Chapter XXIV

THE INTERVAL BEFORE THE ATTACK ON PHILADELPHIA

THE news of the arrival at the Capes of the Delaware of the British fleet bearing Howe's army (July 31, 1777) seemed to presage an immediate attack on Philadelphia. Upon receipt of this information, Washington wrote to Governor Trumbull that no more troops could be sent to the North from Peekskill: 'Not a man more can go, as all Continental troops at that post, excepting two thousand are called to join this army. For I have to inform you that General Howe's object and operations no longer remain a secret. At half after nine this morning, I received an express from Congress, advising that the enemy's fleet, consisting of two hundred and twenty-eight sail, were at the Capes of Delaware yesterday in the forenoon. This being the case, there can be no doubt but he will make a vigorous push to possess Philadelphia, and we should collect all the force we can to oppose him.'

But the 'vigorous push' was to be still longer delayed by Howe. The following is a British account of what happened: 'He [Howe] had made up his mind originally to land in the Delaware, so as to be nearer to New York and to Burgoyne, but gave up the attempt on the remonstrance of the naval officers, and sailed on to the Chesapeake. Whether the naval officers may have exaggerated the risks of disembarkation in the Delaware I cannot pretend to decide; but the fact remains that the voyage to the Chesapeake was disastrous, since contrary winds prolonged a passage of three hundred and fifty miles over no fewer than twenty-four days. Then the army disembarked at the head of Elk River, unopposed indeed, but actually only thirteen miles west of Delaware Bay.' [1]

There is no need of any comment on this statement of the culmination of the almost incredible delays, which postponed Howe's campaign against Philadelphia until so late in the year. Throughout the months of 1777 the city had lain at the mercy of any resolute attack. All that time it had been Howe's one military objective, and the totals of delays can only be called the results of Washington's Trenton-Princeton campaign and his subsequent 'keeping up an appearance' of an American army ready to oppose a march through the country.

It was the dread of a repetition of the British experience in the Jerseys, that compelled Howe to decide on moving by sea. Consequently, the results of Washington's successful strategy had gone far. Instead of capturing Philadelphia early in the year, and being free to coöperate with Burgoyne, Howe was not to be in position to move against the city until the last of August — and this meant that Howe was to be as far from any possibility of helping Burgoyne as if he were not on the same continent. These are merely statements of cause and effect.

The unexpected news, that Howe's expedition had put to sea again, very naturally worried Washington: 'I have this moment received intelligence by express, that the enemy's fleet yesterday morning about eight o'clock sailed out of the Capes in an eastern course. This surprising event gives me

[1] Fortescue: *History of the British Army.*

the greatest anxiety.' [1] To Governor Trumbull he wrote (August 4, 1777): 'They have stood out to sea again, but how far, or where they are going, remains to be known. From their entire command of the water they derive immense advantages, and distress us much by harassing and marching our troops from post to post. I wish we could fix on their destination; in such case I should hope we would be prepared to receive them.'

As a matter of course, with Washington's sound military judgment that the only right strategy for the British would be to combine the efforts of Burgoyne and Howe, the American commander's first impression was that Howe's sailing to the Delaware had been a feint to draw the American army toward Philadelphia, and that the enemy had put back for the North River.

Accordingly, Washington ordered Sullivan and the troops from that region to retrace their steps, and he held his whole army ready to move in whatever direction might be dictated by information of his enemy's intentions.[2] This uncertainty kept Washington 'in a very irksome state of suspense.' [3] However, he soon had cause to doubt that Howe was moving to support Burgoyne: 'But I was last night overtaken by an express from Philadelphia, with an account that they had been seen on the 7th instant off Sinepuxent Inlet, about sixteen leagues to the southward of the Capes of Delaware. Upon this I have halted for further intelligence.' [4]

On August 21 Washington was still obliged to report to

[1] Letter to Putnam, August 1, 1777.

[2] '...Not to proceed any further towards the Delaware, until you had orders from me for that purpose; nor to return towards Peekskill, unless you should have certain information, that the enemy's fleet were arrived at the Hook.' (Letter of instructions to Brigadier General Deborre, August 3, 1777.)

[3] Letter to John Augustine Washington, August 5, 1777.

[4] Letter to Putnam.

the President of Congress: 'We have no other alternative left than to remain here idle and inactive.' But on the next day there was a sudden change in the situation: 'By the inclosed, which has this moment come to hand, you will perceive that the Enemy's Fleet have at length fairly entered the Chesapeake Bay, Swan Point being at least two hundred miles up.' [1] And, in the same letter, the relief to Washington's mind was reflected in an exultant and prophetic message: 'I desire that you will immediately forward this account to Governor Trumbull, to be by him sent on eastward. As there is not now the least danger of General Howe's going to New England, I hope the whole force of that country will turn out, and, by following the great stroke struck by General Stark near Bennington, entirely crush General Burgoyne.'

Washington's exultation was well founded. With Howe a piece off the board, the toils were indeed closing about Burgoyne. At the news of the sighting of Howe's fleet off Sinepuxent, Washington felt free at once to send additional reinforcements to the Northern Department, to give support to the militia he had urged into the field. He ordered up the Hudson two Continental regiments, and he also sent Morgan and the Rifle Regiment. Morgan and his riflemen rendered invaluable service in the ensuing campaign against Burgoyne.

Washington had always refused to act in the vexed question of the command of the Northern Department,[2] but Congress had removed Schuyler and given the command to

[1] Letter to Putnam, August 22, 1777.

[2] Washington to the President of Congress, August 3, 1777: 'At the same time that I express my thanks for the high mark of confidence which Congress have been pleased to repose in me by their Resolve, authorizing me to send an Officer to command the northern army, I should wish to be excused from making the appointment.'

Gates. This was hard measure for Schuyler, whose devoted patriotism and unremitting efforts were deserving of better treatment. But New England was prejudiced against Schuyler, as a result of long friction with New York as to the Hampshire grants, now the State of Vermont, and the New England members of Congress demanded Gates. The removal of Schuyler undoubtedly made it easier to bring out the militia to join the army, and, as the whole success of the campaign against Burgoyne depended upon this, the change must be considered a help. Washington rightly estimated this benefit from the appointment of Gates.[1]

But Burgoyne had no conception of the strong forces that were gathering around him. He had shown his ignorance and overconfidence by his mistake of detaching from his army an expedition of five hundred Hessians and one hundred Indians, to march to Bennington on a foraging mission, under the command of the Hessian Colonel Baum. With this detachment, there actually was sent out a skeleton regimental organization, to receive as recruits the many Loyalists who were expected to rise and flock to the King's standard. To his cost, Baum found that there was indeed an uprising! But it was all hostile, of the men of western New England, who overwhelmed and captured his whole force (Battle of Bennington, August 16, 1777) — and then did the same thing to another detachment under Breyman sent to aid Baum.

This defeat meant a loss of over nine hundred for Burgoyne. But more menacing than the impairment of his numbers was the unmistakable revelation that enemies

[1] 'The excuse of want of confidence in the general officers, which has hitherto been alleged by the eastern States, for withholding those reinforcements from the northern army, which were expected from them, will be obviated by the presence of Major General Gates.' (Letter to Governor Clinton, August 23, 1777.)

were gathering about him, instead of the imaginary Loyalists who were to come to his assistance.

The same upset for the preconceived ideas of the British leaders was happening in the Mohawk Valley, where the supporting inroad of St. Leger was also ending in failure. It had not called forth the response of the Loyalists promised by Sir John Johnson, who was himself with St. Leger's unsuccessful expedition.

This double object lesson ended the British delusion that Burgoyne's invading army would find large bodies of Loyalists rising to its support. Burgoyne himself at last realized that he was in an enemy country. He wrote, 'Wherever the King's forces point, militia to the number of three or four thousand assemble in a few hours.' But, even after this knowledge, Burgoyne did not estimate the full danger of his situation. As a British account has stated, '... he decided to continue his advance after collecting thirty days' provisions, a task which, with his limited resources of transport, occupied him until the 13th of September.' [1] This simply meant that Burgoyne stood still, and allowed all the more time for his enemies to gather around him.

At this interval, when Burgoyne was passive on the east banks of the upper Hudson, Gates took command of the opposing American forces (August 19, 1777). The gathering point of the main American army was on the west side of the Hudson at the junction of the Mohawk. Gates' career afterwards proved that he was lacking in the qualities of a commander of an army. But he did have some talent as an organizer, and that was the one attribute most needed at this time. Actually, it was then more important than anything else, for the hurriedly assembled bands of militia which were arriving to oppose Burgoyne, that they should be blended

[1] Fortescue: *History of the British Army.*

into an army organization. It provided a basis for building them into an army. Without this organization to give direction to their zealous efforts, as has been stated, they would not have been able to render their service in overwhelming Burgoyne.

Consequently, under these unusual circumstances, Gates was playing a useful rôle in the preparations against Burgoyne. A truly formidable array was being brought into the field against the British invading army. This was the state of affairs in the North when Howe's army at last landed to begin his attack upon Philadelphia.

Howe disembarked his troops at Elkton, at the head of the Elk River which flows into Chesapeake Bay (August 25, 1777). As soon as Washington was sure of Howe's actual presence in Chesapeake Bay, he had gathered all his available forces, for an advance to Wilmington to oppose the British army.

Before giving an account of the ensuing campaign, one military condition of the situation must be understood. The circumstances made it mandatory for Washington to fight Howe, and to offer the strongest delaying resistance possible against the British advance on Philadelphia. There can be no question of this, although a review of the facts of the situation is all that is necessary to show that there was no possibility of preventing Howe from capturing Philadelphia. All Washington could do was to harass and delay Howe as long as possible.

In the first place, Washington had less than twelve thousand effectives, including militia and volunteers, while Howe possessed a superiority in numbers of almost three to two. Not only this, but Howe's army was at high efficiency, with complete equipment and supplies. In contrast, a large proportion of Washington's troops were but poorly equipped, from the exigencies of their service, as there was a large proportion of recently joined recruits. Moreover, this was not a case of a British army operating far from its sea base, and thus offering an opportunity for the Americans to resort to the harassing tactics so effective against the Regulars. For Howe's army had been landed, with all its supplies brought by water, at a point from which there was merely a march of about fifty miles through an open country that presented no difficulties.

Yet, in spite of these disadvantages, it was clear that Washington's only course was to fight Howe's advance as best he could. To yield Philadelphia without a battle would have resulted in a bad moral effect everywhere, and would have caused a serious setback for public opinion. Washington's logical strategic aim was, to keep before the eyes of the people the existence of an opposing American army, which would curb the British army and defend the surrounding country, even though Howe's superior forces should occupy Philadelphia.

In order to impress this fact upon the inhabitants of Philadelphia and its neighborhood, Washington had taken pains to march his whole army through the streets of Philadelphia, on his way to oppose Howe. On this occasion (August 24, 1777), although it was true that it was necessary to decorate the American soldiers with sprigs of green for uniformity, no one could help seeing that they had taken on the form of an army.

As has been explained, this change for the better had been the result of Washington's own efforts. He had at last succeeded in his purpose of getting his army on a permanent basis. No longer was he compelled to rely upon short-term enlistments. His recruits were there to stay, and to be made into soldiers. His army had also gained a stable organization, under the new Continental commissions. By this means, Washington had been enabled to give commands to the officers who had won his approbation by their proved services.

Wisely chosen by Washington, and in a close association with him that never was to be broken, were Greene and Knox. These two, each in his own province, were Washington's strongest supports throughout the war. His selection for Adjutant General had been Timothy Pickering, another instance of Washington's good judgment in choice of men. Pickering's military services were of great value, and he was to become the most efficient Quartermaster General of the Continental Army.

It was notable that, in this parade of Washington's army through Philadelphia, the various foreign officers who had joined the Americans were prominent for the first time. Many of those from abroad, seeking commissions, had been merely adventurers, and their presence had been a source of embarrassment to Washington.[1] It had required all his influence and tact to reconcile the jealousies occasioned by their advent. Even Knox and Greene had been offended by their pretensions.

The case of Lafayette was entirely different. Instead of making demands, he modestly asked 'two favors; one is to serve at my own expense; the other to commence serving as a volunteer.'[2] This generous spirit made so great an impression on Congress, that Lafayette was commissioned a major general at once.[3] But this commission was honorary only,

[1] 'Under the privilege of friendship, I take the liberty to ask you what Congress expect I am to do with the many foreigners they have at different times promoted to the ranks of field officers.' (Letter to Richard Henry Lee, May 17, 1777.)

[2] *Mémoires du Général Lafayette.*

[3] July 31, 1777. The veteran de Kalb, who had accompanied Lafayette, was later given a similar commission, to bear the same date.

and it did not imply any command over troops. For this reason, the honor to Lafayette disarmed criticism and had an excellent effect.

When Lafayette first met Washington, the young Frenchman at once felt the spell of the American's impressive personality, and became an ardent admirer who was eager to serve in Washington's military household. It was appropriate that Lafayette rode beside Washington in this march through Philadelphia.

Among the other foreign officers, an enthusiastic volunteer was Count Pulaski,[1] a young Pole serving in the recently organized light horse, with Henry Lee, who was then twenty-two and destined to be known as 'Light Horse Harry.'

After marching through Philadelphia and advancing to Wilmington, Washington was given time to collect the last of his troops, Sullivan's division, as Howe delayed moving toward Philadelphia. Sullivan's troops had been farthest away toward the north, in the interval of doubt as to Howe's intentions.

[1] 'I have brought for Passenger with me one Count Pulaski a Polish Nobleman & General recommended by the Honble Doctor Franklin.

'*Captain* JOHN FISH
'*Brig Massachusetts*

'OFF MARBLEHEAD
'*July* 23, 1777.'

Chapter xxv

THE CAPTURE OF PHILADELPHIA BY THE BRITISH

FROM Elkton, Howe 'moved slowly and cautiously north-eastward,' [1] and it was not until September 3 that the British pushed forward against the advance parties of the Americans. There were only slight clashes, as Washington had decided to fight the battle expected of him at the Brandywine Creek. Along this stream he had chosen his ground in advance, and he was drawing back his army to its designated position. Howe had been moving to turn his right, but on September 9 Washington's army was posted behind the Brandywine Creek.

That the American commander was to make this stand with little or no faith in his ability to stop Howe was clearly shown by Washington's significant act. Before taking position for battle, Washington sent back to Chester all the baggage of his army. The event proved the wisdom of this precaution, as, by so doing, Washington insured its safety from capture by the enemy in the retreat — a most fortunate thing for the Americans.

At the Brandywine, Washington disposed his army in a strong defensive position. The stream was fordable at several points. The American center was at Chad's Ford, and blocked the direct road. There Washington commanded in person, and on heights behind the center Greene's division

[1] Fortescue: *History of the British Army.*

213

was placed in reserve. On the left the stream flowed into rapids, and was so difficult to cross that its defense could be intrusted to militia under General Armstrong.

On the right, the Brandywine did not offer much of an obstacle against an enemy. To guard it Sullivan was given the command of the American right wing, which was made strong. Sullivan had three divisions (his own, Stephen's and Stirling's). But against this American right Howe executed a skillful maneuver.

As he marched forward, Howe had moved his army in two columns. Cornwallis commanded the column on the right, Knyphausen on the left. Each column was approximately half of Howe's army. Upon discovering the American army, disposed as has been explained, Howe decided that a frontal attack was out of the question, and he determined to send Cornwallis' column to turn the American right and take Sullivan in the rear.

With the purpose of masking this plan, at daybreak on September 11 Howe advanced Knyphausen's column, directly against the American center defending Chad's Ford. But, at the same time, he ordered the right column under Cornwallis to file past the rear of Knyphausen, widely to the left, in order to outflank the Americans by crossing the upper fords of the Brandywine,[1] and thus to get to the rear of Sullivan's right wing.

This was actually a repetition of Howe's maneuver at the Battle of Long Island. And it was also a strange fact that this encircling movement was repeated against the same American officer — and with the same success. Sullivan had been the victim in the case of the Long Island maneuver, and he was again to allow the enemy to take him in the rear.

[1] '...At a ford about six miles above us.' (Washington to President of Congress, September 11, 1777.)

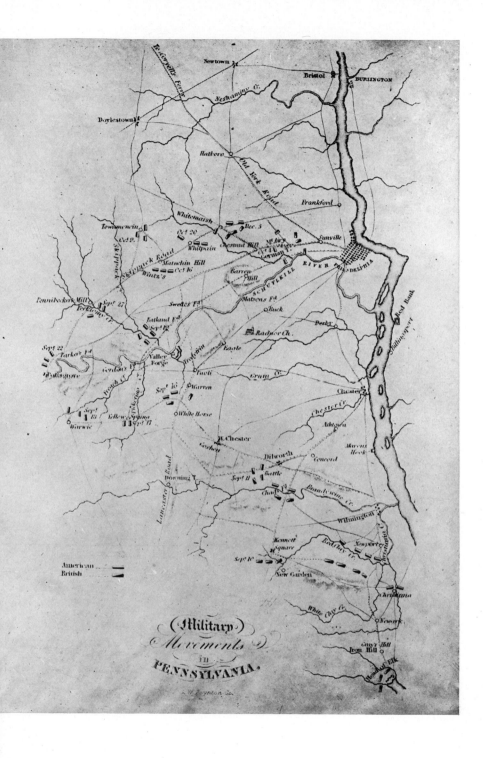

Military
Movements
in
PENNSYLVANIA.

Along the Brandywine Sullivan's troops held posts for two miles. But Sullivan assumed that the enemy would not go beyond these positions, and he did not take sufficient precautions to obtain information of the enemy's movements.

After waiting until about ten o'clock, to give Cornwallis time to be well on his way to turn the American right, the column of Knyphausen approached Chad's Ford, and opened a cannonade as if preparing to force the American center. In the words of the contemporary British account, 'The attention of the Americans was thus amused, in order that Lord Cornwallis might make his passage good.' [1] Cornwallis' troops had discarded knapsacks and the other impedimenta of the Regulars, and they made the encircling march to a successful crossing of the Brandywine. As they crossed far above the positions of Sullivan's troops, they met no opposition, and it was a long time before the truth as to their movement was discovered by the Americans. As a British account has stated, 'So unobservant were Washington's officers that he only by mere chance gained accurate information that Cornwallis' turning movement was not merely in progress but actually accomplished.' [2]

The first information received by Washington was a message from Sullivan, at about noon, that a strong body of the enemy had been seen on the Lancaster road. Washington at once ordered a reconnaissance beyond the right wing, and he made preparations to attack the enemy in his front before the enemy force on the right could come into action. At this stage, came another message which convinced Sullivan there was no enemy threatening his flank and rear. Then came the news of the actual presence of the enemy in Sullivan's rear.

[1] Stedman: *History of the American War.*
[2] Fortescue: *History of the British Army.*

In the midst of these conflicting messages, Washington gave up the design of attacking the enemy across Chad's Ford. This was most fortunate, as Howe's army was so strong that, even after detaching Cornwallis' column Knyphausen's force was too powerful to offer chances of success for an American attack, 'and by Howe's forethought he had been supplied with plenty of guns, so that he could have held his own until Cornwallis came up in the enemy's rear and destroyed the Americans utterly.' [1]

Upon the tardy news from the right of the appearance of Cornwallis' column, Washington ordered Sullivan to oppose him with his whole right wing. Sullivan attempted to do this by forming his three divisions near the Birmingham Meeting House. But Cornwallis' maneuver was too far advanced and in too strong force to be checked. The overwhelming surprise was as complete as at Long Island.

Washington's own dispatch to Congress told the true story: 'Unfortunately the intelligence rec'd., of the enemy's advancing up the Brandywine & crossing at a ford about six miles above us, was uncertain & contradictory, notwithstanding all my pains to get the best. This prevented my making a disposition adequate to the force with which the enemy attacked us on our right; in consequence of which, the troops first engaged were obliged to retire before they could be reinforced.' [2] This unexpected strength of Cornwallis' attacks overwhelmed Sullivan's divisions before they could be formed for defense, and his whole force was compelled to retreat toward Dilworth.

But Washington had also ordered Greene, with the American troops which had been held in reserve behind the center,

[1] Fortescue: *History of the British Army.*

[2] To the President of Congress, Chester, twelve o'clock at night, September 11, 1777.

to the aid of Sullivan. And here was in evidence another benefit from the sound military instinct of Washington, which had warned him to provide for the contingencies of what was bound to be a campaign of retreat. At the time he was selecting the Brandywine positions, and when he was studying his dispositions for their defense, Washington had pointed out to Greene a place about a mile beyond Dilworth as well adapted for a second position, to make a stand in case the Americans should be obliged to fall back.

At the emergency of Cornwallis' overwhelming attack, such a rallying point was just what was needed, and Washington ordered Greene to occupy this chosen position in support of Sullivan. It saved the situation, after Greene had hurried his troops by a wonderfully quick march to this designated place.[1] Thus strongly posted, Greene was able to cover the retreat of Sullivan's broken divisions. Greene also repulsed the assaults of Cornwallis, and held him back from any pursuit.

In the mean time, after these American forces had been diverted to oppose Cornwallis' column, the position at Chad's Ford was left inadequately defended under the command of Wayne. Taking advantage of this, Knyphausen, when he knew from the sound of guns that Cornwallis was attacking the American right and rear, made an attack in force at Chad's Ford. Wayne put up a good resistance, but he was unable to prevent the enemy from forcing a crossing, and Knyphausen's column also pressed upon the Americans.

However, Greene's skillful defense, in the wisely chosen position, held back Cornwallis until nightfall. Consequently, the two British columns did not unite their attacks until it was thought too late to pursue the retreating Amer-

[1] 'It is said, on good authority, his division accomplished the march, or rather run of five miles, in less than fifty minutes.' (Irving: *Life of Washington*.)

icans, who gained safety at Chester. To that place the baggage of the American army had been sent in advance, as has been stated, and the army could be reorganized after its retreat. The divisions which had been put to flight by Cornwallis were in disorder, but, on the arrival of Washington himself with Greene's unbroken troops, order was restored, and the American army was placed in a good position near Chester.

In his report to Congress, Washington stated: 'The baggage having been previously moved off, all is secure, saving the blankets, which being at their backs, many of them doubtless were lost. I have directed all the troops to assemble behind Chester, where they are now arranging for the night. Notwithstanding the misfortunes of the day, I am happy to find the troops in good spirits and I hope another time we shall compensate for the losses now sustained.' [1]

The losses of the Americans in the Battle of the Brandywine were about one thousand, in killed, wounded, and prisoners. The British stated that the total of their losses amounted to five hundred and seventy-five.

The contemporary British account complained that the British commander missed an opportunity for the total destruction of the American army [2] by failing to follow up this victory promptly. But, in addition to the fact that the Americans had checked the enemy until nightfall, Cornwallis' troops were fatigued by their long march, and they needed rest. Beside this, even if the British had hastened to follow up their victory,[3] it would not have been a case of

[1] Chester, twelve o'clock at night, September 11, 1777.

[2] 'Any one of these movements, it was thought, might have been attended with the total destruction of the American army.' (Stedman: *History of the American War.*)

[3] 'They dared not pursue a single step.' (General Knox to his wife, September 13, 1777.)

218

pressing a broken army. The retreat of those of the American troops who had been thrown into disorder was being covered by other American troops, who were in good order and able to offer a strong defense.

In regard to this battle, it also should be noted that Washington showed his freedom from any small quality of mind by protecting General Sullivan, when Congress was about to suspend him for his failure on the Brandywine,[1] and by absolving Sullivan from blame,[2] instead of attributing the defeat to his conduct.

As the results of this battle made it evident that Howe could not be prevented from capturing Philadelphia, Congress resolved to move to Lancaster. From there they afterwards removed to Yorktown. And again, as after the retreat in the Jerseys, Congress voted extraordinary powers to Washington, especially as to officers under his command and in conferring authority over all matters within seventy miles of his headquarters.[3]

Although Washington was still resolved to oppose Howe to the utmost, he showed clearly he thought Howe would occupy Philadelphia, by advising Congress that 'every species of food should be moved from the city.' [4] As to projected fortifications for the defense of Philadelphia, Washington's statement to Congress was strikingly in accord with the most modern military doctrine, 'If we should be able to oppose General Howe with success in the Field, the works will be unnecessary; if not, and he should force us from hence, he will certainly possess himself of 'em.' [5]

[1] To the President of Congress, September 15, 1777.

[2] To Sullivan, October 24, 1777.

[3] '... for the space of sixty days, unless sooner revoked by Congress.' (Journals, September 17, 1777.)

[4] To the President of Congress, September 15, 1777.

[5] Ibid., September 13, 1777.

Although it must be considered an exaggeration for the British historian to write that Howe might have destroyed Washington's army immediately after Brandywine, yet it was undoubtedly true that Howe's habitually slow and cautious movements continued to afford Washington the opportunity to rest and refresh the American troops, and also to make defensive preparations which still farther delayed Howe's occupation of Philadelphia. Washington was given time to station militia to defend the crossings of the Schuylkill on Howe's direct route, while he advanced his army against Howe's left on the Lancaster road toward Derby. Upon this, Howe moved his army to the northeast to strike to the right of Washington.

Washington's army had been reinforced by militia, and was 'more numerous after the battle of Brandywine than before.' [1] As to the ensuing events, Washington's own account should be quoted. He reported that he had moved his army 'with a firm intent of giving the Enemy Battle whenever I should meet them; and accordingly advanced as far as the Warren Tavern upon the Lancaster road, near which place the two armies were upon the point of coming to a General Engagement, but were prevented by a most violent flood of Rain, which continued all day and following night. When it held up, we had the mortification to find that our ammunition, which had been compleated to forty rounds a man, was entirely ruined; and in that situation we had nothing left for it but to find out a strong piece of Ground, which we could easily maintain until we could get the Army put in order, and a Recruit of Ammunition.' [2]

At this disadvantage, Washington could do little to retard

[1] General Knox to President of the Council of Massachusetts Bay, October 7, 1777.

[2] To the President of Congress, September 23, 1777.

Howe's progress. He detached a force under Wayne to harass the British left. Wayne moved his division into a concealed position in the woods near Howe's flank, and reported to Washington, 'I believe he knows nothing of my situation.' But, in the night of September 20, a British force under Major General Grey surprised Wayne's command and defeated it, with a loss of three hundred killed and wounded, and eighty prisoners. General Grey, in order that he might be sure no stray shot would betray his approach, had the flints removed from the muskets of his soldiers and directed them to rely entirely on the bayonet. For this reason he was called afterwards 'No flint' Grey.

There were more maneuvers, but nothing approaching a battle, as there was no longer anything to prevent Howe from occupying Philadelphia. He established his headquarters in Germantown, and the troops of Cornwallis took possession of Philadelphia on September 25. At last General Howe was in Philadelphia. He had occupied the 'rebel capital.' But he was to find it a barren victory. In the first place, this newly constituted meeting place of Congress had nothing of the importance of a European capital. Howe had taken the European point of view, and had magnified the value of the city as a military objective. The fact was, it was merely a repetition of the New York situation. Control of the city did not mean control of the surrounding country.

As at New York, Howe's army was curbed by Washington's army. Outside of the city Howe had no hold, so long as this American army remained unbroken. In view of the lessons of New York, Howe's logical objective was to break Washington's army — and that should have been the central idea of his campaign, instead of his obsession for the mere capture of Philadelphia. But no trace of this can be found in Howe's strategy.

There could be no question as to this lack in General Howe's conduct of military operations. After Brandywine, instead of following up and attacking Washington, Howe simply marched and maneuvered to get into Philadelphia. After the capture of the city, the British general did not make any move against Washington. Howe restricted his efforts to safeguarding himself in the city. Moreover, he sought only to make his communications safe by water, and actually conceded control of the countryside to Washington.

Instead of any British attacks on Washington's army, it was the American army that took the offensive.

Chapter XXVI

THE FALL OF 1777

AFTER occupying Philadelphia, General Howe devoted his attention to opening the Delaware River for communication by water. When Howe's army was on its way to Philadelphia, the British fleet had been sent back from the Chesapeake to the Delaware. But the Americans had placed obstructions in the river, which the contemporary British historian described as 'three rows of chevaux de frize, composed of immense beams of timber bolted and fastened together, and stuck with iron pikes fastened in every direction.' [1] The same British narrative stated: 'To remove these obstructions, so as to open a communication between the fleet and the army, was an object of the utmost importance, but which could not be accomplished without previously reducing the forts by which they were defended.' [2]

These American works, built to defend the obstructions in the Delaware River, were Fort Mercer, at Red Bank on the New Jersey side of the river, and Fort Mifflin, on an island in the same stretch of the river, about seven miles below Philadelphia. In addition, American troops had constructed works at Billingsport, on the New Jersey side, and there was a small flotilla of naval vessels. These last defenses were not of much value. The frigate *Delaware* was

[1] Stedman: *History of the American War.*   [2] *Ibid.*

223

lost, by going aground under the guns of the enemy and falling into their hands, and the works at Billingsport were razed and abandoned at the approach of a British expedition of three battalions sent out by Howe on September 29.

But Washington decided to persist in holding Fort Mifflin and Fort Mercer, and, 'as the navigation of the river was still blocked, Howe was obliged further to detach three thousand men, to escort his supplies overland from the Chesapeake.'[1] Having received information that the enemy had been thus temporarily weakened,[2] Washington resolved 'to make an attack upon the troops, which were at and near Germantown.'[3]

Washington's own report of his dispositions for this attack should be quoted, as there have been many erroneous versions of this battle. 'The divisions of Sullivan and Wayne, flanked by Conway's brigade, were to enter the town by the way of Chestnut Hill, while General Armstrong with the Pennsylvania militia should fall down the Manatawney road by Vandeering's Mill, and get upon the enemy's left and rear. The divisions of Greene and Stephen flanked by McDougall's brigade, were to enter, by taking a circuit by way of the Lime-kiln road at the Market-house, and to attack their right wing; and the militia of Maryland and Jersey, under Generals Smallwood and Forman, were to march by the old York road, and fall upon the rear of their right. Lord Stirling, with Nash's and Maxwell's brigades, was to form a corps de reserve.'[4]

The troops which were to carry out these plans made night marches into position for the attack, which was to

[1] Fortescue: *History of the British Army.*

[2] 'Having received intelligence through two intercepted letters, that General Howe had detached a part of his force....' (To the President of Congress, October 5, 1777.)

[3] To the President of Congress, October 5, 1777.   [4] *Ibid.*

take place at sunrise October 5, 1777. The contemporary British account has stated that General Howe had information 'the evening before the attack,' and neglected to make preparations against it.[1] There is no doubt of the fact that the first assault of Sullivan's column effected a surprise, as it drove the enemy from their ground. But, as they retreated, a strong party of the enemy took position in the large stone house of Judge Chew in Germantown. This served as an improvised fortress for the enemy, who, in the words of Washington, 'were in a situation not to be easily forced, and had it in their power, from the windows, to give us no small annoyance, and in a great measure to obstruct our advance.'[2]

Washington reported: 'The attack from our left column, under General Greene, began about three quarters of an hour after that from the right, and was for some time equally successful.'[3] But all these first promises of victory were spoiled by a thick fog, which made it impossible to coördinate the assaults of the American troops. As their attacks were made from different directions, it was essential that they should be in combination. But the fog became so dense that the Americans could see neither friends nor foes.

Under these circumstances, the whole scheme of attack was thrown into confusion. In spite of the resistance of the six companies of British troops under Colonel Musgrave in the Chew house, the British left was falling back. But the advance of Greene's force against the British right, which was intended to be the main attack, went astray, even to the extent of mistaking the American troops for the enemy and

---

[1] 'The neglect of the commander in chief in this action at Germantown was extreme. He was acquainted with the intentions of General Washington on the evening before the attack, and therefore could have provided against it.' (Stedman: *History of the American War.*)

[2] To the President of Congress, October 5, 1777.   [3] *Ibid.*

attacking them. Stephen's brigade, of Greene's command, and Wayne's troops, which were with Sullivan's attacking force, were thus involved in fighting against one another.

From this contretemps, disorder spread through the American troops, and their attack fell to pieces. The British were given the opportunity to rally their retreating troops, and the bewildered Americans in turn retreated from the action which had opened so favorably. The British contemporary account stated: 'They attempted to rally upon some rising ground; but this was only a feint to secure a retreat. This they effected, with all their artillery, under cover of the fog, which rendered it difficult for the British troops to discover their movements. This fog, which had at first been so advantageous to the Americans, was alleged to have greatly contributed to the disappointment of the scheme, inasmuch as it prevented the different bodies of the American army from discovering each other's operations.' [1]

This British account in reality gave a true summary of the essentials of the Battle of Germantown, about which many fables have been entwined. On the part of Washington, it was a bold project, an attack that Howe thought out of the question, 'as he frankly confessed he did not look for so vigorous an onslaught after such a success as Brandywine.' [2] That it came so near success was ample justification for the venture.

Washington himself always felt that the Americans had 'retreated at the instant when victory was declaring herself in our favor.' [3] But, when one takes into account the diffi-

[1] Stedman: *History of the American War.*

[2] Fortescue: *History of the British Army.*

[3] 'It is with much chagrin and mortification I add, that every account confirms the opinion I at first entertained, that our troops retreated at the instant when victory was declaring herself in our favor.' (To the President of Congress, October 7, 1777.)

culties of carrying out such operations in the dense fog,[1] it seems impossible that full success could have been attained. However, although the attack failed to accomplish decisive results on the field, Washington's boldness produced an effect that was in itself a victory. This good effect was marked, upon the troops of Washington's army. Knox wrote: '... we have gained considerable experience, and our army have a certain proof that the British troops are vulnerable.'

To the American public this battle also furnished proof that Howe's army was not dominating the situation. At Germantown Washington had shown that the American army remained an active factor in the field, and was strong enough to take the offensive against Howe — 'the first attack made during the war by the American troops on the main body of the enemy.'[2] But in Europe the effect of the Battle of Germantown was most significant. Arthur Lee wrote that, at the first interview with Vergennes on the subject of a French alliance (December 12, 1777), the French Minister said, 'that nothing had struck him so much as General Washington's attacking and giving battle to General Howe's army; that to bring an army, raised within a year, to this promised everything.' For this reason, the Battle of Germantown was of importance as an influence favorable to the Americans.

The losses in killed and wounded were: British 537, Americans 673. But the Americans lost four hundred in prisoners, as one regiment of Greene's force had been cut off in the fog and surrendered. The British lost very few prisoners, as most of these, who had been captured in the

---

[1] 'Had it not been for the unlucky circumstance of the fog....' (General Knox to President of Council of Massachusetts Bay, October 7, 1777.)

[2] General Knox, October 7, 1777.

227

first successful advances of the Americans, escaped when the Americans were thrown into confusion in the fog.

The British fleet anchored in the Delaware below Newcastle, and Howe withdrew his army to Philadelphia, gathering his whole force for operations to open the navigation of the river for the fleet. With his army thus concentrated, Howe had a superiority which rendered him safe from any serious attacks on the part of Washington. On the other hand, this British superiority prevented Washington from giving support to the forts which defended the obstructions in the river.

All Washington could do was to reinforce the garrisons at Fort Mifflin and Fort Mercer, and put them in condition to make as strong a defense as possible, to delay the enemy from gaining command of the Delaware. Consequently, in spite of their isolation, these American forts were able to give Howe a great deal of trouble, and occupied all his efforts for six weeks.

In conjunction with attacks by the warships of the fleet, the enemy first attempted to carry Fort Mercer by storm (October 22, 1777). This assault was undertaken by Colonel Donop with a strong force of veteran Hessians. But the garrison beat off the enemy and inflicted a loss of nearly four hundred, with a loss of only thirty-seven for the Americans. Colonel Donop was mortally wounded, and was left in the hands of the Americans. The attacking warships also met losses, as two of them went aground and were destroyed. After this repulse, Howe resorted to bombardment from shore batteries and the fleet. 'Howe had already sent to Clinton for five additional battalions from New York; but it was not until the 15th of November, and after immense labour, that the Americans were driven by the British batteries from Mud Island and Red Banks, and that the navigation of the Delaware was opened for the supply of the army.'[1]

In the mean time the final curtain had been rung down upon Burgoyne's invasion. There never was a more helpless and hopeless ending of an overconfident undertaking. The way from Canada, that had looked so easy on the map in London, had closed into a trap from which he could see no escape. Harassed and beset by constantly increasing numbers, his army was actually mobbed. That is the only term to describe the plight of the British and Hessians, and the end was a general collapse. Clinton had captured Fort Clinton and Montgomery on the Hudson (October 6, 1777), but Burgoyne's army was 'not only surrounded but starving.'[2] Clinton could not get to Burgoyne — and Burgoyne could not break through the surrounding hoards of enemies to join Clinton. On October 17, 1777, Burgoyne's exhausted and depleted army surrendered.

Burgoyne's campaign cannot be described in any terms of the European operations of the day. He had been defeated because he encountered problems that European soldiers were unfit to solve. The actual military operations were buried under the accumulating difficulties of his situation. The one military factor, which was decisive, was the gathering of the militia, made effective by the organization that welded them into the overwhelming army to smother Burgoyne. The fact, that this necessary organization was at hand for the Americans, must be attributed to Washington's efforts. It also was true that the executives Washington sent to the northern army provided its leadership. No one can think there was any military skill shown by Gates. In the actual battles he was passive, to say the least, and Arnold and Morgan commanded on the field.

[1] Fortescue: *History of the British Army.*   [2] *Ibid.*

After the first exultation over the capture of Burgoyne's army, it was evident to Washington that his troops should be returned from the northern army to strengthen his forces about Philadelphia. As has been explained, Washington had diverted to the campaign against Burgoyne more troops than he could readily spare.[1] These had performed their task, and they were needed to oppose Howe. But Gates delayed sending back troops to Washington and insisted on holding together his army on the Hudson. There was no sense in retaining so large a force there, and a reinforcement would have made Washington strong enough to support the forts on the Delaware and save them from capture.

Congress made it difficult to detach troops from Gates by an order that Washington should not withdraw more than twenty-five hundred troops without consulting Gates and Governor Clinton. It was only by sending his most trusted aide, Colonel Hamilton, to Gates that Washington could obtain the return of Morgan and the Rifle Regiment. When reinforcements at last came to Washington, it was too late, and the British had gained full control of the Delaware.

But, underneath this reluctance of Gates to send troops to Washington's army, there lay another intrigue, similar to that of Lee, to undermine and supplant Washington. Gates actually thought that he would be borne to the chief command on the wave of popularity due to the victory over Burgoyne. As before, there were other officers ready to join in this scheme, which developed into the most dangerous move that was directed against Washington in the whole Revolution. For this intrigue could assume a guise that was plausible on the surface, because Congress and the public

[1] '...The extra aid of Continental troops which the gloomy prospects of our affairs in the north, immediately after the reduction of Ticonderoga, induced me to spare from this army.' (To Patrick Henry, November 13, 1777.)

did not realize the small share of Gates in securing the victory.

The contrast between the surrender of Burgoyne and the loss of Philadelphia was used to put Washington in a false light, and again the impatient members of Congress began to complain of the 'Fabian policy' of Washington.[1] This honest but altogether mistaken impulsiveness of well-meaning men, who knew nothing of military matters, was played upon by the intriguing schemers who sought advancement. The first result was a reorganization of the Board of War, with Gates as President. Another member of the Board was General Mifflin, who was one of those most active in the plot against Washington.

The appointment of Mifflin, who was a commissary general, aggravated an unsatisfactory situation, which had been created in the commissary department earlier in the year through the meddling of Congress. By the choice of Washington, this department had been put on an efficient basis under the able management of a single commissary general, Colonel Joseph Trumbull of Connecticut. But, in spite of the opposition of Washington, Congress had made a most unfortunate change at the time of Howe's expedition against Philadelphia. In fact, Congress assumed complete charge of the commissariat and reorganized its administration.

By act of Congress, there were to be two commissary generals, one of purchase and one of issue, both to be appointed by Congress. Their subordinate officers were also to be appointed by Congress, and all were accountable to Congress. This meant the separation of the commissariat from the military organization of the army, a clumsy un-

---

[1] John Adams, at this time, expressed himself as 'sick of Fabian policies' and in favor of 'a short and violent war.'

Chapter XXVII

VALLEY FORGE

IT WAS a tragic fact that, when Washington's army went into winter quarters at Valley Forge, there was a period of the worst mismanagement of military affairs on the part of Congress. Never, in the whole course of the Revolution, was the influence of Washington at so low an ebb among its members. Congress no longer was guided by Washington's advice in military matters. Instead of relying upon Washington, and upon the able officers Washington had associated with himself, the members of Congress gave their ears to the clique of self-seeking plotters who were banded together in an intrigue against Washington.

The amount of harm, caused by the unwise military control usurped by Congress, can only be measured in terms of the appalling sufferings of the American soldiers at Valley Forge, which Washington was powerless to prevent. This was a sad chapter in our history. But the hostile group of unworthy opponents of Washington were destined to be defeated in their base aims by the very baseness of their methods.

Among those most active in this sordid intrigue was Thomas Conway. He had come to America from France, after service in the French Army, and he had been made a brigadier general by Congress. He was untiring in pushing himself forward for a higher rank. Washington had

234

rightly estimated Conway's character,[1] and had written that to give him a commission as a major general would be 'as unfortunate a measure as ever was adopted.' [2] But Conway joined the faction that was taking advantage of the prominence of Gates, and, under their influence, Congress actually made him an inspector general with the rank of major general. This unscrupulous adventurer, in his eagerness to advance his own interests, conspired with Gates, and one of his letters to Gates proved to be the undoing of the plotters.

In this letter Conway had written disparagingly of Washington, and Gates foolishly showed it to his associates. Still more foolishly, Gates' own personal aide Wilkinson quoted passages from this Conway letter to other officers, and General Stirling, who was unswervingly loyal to Washington, reported Wilkinson's act to the Commander in Chief.[3] Upon receipt of Stirling's report, Washington wrote the following laconic note to Conway (November 9, 1777): 'Sir, A letter, which I received last night, contained the following paragraph. "In a letter from General Conway to General Gates he says, '*Heaven has been determined to save your country, or a weak General and bad counsellors would have ruined it.*'" I am, Sir, your humble servant.'

This 'eclaircissement,' as Gates himself called the revelation of the intrigue,[4] threw into confusion the whole plot, which has been called in consequence the 'Conway cabal.'

[1] 'His importance in this army exists more in his imagination than in reality.' (Letter to Richard Henry Lee, October 17, 1777.)

[2] *Ibid.*

[3] Stirling, in this report to Washington, wrote with indignation, 'Such wicked duplicity of conduct I shall always think it my duty to detect.'

[4] 'This moment I received a letter from our worthy friend, General Mifflin, who informs me, that extracts from your letters to me had been conveyed to General Washington, and, that it occasioned an eclaircissement....' (Gates to Conway, December 3, 1777.)

The shallow Gates, who was panic-stricken on being informed of the intercepted letter by his fellow schemer Mifflin, followed his first mistaken impulse to attempt a retort by claiming that his private papers had been 'stealingly copied.' He used this phrase in a letter written to Washington.[1] And he committed the additional blunder of sending to Congress a copy of this letter to Washington, in the vain hope of creating an impression unfavorable to Washington by imputing 'the treachery which occasioned my writing to General Washington.'[2]

But, instead of producing any ill effect against Washington, Gates only put himself in the worst possible light. For, as Gates himself had made the whole matter public by writing to Congress, he had also made it necessary that Washington should transmit his reply to Congress,[3] although, as he stated in this reply, he had been 'desirous of concealing every matter that could, in its consequence, give the smallest interruption to the tranquillity of this army, or afford a gleam of hope to the enemy by dissentions within.'[4] Washington then gave a straightforward account of Stirling's report of Wilkinson's quotations from Conway's letter.[5]

It thus became public, through the foolish course of Gates himself, that Gates' own aide had babbled the discreditable secret. Moreover, Gates managed to make things still worse for himself, by a stupid attempt to deny the words he had unwittingly admitted when he charged that his

[1] 'These letters have been stealingly copied....' (Gates to Washington, December 8, 1777.)

[2] Gates to the President of Congress, December 11, 1777.

[3] 'I am laid under the disagreeable necessity of returning my answer through the same channel, lest any member of that honorable body should harbour an unfavorable suspicion of my having practised some indirect means to come at the contents of the confidential letters between you and General Conway.'

[4] Letter to Gates, January 4, 1778.   [5] *Ibid.*

236

papers had been 'stealingly copied.' If the words had not been there, how could they have been 'copied' — 'stealingly' or otherwise?

Gates' shameless equivocations drew him into an open quarrel with Wilkinson, which even came to the point of arranging a duel. Gates avoided the duel, by going to the place of meeting and assuring Wilkinson with tears that he never had made any statements derogatory to his favorite aide — only for Wilkinson to see a letter written by Gates which contained the slanderous charge that Wilkinson had attempted to throw suspicions on another officer.[1]

This damning proof of the treachery of Gates so enraged Wilkinson that he wrote to the President of Congress the following letter: 'Sir; While I make my acknowledgements to Congress for the appointment of secretary to the Board of War and Ordnance, I am sorry I should be constrained to resign that office; but, after the acts of *treachery* and falsehood in which I have detected Major General Gates, the president of that board, it is impossible for me to reconcile it with my honor to serve with him.'

It also transpired that the schemers had made use of the Board of War, in an attempt to detach Lafayette from Washington by offering the young Frenchman the command of an imaginary expedition against Canada, which would put him under the influence of Conway, who was to be associated with him. But this was a fiasco. Lafayette found that the promised troops were not available, and returned to Washington at Valley Forge. Lafayette had fathomed the true character and aims of Conway,[2] who remained on the Hudson.

[1] Gates to Washington, January 23, 1778.

[2] 'He has done all in his power to draw off my confidence and affection from you.' (Lafayette to Washington, December 30, 1777.)

237

All of this had opened the eyes of Congress, and of public opinion, to the utter worthlessness of the self-seeking group who were plotting against Washington. Their intrigue stood revealed in its true colors, and they lost all caste in Congress and in the estimation of the public.

Their downfall was immediate and complete. Conway, before he realized that the tide of sentiment had turned, was unwise enough to try to enforce a complaint by threatening to resign. This was at once seized upon by Congress and accepted as a resignation. Conway frantically protested that he had not intended to resign. But Congress adhered to its action, and Conway was ignominiously shunted out of the army. Both Gates and Mifflin were removed from the Board of War, and, so strong was the reaction against Gates, that he was relegated to the command of the forts on the Hudson — with the special provision that he was to be definitely under Washington. All the adherents of Gates and his coterie, in Congress and elsewhere, fell away from them and hastened to disown them.[1]

This was the end of the attempt to supersede Washington. The 'cabal' had been thus discredited and broken up before it could attain its unworthy object. In spite of the harm it had done, through the misuse of Congress and the Board of War, in upsetting the military organization painstakingly built up by Washington, its actual result was to insure the domination of Washington. Its object lesson of selfish ambitions, in contrast with the high aims of Washington, had been too evident for any one to miss.

Even the most prejudiced members of Congress, who had feared the imaginary evils of the 'standing army,' and of

---

[1] Significant of the eclipse of Gates in the estimation of the public was a cartoon, circulated at this time, showing Gates on his back after a fall from his 'high horse.'

the 'idolatry' of Washington,[1] could not help seeing that the high esteem, so widely accorded to Washington, had been well earned — that Washington was the only man who could be entrusted with the control of military affairs. Of course, it was too much to expect great and guiding wisdom in this newly fledged and ill-organized body, but, from this time on, the influence of Washington in Congress was established on a strong basis.

However, it was too late to repair the damage done by Congress, in demoralizing the service of supply of the army. As should be stated at once, it was not until Washington induced Congress to appoint Greene quartermaster general (March 3, 1778) that this department was put on a different basis. All through the winter Washington was obliged to contend with the disorder and confusion, into which the control by Congress had thrown its administration. Often Washington himself was obliged to undertake the duties of this department. But all his efforts could not do away with the hardships that followed in the train of the incompetents imposed by the mistaken policy of Congress.

For this reason, the name of Valley Forge has become a synonym for hardship in the history of the Revolution. In his first letters to Congress, after going into winter quarters at Valley Forge, Washington described conditions there in terms that gave a picture of the sufferings of his army more true than any account that could be written: 'Full as I was in my representations of the matters in the commissary's department yesterday, fresh and more powerful reasons oblige me to add, that I am now convinced beyond a doubt, that, unless some great and capital change suddenly takes place in that line, this army must inevitably be reduced to one or the other of these three things; starve, dissolve, or dis-

[1] These are often found cited by well-meaning patriots as dangers for America.

perse in order to obtain subsistence in the best manner they can. Rest assured, Sir, this is not an exaggerated picture, and that I have abundant reason to support what I say.... Since the month of July we have had no assistance from the quartermaster-general, and to want of assistance from this department the commissary-general charges great part of his difficiency.... We have by a field-return this day made, no less than two thousand eight hundred and ninety-eight men now in camp unfit for duty, because they are barefoot and otherwise naked.' [1]

Under these conditions of hardship, it is no exaggeration to state that the army was held together solely by the personal influence of Washington. The most impressive testimony of this was from the pen of an enemy: 'And it is perhaps one of the most striking traits in General Washington's character, that he possessed the faculty of gaining such an ascendency over his raw and undisciplined troops, most of whom were destitute of proper winter clothing, and otherwise unprovided with necessaries, as to be able to prevail upon so many of them to remain with him, during the winter, in so distressful a situation.... In three months he had not four thousand men, and these by no means to be termed effective. He had often not three days provision in his camp, and at times not enough for one day. In this infirm and dangerous state he continued from December to May.' [2]

Yet it was characteristic of the indomitable spirit of Washington that he made this winter of privation a period of great improvement of the army organization for which he had labored so long. He collected from his officers opinions and suggestions as to reforms and improvements.

[1] To the President of Congress, December 23, 1777.
[2] Stedman: *History of the American War.*

In CONGRESS, 29th March, 1779.

CONGRESS *judging it of the greateſt importance to preſcribe ſome invariable rules for the order and diſcipline of the troops, eſpecially for the purpoſe of introducing an uniformity in their formation and manœuvres, and in the ſervice of the camp:*

ORDERED, *That the following regulations be obſerved by all the troops of the United States, and that all general and other officers cauſe the ſame to be executed with all poſſible exactneſs.*

By Order,

JOHN JAY, PRESIDENT.

Atteſt.

CHARLES THOMPSON,
Secretary.

PAGE IN WASHINGTON'S OWN COPY OF STEUBEN'S BOOK, WHICH WAS
THE RESULT OF THE DRILLING AT VALLEY FORGE

He then had drawn up a scheme for the changes deemed necessary. In order to be sure of the prompt coöperation of Congress, he induced that body to appoint a 'Committee of Arrangements' [1] to come to Valley Forge and to remain there while he was working out his reforms. In addition to better methods in military affairs, Washington influenced Congress to adopt a provision for his permanent army, by which officers were to receive half pay for seven years after the war, and non-commissioned officers and privates eighty dollars each. This had a good effect upon the army.

But a most notable element in the improvement of Washington's army was the result of the arrival at Valley Forge of Baron von Steuben, a skilled Prussian officer of the wars of Frederick the Great. He had been retired when Frederick cut down his army. In Paris he met Franklin and Beaumarchais, and, at the instance of Vergennes, he agreed to come to America to drill the American troops. He arrived at Valley Forge in February, 1778, and at once made a favorable impression upon Washington [2] and won his confidence.

Steuben soon proved that he was an extraordinary genius, by his able performance of his difficult task. It required almost a miracle to adapt the formal school of Frederick the Great to such a novel situation, but this Steuben soon accomplished. He actually devised a system of drill and tactics that modified the Prussian system to American conditions. This was so excellent that it remained in force long after the Revolution. It was a wonderful achieve-

[1] General Reed, Nathaniel Folsom, Francis Dana, Charles Carroll, Gouverneur Morris.

[2] 'Baron Steuben has arrived at camp. He appears to be much of a gentleman, and, as far as I have had an opportunity of judging, a man of military knowledge, and acquainted with the world.' (To the President of Congress, February 27, 1777.)

ment, for it showed a breadth of mind rarely found in the formal officer of the day. But the influence of Steuben's own personality was even more remarkable. He had soon realized that in the unkempt American soldiers there were surprising possibilities, and he threw himself into his task with contagious enthusiasm. He drilled the men himself, and aroused the officers to zeal like his own. Soon officers and men were at work with equal enthusiasm, inspired by a real fondness for their eager instructor, and the whole camp became a school for drill.

In fact, and this was one of the many paradoxes of the American Revolution, the forlorn cantonment of starved and ragged men became one of the most efficient schools of the soldier in all history. It was a well-earned recognition of the value of Steuben, that he was made Inspector General with the rank of major general. For, from the privations of Valley Forge, there emerged a tried and disciplined army, with a drilled organization that embraced the troops who increased its numbers — an army that could hold its own with any drilled troops on the field of battle.

Chapter XXVIII

THE SITUATION AT THE BEGINNING OF 1778

THE result of the campaigns of 1777 can only be described as a stunning shock and setback for the King's Ministers. They had failed in all their objects in America. The northern army of invasion had been lost, and, as the contemporary British historian stated, all the efforts of their main army under General Howe 'amounted to no more than the acquisition of good winter-quarters for the British army in Philadelphia.'[1] The first of the year 1777 had seen Washington, with only a hopelessly inferior force, holding Howe's main British army restricted to New York. The beginning of 1778 found again the same situation, as at that time Howe's superior army was restricted to Philadelphia by Washington's army.

The great effort of the King's Ministers had been made, and nothing had been accomplished. The Royal troops were still confined to their bases where they could be maintained by sea. All the rest of America in revolt was free from any semblance of Royal authority. It was a situation of military failure, which was beyond concealment or palliation. Naturally there was an immediate reaction in Great Britain, where the opinion had been general that the Americans would not be able to resist the forces employed against them in 1777.

[1] Stedman: *History of the American War.*

There was the other adverse element, which always had a strong effect upon the public mind in Great Britain. The losses on the sea were counting more heavily against Great Britain as the war went on. In the year 1777 the British lost 467 sail of merchantmen. Those captured by the Americans were almost wholly due to the operations of the privateers. After the first stimulus of Washington's initiative at the siege of Boston, Congress had kept on in efforts to create an American navy. Regular commissions were issued, and attempts were made to construct naval vessels. Few of these got to sea, as most of them were captured, or destroyed by the Americans to prevent them from falling into the hands of the enemy.[1] But the infant United States Navy must be considered as joined up with the privateers,[2] and these continued to be unexpectedly successful in destroying British shipping.

Most significant of all the results of 1777 was the fact, which had become only too apparent to the British, that the failure of the King's Ministers in America was leading inevitably to the alliance of France with the Americans. And this meant that Great Britain was facing another European war.

The first instinct of the panic of the King's Ministers, after realizing that everything had gone against them, was to make a desperate attempt to conciliate the Americans — a complete reversal of their previous policies. Before the adjournment of Parliament for the Christmas holidays of 1777, Lord North had announced that he would introduce measures to pacify America. But what he actually pro-

[1] Many of the projected naval craft were thus destroyed, after being shut into the Delaware by the British fleet.

[2] Captain John Barry, after serving in the defense of the Delaware River and going to sea as a naval officer, made cruises in a privateer, and then returned to finish out the war in the United States Navy.

posed in February, 1778, went beyond anything that would have been thought possible a few months before.

Lord North's 'Conciliatory Bills' repealed practically all of the measures that had caused the obnoxious imposition of taxes, and authorized the appointment of a commission to treat with Congress and negotiate a peace, with power to grant amnesty to the Americans in revolt. These bills were passed with very little opposition, for all parties were dazed by the unexpected situation as to America.

But, while these bills were pending, the alliance between France and the United States became an accomplished fact. The situation in America had convinced the French leaders that it was the right move. And, if anything, the announcement by the British Ministers of a program of conciliation only hastened the French to seize upon the opportunity for a stroke against Great Britain. Accordingly the treaties with the United States were signed on February 6, 1778. Soon after the passage of Lord North's conciliatory measures, the King's Ministers received official notice of these treaties, and war was declared against France (March 13, 1778).

In the reaction against Great Britain in Europe, it was evident that Spain also would be aligned as an enemy. It was another sign of the times that Frederick the Great opened the port of Dantzig to American privateers, and forbade the passage of German troops to aid Great Britain. In this adverse situation, the King's Ministers made every haste to send copies of the 'Conciliatory Bills' to America, in order to have them circulated as soon as possible among the people. Their object was to counteract the alliance with France, and to induce the Americans to turn from this to the offers of Great Britain.

But it was too late for any such appeal to be effective.

The contemporary British historian gave the reason in one sentence: 'If what was now proposed was a right measure, it ought to have been adopted at first and before the sword was drawn.' [1] In 1778 it was too obviously a concession forced from the King's Ministers by the unfavorable course of events. And these events had moved too far for any such readjustment. Washington's comment on this offer of the King's Ministers stated the case: 'Nothing short of independence, it appears to me, can possibly do. A peace on any other terms would, if I may be allowed the expression, be a peace of war.'

And here the 'Conciliatory Bills' can be dismissed, as having no effect whatever upon the military situation. Tryon had copies of them printed in New York and circulated throughout the country, but they only met hostility and derision. Congress unanimously resolved not to treat with the commissioners of Great Britain, unless the British forces should be withdrawn and the independence of the United States acknowledged.

Congress made a very apt rejoinder to the British offer of pardon, by passing a resolution (April 23, 1778), advising the different States to grant amnesty to their citizens who had been in arms against them, on condition that these should return to their allegiance to the United States before June 16. Copies of this resolution were struck off and transmitted to Tryon, in return for the British copies sent by him, with a gravely ironical letter from Washington, who wrote: 'I take the liberty to transmit to you a few printed copies of a resolution of Congress of the 23d instant, and to request that you will be instrumental in communicating its contents, so far as it may be in your power, to the persons who are the objects of its operation. The benevolent purpose it is

[1] Stedman: *History of the American War.*

intended to answer will, I persuade myself, sufficiently recommend it to your candor.'

Ten days after Congress had passed this resolution, a messenger arrived bringing the treaties with France. Congress promptly ratified these treaties, and the United States and France stood pledged to make peace only by mutual con-

I *William Alexander Earl of Stirling, major General in the armies of the United States of America,*
do acknowledge the UNITED STATES of AME-
RICA, to be Free, Independent and Sovereign States, and
declare that the people thereof owe no allegiance or obedience to George the Third, King of Great-Britain; and I re-
nounce, refufe and abjure any allegiance or obedience to him;
and I do *Swear* that I will to the utmoft of
my power, fupport, maintain and defend the faid United
States, againft the faid King George the Third, his heirs and
fucceffors and his or their abettors, affiftants and adherents,
and will ferve the faid United States in the office of *Major
General* ———— which I now hold, with fidelity,
according to the beft of my fkill and underftanding.

Sworn before me at the Camp at Valley forge the 12th may 1778 *Stirling,*
G. Washington

OATH OF ALLEGIANCE AT VALLEY FORGE, SPRING OF 1778

sent — and not until the independence of the United States was established. Consequently, the mission of the British commissioners was hopeless — even for getting a hearing. They lingered in America until October, and then departed for England, leaving a foolish manifesto of threats against the Americans, which only aroused greater resentment against the King's Ministers.

May 6 was made a day of rejoicing at Valley Forge, with a military celebration of the French alliance. The situation as to Philadelphia had remained unchanged, and the

British army was still passive in its rôle of being beleaguered in Philadelphia. Throughout the winter Washington's forlorn army at Valley Forge had been as safe from British attacks as if it had been an overpowering host. The British historian was very bitter in his criticism of Howe, for not attacking Washington when the American army was at such a low ebb.[1] But we must not forget that, to the mind of Howe, winter operations were out of the question. It was inconceivable that the British general could undertake anything resembling Washington's Trenton-Princeton campaign. However, when the inactivity of the British army went to the extent of leaving Washington free from attacks all through the spring — and free to recruit his depleted army — it was a different matter. There was no military excuse for this indolence on the part of Howe.

The explanation lay in Howe's situation at Philadelphia. In the whole operation, which he had fondly imagined would give the final blow to the rebellion, General Howe was a self-confessed failure. His resignation was in the hands of the King's Ministers, and, in his own eyes, he was only waiting for his successor, and, in the mean time, he was commanding an army that was committed to the abandonment of Philadelphia as a useless base of operations. Howe's horizon was limited to these dimensions, and he remained incapable of taking advantage of Washington's weakness to destroy or disperse the American army.

Throughout the winter Washington had realized that his safeguard was the incapacity of the British to undertake winter operations. But, in the spring, his letters revealed great anxiety lest the British commander might be 'medi-

---

[1] 'Under such propitious circumstances what mortal could doubt of success? But our army neglecting all these opportunities, was suffered to continue in Philadelphia.' (Stedman: *History of the American War.*)

tating a stroke against this army.' [1] On March 27 Washington wrote, 'If General Howe draws his strength together before we have collected ours, nothing can hinder him from moving against us but ignorance of our numbers.' [2] But nothing was farther from Howe's intention. As late as April 19 he wrote to the King's Ministers giving the excuse of 'the want of green forage' as preventing him from taking the field, and also stating that 'their situation is too strong to hazard an attack.' This last gave the true reason. To the mind of Howe, the Americans were again in a 'stronghold,' and again the specter of Bunker Hill was before his eyes. As a result, Washington remained free from British attacks throughout the whole period of the weakness of his army.

While the British army remained idle in Philadelphia, the British account stated, 'A want of discipline and proper subordination pervaded the whole army,' [3] and the character of its general was reflected in the 'indolence and luxury' of his troops. On May 8 General Clinton arrived to relieve General Howe of his command. Before Howe left for England there was 'a very ridiculous festival held by his officers and by the prettiest women in Philadelphia in his honor.' [4] This was the 'Mischianza,' of which Irving wrote: 'At the time of this silken and mock heroic display, the number of British chivalry in Philadelphia was nineteen thousand five hundred and thirty, cooped up in a manner by an American force at Valley Forge, amounting, according to official returns, to eleven thousand eight hundred men. Could any triumphant pageant be more ill-placed and ill-timed!' [5]

[1] To General Cadwalader, March 20, 1778.
[2] To General Armstrong, March 27, 1778.
[3] Stedman: *History of the American War.*
[4] Fortescue: *History of the British Army.*   [5] Irving: *Life of Washington.*

This was the end of Howe's command of the British forces in America. The British historian was very severe in his condemnation of Howe's excuse for his failure, in claiming that the troops given to him were insufficient: 'The account of the armed forces in 1777 stood thus: British, forty thousand eight hundred and seventy four, veteran troops.' And, after stating the small numbers in Washington's army, he asked, 'With what justice, then, it was said, could the general complain of his want of force?' [1]

The first instructions of the King's Ministers to General Clinton, the successor of General Howe,[2] reflected their sense of defeat in the Northern States: 'Should you not succeed in bringing Washington to a general and decisive action early in the season, it is recommended not to pursue an offensive warfare against the interior, but to leave men enough to defend the posts, and embark a detachment on board the King's ships, and attack the harbours along the coast between New York and Halifax.' This was admitting that British operations were restricted to those based upon the sea. The evacuation of Philadelphia was authorized 'on the condition that the northern service cannot be effected without it.' And it was announced that 'an attack will be made on the southern colonies in the winter, with a view to the conquest and possession of Georgia and South Carolina.'

Two weeks afterwards (March 21, 1778) these instructions were changed. In view of the fact that France had 'signed a treaty with the agents of the revolting colonies, it is resolved to make a prompt attack upon the Island of St. Lucia in the West Indies.' A descent upon Florida was also planned, and 'when these detachments shall have been

[1] Stedman: *History of the American War.*
[2] Lord George Germaine to General Clinton, March 8, 1778.

made, or while they are making, Philadelphia is to be evacuated; all the troops to be embarked, with everything belonging to the army, and to proceed thence to New York.'

These instructions proved that the King's Ministers shared with Howe and Clinton the conviction that the 'rebel capital' should be abandoned. The new British commander devoted all his attention to preparations for the British withdrawal to New York. He never at any time had the slightest intention of taking the field against Washington. This meant that the whole British army, of more than thirty-three thousand, had lost the offensive and had lapsed into the defensive.[1]

[1] The British Army in America March 26, 1778, consisted of:

	At Philadelphia	At New York	At Rhode Island
British.......	13,078	3,486	1,610
German......	5,202	3,689	2,116
Provincial....	1,250	3,281	44
	19,530	10,456	3,770

Total of the Army, 33,756.

Chapter XXIX

THE BRITISH RETREAT TO NEW YORK

ON MAY 8, 1778, the day that Clinton assumed command of the British army at Philadelphia, there was a council of war of the general officers of the American Army. This council had been convened by the order of Congress to discuss the military policy for the army.[1] As Washington's whole force at Valley Forge was eleven thousand and eight hundred, and the total of the American Army, including troops on the North River and at other distant posts, was not more than twenty thousand, it was 'the unanimous opinion of the council that the line of conduct most consistent with sound policy, and best suited to promote the interests and safety of the United States, was to remain on the defensive and wait events, and not to attempt any offensive operations against the enemy till circumstances should offer a fairer opportunity of striking a successful blow.'

At this time the American Army had become, in every sense of the word, Washington's army. The opposing elements, after losing all their influence in Congress, had sunk back to their proper level, and were powerless to do any further harm. The organization of the army had passed al-

[1] There were present: Major Generals Gates, Greene, Stirling, Mifflin, Lafayette, Kalb, Armstrong, Steuben; Brigadier Generals Knox, Duportail. Major General Lee was not at this council, but he signed his name to its written decision.

together into the hands of Washington's trusted officers, and all departments were under men of his own choice. Greene was acting as Quartermaster General, Pickering was Adjutant General, General Knox was Chief of Artillery, and Steuben, the new Inspector General, had already earned the right to take his stand beside these well-tested supporters of Washington. Reed had forfeited his standing as the confidential staff officer of Washington, through allowing himself to be drawn into Lee's intrigue. Hamilton had become Washington's confidential aide, and Lafayette was also in close personal relationship with Washington.

The army which owed its permanent organization to the efforts of Washington, and then had been held together through the winter of hardships by his influence alone, had emerged a body of tried soldiers — and this too in every sense of the word. It was one of Washington's 'rules of war' [1] that 'the first qualification of a soldier is fortitude under fatigue and privation; courage is only the second.' Napoleon afterwards adopted this maxim — and it stands true to-day. Washington's army had undergone this supreme test. In addition, as has been explained, the army had been thoroughly drilled at Valley Forge. In this regard, it was noticeable that a British historian called Washton's troops 'well-trained and well-equipped men' for the

[1] Washington's 'Six Rules of War':
1. Never attack a position in front which you can gain by turning.
2. Charges of cavalry should be made, if possible, on the flanks of the enemy.
3. The first qualification of a soldier is fortitude under fatigue and privation; courage is only the second. Hardship, poverty and actual want are the soldier's best schools.
4. Nothing is so important in war as an undivided command.
5. Never do what the enemy wants you to do.
6. A general of ordinary talent, occupying a bad position and surprised by a superior force, seeks safety in retreat, but a great captain supplies all deficiencies by his courage, and marches boldly to meet the attack.

first time, when he was writing of this stage of 1778.[1] This reflected the general recognition among the British that the Americans had grown really formidable in the field.

It was an interesting detail that Pulaski, through the intercession of Washington, had been given the authority 'to raise an independent corps.'[2] This was afterwards called 'Pulaski's Legion.' At Washington's request, 'Light Horse Harry' Lee was also authorized to command two troops of horse 'to act as an independent partisan corps.'[3]

Washington had exerted himself to bring about the exchange of General Charles Lee, and this was at last effected by the British exchanging Lee for the British General Prescott, who had been captured in Rhode Island in somewhat the same manner as the capture of Lee.[4] The traitorous ingrate Lee thus returned before the British evacuated Philadelphia, and resumed service as second in command of Washington's army, an unsuspected element of great danger for the Americans.

When Clinton was preparing for the evacuation of Philadelphia, he soon perceived that the British army must make its retreat to New York by land. There were not transports enough to convey by sea the troops and the refugees from Philadelphia. In general, as British authorities stated, the conduct of the British troops in Philadelphia had not won over the inhabitants of that region. But, in the city itself, there was the same tragic situation as at the time of the

[1] Fortescue: *History of the British Army.*

[2] To the President of Congress, March 14, 1778.

[3] To the President of Congress, April 3, 1778. Three companies were organized, instead of two.

[4] General Prescott, British commander in Rhode Island, was captured in his quarters four miles from Newport by a daring raiding party under Colonel Barton.

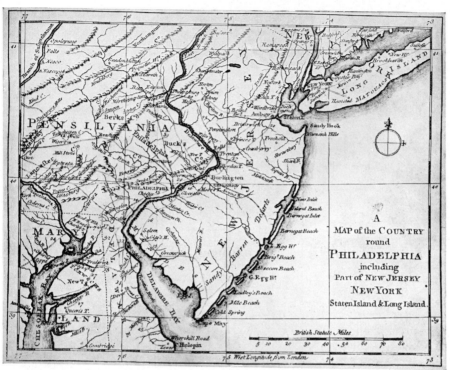

SCENE OF OPERATIONS, 1778

evacuation of Boston. There were Loyalists who had cast their lot with the British, and had never imagined that the British troops would be forced to abandon Philadelphia. These unfortunates went away in the British transports.

Clinton's evident preparations for evacuating Philadelphia revealed to Washington that the British were about to move, and he sent forward Lafayette with a detachment of about twenty-one hundred, to take position at Barren Hill, some ten miles from Philadelphia (May 18, 1778), as an advanced force 'for restraining the enemy's parties and procuring intelligence, and to act as circumstances may require.'[1] Clinton, on learning from spies the position of Lafayette's detachment, sent out a British force of five thousand to surround and destroy it. This was attempted by encircling marches under General Grant and General Gray. But Lafayette received information of his danger just in time (May 20, 1778). Thereupon, he very skillfully held up the march of Grant by a feint of attack made by a few scattered troops, and gained time to reach Matson's Ford on the Schuylkill. This he crossed in safety, and took up so strong a position behind the Schuylkill that the enemy gave up their attempt, after only a slight skirmish, and returned to Philadelphia.

At the time the British commander was making his final arrangements for evacuation, the British commissioners arrived in Philadelphia (June 6, 1778) on their fruitless errand, which has been described. Any delusive hopes these British commissioners may have entertained, as to the success of their mission, were soon destroyed. They not only perceived, from the attitude of Congress and the people, that their presence 'produced in America no good conse-

[1] To the President of Congress, May 18, 1778.

quences whatever,' [1] but they also met the disheartening news that 'the orders for the evacuation had been made public.' [2]

In the early morning of June 18 Clinton began to move his troops across the Delaware, by crossing in boats below Philadelphia at the junction of the Delaware and the Schuyl-kill, where he was safe from being harassed by the Americans. Upon information 'confirming the evacuation,' [3] received the same day, Washington in the north moved to cross the Delaware into New Jersey at Coryell's Ferry, not far from where he had crossed to attack Trenton.

On June 18 Washington also reported to Congress. 'I have appointed General Arnold to command in Philadelphia, as the state of his wound will not permit his services in a more active line. Colonel Jackson, with a detachment of troops, is to attend him.' Washington's instructions to Arnold directed, 'You will take every prudent step in your power to preserve tranquillity and order in the city, and to give security to individuals of every class and description, restraining as far as possible, till the restoration of civil government, every species of persecution, insult, or abuse, either from the soldiery to the inhabitants, or among each other.'

After landing in New Jersey, Clinton was retreating 'with his fifteen thousand men and an immense train of bag-

---

[1] Stedman: *History of the American War.*

The contemporary British historian also stated that 'the second attempt to bring about a reconciliation...flattered the pride of the American republicans, confirmed them in pursuing the measures they had adopted, and finally established the authority of Congress, which the commissioners had in fact recognized by offering to treat with them. On the other hand...the active and persecuted loyalist was plunged into the deepest despair.'

[2] Johnstone to Parliament. He added, 'The city was in the utmost consternation; a more affecting spectacle of woe I never beheld.'

[3] To the President of Congress, June 18, 1778.

gage.'[1] The contemporary British historian stated that, in view of 'difficult passes' which might be 'occupied by the enemy,' 'Sir Henry Clinton thought it necessary, in order to guard against the consequences of such obstructions, to carry along with him a considerable quantity of baggage and a large supply of provisions. The progress of the army, thus heavily encumbered, was uncommonly slow.'[2]

Washington, by gathering all available detachments, had an army of almost equal size. He had been 'a good deal impeded in his march by rainy weather,'[3] but he proposed 'moving toward Princeton in order to avail ourselves of any favorable occasions, that may present themselves of attacking or annoying the enemy.'[4] Washington was thus moving on a route north of that taken by Clinton, but the march of the 'encumbered' British army was so slow that the two armies were drawing into striking distance of one another.

This situation, as the two armies came to a clash, has been a matter of much controversy, but it cannot be misunderstood if only facts are considered. Successive councils of officers had reaffirmed the policy, agreed upon for the American Army, of avoiding a general engagement. This was wise, as the Americans were not strong enough to stand any chance of destroying Clinton's army. But an American advanced force had been constituted 'to act, as the occasion may serve, on the enemy's left flank and rear, in conjunction with the other Continental troops and militia, who are already hanging about them.'[5]

Lee, who was playing his unsuspected double part, had on all occasions protested against any attacks upon the

[1] Fortescue: *History of the British Army.*
[2] Stedman: *History of the American War.*
[3] To the President of Congress, June 22, 1778.   [4] *Ibid.*
[5] Decision of Council of Officers, June 24, 1778.

British. But Washington determined to make this advance force strong, and to send it forward to attack the enemy. In this decision he was abetted by Greene, Lafayette, and Wayne. As Lee was second in rank in the army, he was entitled to the command of this important detachment under ordinary circumstances. But, as Lee always had been opposed to the purpose of this force, Washington gave the command of it to Lafayette, on condition that he obtained the consent of Lee. At first Lee readily consented to this, and Lafayette went out in command. His instructions from Washington contained the following: 'All Continental parties, that are already in line, will be under your command, and you will take such measures, in concert with General Dickinson, as will cause the enemy the greatest impediment and loss in their march. For these purposes you will attack them as occasion may require by detachment, and, if a proper opening should be given, by operating against them with the whole force of your command. You will naturally take such precautions, as will secure you against surprise, and maintain your communication with this army.'

These instructions were dated June 25. But Lee changed his mind and wrote to Washington, claiming that 'a corps consisting of six thousand men, the greater part chosen, is undoubtedly the most honorable command next to the Commander-in-Chief,' and, if this force remained under the command of Lafayette, Lee himself would be 'disgraced.' Upon this Washington felt obliged to give the command to Lee, with only the condition that Lee should not interfere with any plan Lafayette might be carrying out 'for the purpose of attacking or otherwise annoying the enemy.' [1] But, as Lafayette was not yet in contact with the enemy, he

[1] Washington to Lafayette, June 16, 1778.

turned over the command to Lee. On June 28 Washington made the specific report to Congress, 'We have a select and strong detachment moving forward, under the command of Major General Lee, with orders to attack their rear if possible.'

In the mean time, Clinton had decided to take his army to Sandy Hook, instead of Perth Amboy. On June 27 he encamped near Monmouth Court House on the Allentown road. Clinton had feared attacks on his baggage train, and he had formed one force of about half his army to guard it. This was largely made up of Hessians, and was under the command of Knyphausen. The other half of his army was put under the command of Cornwallis, to serve as a force to cover the march of Knyphausen.

On the morning of June 28, Knyphausen, with the baggage train, had moved off on the Middletown Road. Cornwallis was following beyond the Monmouth Court House, and there he came in contact with Lee's advance force, which had come from the north, and was in position on the British left flank, with Wayne next, and Lafayette pressing to the south of the British. But at the first attacks of the enemy, in the words of a British historian, 'the Americans thereupon fell back, in obedience to Lee, who, it appears, was still playing a traitorous game.' [1] This general retreat, ordered by Lee, cannot be explained on any other ground. Lee's advance force was in no danger of envelopment or destruction, as Washington's main army was advancing to Lee's support, and Clinton could not gather quickly sufficient numbers to overwhelm Lee. On the other hand, Lee might have done the enemy a great deal of harm by a harassing action, in obedience to his orders.

But Lee continued the retreat, to the astonishment of

[1] Fortescue: *History of the British Army.*

Wayne and Lafayette, passing over a high ridge that was an advantageous position for making a fight, and across a marshy ravine that was throwing his ranks into disorder. At this stage Washington came riding to meet Lee. Washington was in a towering rage, and his rarely aroused anger was a fearful thing to encounter. Its flame withered Lee, as Washington reprimanded him[1] and took charge of the situation. Washington rallied the retreating Americans, who, even at this disadvantage, showed the steadiness and good training of the Steuben drill, and he then hastened to bring up reinforcements from the main army. This 'turned the fate of the day,'[2] and the enemy, as the British account expressed it, 'were obliged to retire, heavily pressed in front and flanks, until night put an end to the combat.'[3]

In the night the British retreated on the road to Sandy Hook. The next day Washington reported: 'We forced the enemy from the field, and encamped on the ground. They took a strong post on our front secured on both flanks by morasses and thick woods, where they remained till about twelve at night, and then retreated.'[4] In his later detailed report Washington stated: 'In the mean time the enemy were employed in removing their wounded, and about

[1] Lee's own words proved that the reprimand was severe. The proceedings of the Court Martial showed that he stated in his defense: 'The terms I think were these — "I desire to know, sir, what is the reason — whence arises this disorder and confusion?" The manner in which he expressed them was much stronger and more severe than the expressions themselves.' Nothing more is needed to complete the picture of the wrathful Washington.

[2] On July 5 Hamilton wrote in regard to Washington's conduct: 'A general rout, dismay, and disgrace would have attended the whole army in any other hand but his. By his own good sense and fortitude he turned the fate of the day. ... He did not hug himself at a distance, and have an Arnold to win laurels for him; but by his own presence he brought order out of confusion, animated his troops, and led them to success.'

[3] Fortescue: *History of the British Army.*

[4] To the President of Congress, June 29, 1778.

twelve o'clock at night marched away in such silence that, though General Poor lay extremely near them, they effected their retreat without his knowledge.... The extreme heat of the weather, the fatigue of the men from their march through a deep sandy country almost entirely destitute of water, and the distance the enemy had gained by marching in the night, made a pursuit impracticable and fruitless.' [1]

The day of the battle had been fearfully hot, and many of both sides had died of the heat. The totals of losses of both armies have been stated as almost equal (British 358, American 362). But Clinton's army was diminished by desertions in its retreat. The British placed these desertions at six hundred, but they probably were more numerous. Washington reported: 'Being fully convinced by the gentlemen of this country, that the enemy cannot be hurt or injured in their embarkation at Sandy Hook, the place to which they are going, and unwilling to get too far removed from the North River, I put the troops in motion early this morning, and shall proceed that way, leaving the Jersey brigade, Morgan's corps, and other light parties (the militia being all dismissed) to hover about them, to countenance desertion, and to prevent depredations as far as possible.' [2]

Clinton arrived at the Navesink, and encamped there two days, while the British fleet, which was ready to receive him, provided transportation for his troops and baggage. On July 5 his army was transported from Sandy Hook to New York. Washington was soon on the North River and again was encamped at White Plains. This meant that, after two years, the armies had returned to the same positions they occupied when the British began offensive operations in 1776 — and this situation was the measure of the

[1] To the President of Congress, July 1, 1778.   [2] *Ibid.*

complete failure of two years of British offensives against the Americans.

After reviewing the facts of the Battle of Monmouth, it must be evident that there was no possibility of a decisive action on that field. Clinton was committed to dispositions for a retreat, and Washington was not strong enough to hope to destroy the British army in its retreat. But this British retreat, of which Monmouth was only an incident, was decisive in the broadest sense of the word. It signified, as was exemplified by a British army of fifteen thousand men intent only on retreat, that the British had been defeated in their effort to conquer the northern part of the new United States. In fact, it meant that the British abandoned their hope of conquering the Northern States — the end of the war of conquest in the North.

This was a complete overturn of previous ideas. It had been demonstrated that the army created by Washington, and built up by his constancy through reverses and hardships, had sent the main British army to cover in New York. It was no wonder that Knox exulted: 'Indeed, upon the whole, it is very splendid. The capital army of Britain defeated and obliged to retreat before the Americans whom they dispised so much!' [1]

But an important result of the battle itself was the fact that at Monmouth Lee provided the opportunity for ejecting him from the American Army. This was a fortunate thing for the Americans. For there is no measuring the amount of harm that might have been done, if this unsuspected traitor had remained with so high a rank in the army. But Lee's whole career showed he was as much a fool as a knave. And his own folly brought about his removal in this very first campaign after his exchange, before he had

[1] Letter to Mrs. Knox, June 29, 1778.

been able to do any damage beyond spoiling what only could have been a harassing operation at the best.[1]

The day after the battle, Lee, who had a self-sufficient conceit in his imaginary skill with his pen, concocted a letter to Washington, with a pompous argument as to 'making use of very singular expressions,' 'reparation for the injury committed,' and 'justification... to the army, to the Congress, to America, and to the world in general.' In answer Lee received a letter that was a notable example of Washington's real ability to wield a pen:

'*Sir*, I received your letter (dated through mistake the 1st July), expressed as I conceive it in terms highly improper. I am not conscious of having made use of any singular expressions at the time of meeting you, as you intimate. What I recollect to have said was dictated by duty, and warrented by the occasion. As soon as circumstances will permit, you shall have an opportunity of justifying yourself to the army, to Congress, to America and to the world at large, or of convincing them that you are guilty of a breach of orders, and of misbehavior before the enemy, on the 28th instant, in not attacking them as you had been directed, and in making an unnecessary, disorderly, and shameful retreat.

'I am, sir, your most obedient servant,

GEORGE WASHINGTON'

Upon receipt of this scathing letter, which he had brought upon himself, Lee lost his head completely. He sent to Washington, by the hand of Colonel Fitzgerald, a hysterical

---

[1] At Lee's court martial, Steuben testified that, when he was leading forward reinforcements at Washington's order, Lee had tried to dissuade him by saying, 'I am sure there is some misunderstanding in your being to advance with these troops.' This was after Lee had made his retreat and had been sent from the front. This testimony, as to Lee's continuing to make trouble, so enraged Lee that he insulted Steuben, who challenged Lee to a duel, which Lee evaded.

note which contained this outburst of folly: 'I trust that temporary power of office, and the tinsel dignity attending it, will not be able, by all the mists they can raise, to obfuscate the bright rays of truth.' After he had sent this, and 'reflected,' Lee wrote on the same day a chastened note, asking for a court, and Washington put him in arrest to be tried by court martial.

The charges were:

'First; Disobedience of orders in not attacking the enemy on the 28th of June, agreeably to repeated instructions.

'Secondly; Misbehavior before the enemy on that same day, by making an unnecessary, disorderly, and shameful retreat.[1]

'Thirdly; Disrespect to the Commander-in-Chief, in two letters dated the 1st of July and the 28th of June.' [2]

Lee was convicted on all three charges, and sentenced 'to be suspended from any command in the armies of the United States of North America for the term of twelve months.' [3] After Congress had confirmed this sentence, Lee indulged in a controversy in the newspapers, and, after a vindictive letter to Congress, he was expelled from the army. Thus happily a most dangerous factor was taken out of the war.

[1] This charge was modified to read 'unnecessary, and in some instances a disorderly retreat.'

[2] It was characteristic of Lee that both these letters were misdated.

[3] Proceedings of the Court Martial.

Chapter xxx

THE ARRIVAL OF FRENCH TROOPS AND NEWPORT

WASHINGTON'S own description of the military situation, in the midsummer of 1778, was striking: 'It is not a little pleasing, nor less wonderful to contemplate that after two year's manœuvring and undergoing the strangest vicissitudes, that perhaps ever attended any one contest since the creation, both armies are brought back to the very place they set out from, and that the offending party at the beginning is now reduced to the use of the spade and pickaxe for defense.' [1] It was at this stage that the first forces from France arrived in America.

On April 13, 1778, an expedition commanded by the Count d'Estaing had sailed from Toulon. It consisted of twelve ships of the line and six frigates, and the fleet carried a landing force of four thousand French troops. This French fleet had a hard struggle against head winds throughout its passage. Consequently, it did not arrive at the mouth of the Delaware until July 8. As has been described, the British fleet had left the Delaware for New York. Upon information that the British had evacuated Philadelphia, the French fleet left for the vicinity of New York.

When Washington received 'intelligence tolerably authentic of its arrival off Sandy Hook,' [2] he at once wrote to

[1] To Brigadier General Nelson, August 20, 1778.
[2] To Governor Trumbull, July 14, 1778.

Count d'Estaing, on board the flag ship, of his intention to take position on the North River, and 'then move down before the enemy's lines, with a view of giving them every uneasiness in my power.' [1] Washington was eager to attack the enemy, and two plans 'seemed to present themselves; either an attack upon New York, or one upon Rhode Island.' [2] He sent his aide Lieutenant Colonel Laurens, and afterwards his confidential aide Hamilton,[3] to confer with d'Estaing.

Washington was informed that 'the Count's first wish was to enter at Sandy Hook, in order to possess himself of, or to destroy if possible, the whole of the British fleet lying in the bay of New York; and that, for this purpose, he had been much engaged in his inquiries about the depth of water, and in sounding the channel to ascertain it; the result of which was, that the water, from the experiments made, was too shallow at the entrance to admit his large ships; or, if they could be got in, it appeared that it would not be without a great deal of difficulty and risk.' [4]

As a result of these unfavorable views of d'Estaing, Washington reported to Congress, 'After this disappointment,[5] the next most important object which seemed to present itself was an attempt against Rhode Island.' [6] Count

[1] To Count d'Estaing, July 14, 1778.

[2] To Major General Sullivan, July 17, 1778.

[3] 'The difficulty of doing justice by letter to matters of such variety and importance... has induced me to send to you Lieutenant-Colonel Hamilton, another of my aids, in whom I place entire confidence... and I would wish you to consider the information he delivers as coming from myself.' (To Count d'Estaing, July 17, 1778.)

[4] To the President of Congress, July 22, 1778.

[5] 'I offered in vain a reward of fifty thousand crowns to anyone, who would promise success. All refused and the particular soundings, which I caused to be made myself, too well demonstrated that they were right.' (D'Estaing to Congress, August 26, 1778.)

[6] To the President of Congress, July 22, 1778.

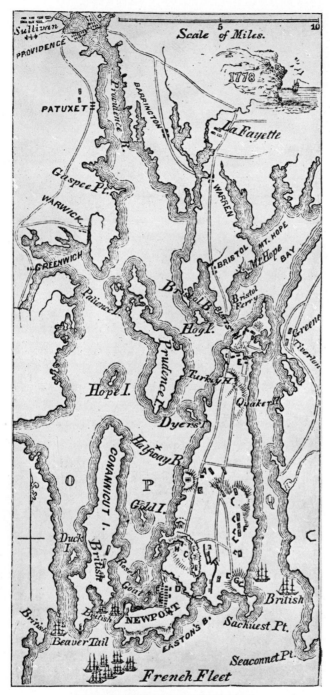

THE FAILURE AT NEWPORT

d'Estaing agreed with Washington, and both 'coincided so exactly in the importance of this expedition.' [1] The British forces were stationed on the Newport island, and had been reinforced to about six thousand troops under General Pigott. An American force under General Sullivan had been in position near Pigott, but Sullivan had never been strong enough to venture an attack.

For this new undertaking against the British, New England militia companies were called out, and Washington sent Greene, Lafayette, and Glover, with fifteen hundred Continental troops. Washington very wisely 'directed General Sullivan to throw all the American troops, both Continental, State, and militia, into two divisions, making an equal distribution of each.' [2] Washington stated, as his reason for this: 'The Continental troops being divided in this manner with the militia, will serve to give them confidence, and probably make them act better than they would alone.' [3]

In these words Washington reaffirmed the working principle of the organization he had given to the army. His method of gaining efficiency was, to use the Continentals he had created as a nucleus for stiffening the raw levies into troops able to take the field against the British. It was his application of this principle, in 1777, that had transformed the gathering of militia into the formidable American army that had overwhelmed Burgoyne. All through the Revolution, this value of Washington's own Continental Army was in evidence.

This permanent military organization had proved its value in insuring the means of quickly rallying increased forces after the depletions from the hardships of winter. This

[1] To the Count d'Estaing, July 22, 1778.
[2] To the Marquis de Lafayette, July 27, 1778.   [3] *Ibid.*

267

continued through the war. The Continentals also provided the basis for any gathering of American forces in other fields. If Washington had not succeeded in his indomitable efforts to create his Continental Army, it would be difficult to find any means by which the Americans could have fought out the Revolution.

The act of Washington in designating Lafayette for the command of one of the divisions of Sullivan's Rhode Island force was significant. It meant Washington's formal acknowledgment that Lafayette, in the test of actual service, had proved himself worthy of a high command over American troops in the field. Its special significance lay in the fact that, at this very time, Washington was undergoing a renewal of the trouble caused by the importunate demands of foreign officers for high commissions in the American Army. It was only natural that this should happen, as the alliance with France had given a new excuse for pressing their claims.

The patience of Washington was tried almost to the point of exasperation.[1] But he made the case of Steuben, who wished to have his temporary command in the field [2] made permanent, an occasion for defining to Congress the evil of granting these high commands to foreign officers.[3] Washington stated emphatically to Congress that the 'desire of having an actual and permanent command in the line cannot be complied with, without wounding the feelings of a number of officers, whose rank and merits give them

[1] 'I do most devoutly wish that we had not a single foreigner among us, except the Marquis de Lafayette, who acts upon a very different principle from those which govern the rest.' (To Gouverneur Morris, July 24, 1778.)

[2] 'I appointed him *pro tempore*, and so expressed it in orders, to conduct a wing to the North River.' (To the President of Congress, July 24, 1778.)

[3] 'An evil more extensive in its nature and fatal in its consequences.' (To Gouverneur Morris, July 24, 1778.)

every claim to attention; and that the doing of it would be productive of much dissatisfaction and extensive ill consequences.' [1]

In this way Washington expressed a rule of conduct that was a restraint upon such commissions to foreign officers throughout the war. The case of Steuben, who of course had real merit, was well adjusted by assigning him 'to repair to Rhode Island, and give his advice and assistance to General Sullivan and the army under his command.' This assignment was accepted by Steuben as satisfactory to himself.

The operation against Rhode Island seemed to promise success. American pilots were secured, to safeguard the French fleet in those waters, and the French fleet arrived there July 29. General Sullivan at once went on board, for an interview with d'Estaing to arrange their joint plans. There was a delay while the American forces were being assembled, and it was agreed that the American and French troops should land August 10 on the island held by the British.

In the mean time, General Pigott had concentrated all the British troops near Newport. This left undefended a strong position at Butt's Hill on the northern part of the Island. Sullivan took advantage of this, to send American troops across in advance and seize Butt's Hill. With the hill in his possession, Sullivan was ready to coöperate with the landing of the French troops, which had been set for August 10. But unforeseen circumstances prevented this promised landing of the French troops.

The French fleet had passed in, through the middle channel, on August 8. But suddenly Lord Howe's fleet appeared on August 9. The British fleet had been reinforced,[2]

[1] To the President of Congress, July 26, 1778.

[2] '...Increased to eight line-of-battle ships, five ships of fifty guns, two of forty-four guns, and four frigates.' (Stedman: *History of the American War*.)

and d'Estaing did not wish to fight 'between two shores, in such an unequal combat.' [1] Consequently he took advantage of a favorable wind, and put to sea, to offer battle in the open. The two fleets were maneuvering for position, but, on the third day, there was a fearful gale, which was known for years as 'the great storm.' This gale ended any possibility of a sea fight by scattering the opposing fleets far and wide on the ocean. It also ended any possibility of landing the French troops to coöperate with the Americans. For, when after many days d'Estaing gathered his ships, he found they had been so greatly damaged by the buffeting of the sea, that he was obliged to take the French fleet to Boston to refit.

This meant that the French troops also were taken away, and their withdrawal aroused much bitterness among the Americans. The American general officers had signed a 'Protest' against the departing of the French troops. [2] But it was too much to expect of the shattered and demoralized French fleet, that it should go into narrow waters and attempt to land the French troops. Washington rendered justice to d'Estaing in this misfortune, as he reported to Congress: 'This accident has much deranged our views; and I shall be happy if it does not totally defeat our enterprise against Rhode Island. I feel much for the Count. He has been peculiarly unfortunate in the combination of several untoward circumstances to frustrate his plans.' [3] Washington wrote to d'Estaing, 'If the deepest regret, that the best concerted enterprise and bravest exertions should have been rendered fruitless by a disaster, which human prudence was incapable of foreseeing or preventing, can al-

[1] D'Estaing to Congress, August 20, 1778.
[2] Lafayette did not sign this 'Protest.'
[3] To the President of Congress, April 16, 1778.

leviate disappointment, you may be assured, that the whole continent sympathizes with you.' [1] And he added: '... the adverse element, which robbed you of your prize, can never deprive you of the glory due to you.' [2]

There was soon an end to the operations of the Americans against Newport after the departure of the French. Sullivan had pushed his lines closer to the British. But, after the supporting French fleet had left Rhode Island, the way was open for the British to reinforce Pigott, and Sullivan's militia were returning to their homes. Consequently, Sullivan withdrew his forces to Butt's Hill in the night of August 28. There the British attacked him the next day, but were beaten back with losses. However, on the following day Sullivan received timely warning from Washington that Clinton was to reinforce Pigott. Upon this, Sullivan withdrew to the mainland. His troops and stores were ferried across without damage in the night, and the Americans thus escaped Clinton's reinforcement of five thousand, which arrived the day after the withdrawal. In their night retreat to the mainland, the Americans were again transported by making use of General Glover and his amphibious soldiers.

The failure of this expedition against Newport aroused much dissatisfaction against the French among the American officers. Washington's letters show that one of his cares at this time was 'to combat these effects.' [3] He wrote to Sullivan, 'The disagreement between the army under your command and the fleet has given me very singular uneasiness.' [4] And he gave earnest instruction, 'Permit me to recommend, in the most particular manner, the cultivation of

[1] To the Count d'Estaing, September 11, 1778.　　　　[2] *Ibid.*
[3] To General Sullivan, August 28, 1778.
[4] To General Sullivan, September 1, 1778.

harmony and good agreement, and your endeavors to destroy that ill humor, which may have got into the officers.' To Greene Washington wrote in the same spirit, 'I depend much upon your temper and influence to conciliate that animosity.' [1]

It was only through Washington's efforts that a serious break was averted, for the discontent even went to the extent of a riot on the wharves in Boston, where the French fleet was for a long time refitting. From Boston, d'Estaing sailed for the West Indies on November 4. This caused more dissatisfaction with the French.

But in this case it was obviously unjust, for the British fleet had been reinforced to a superior strength over the French fleet, by the arrival of Admiral Byron's squadron from England. As a result, the French no longer could hope for control in American waters, and it is hard to imagine anything d'Estaing could have accomplished here. Whereas, the active operations conducted by the French in the West Indies were of actual help to the Americans. These French operations not only diverted British forces, from being sent to America, but also drew British forces away from America, as in November Clinton detached over five thousand troops to be sent to the West Indies. From this time on, the hostilities in the West Indies must be counted as an element in the military situation strongly in favor of the Americans.

[1] 'I fear it will sow the seeds of dissention and distrust between us and our new allies, unless the most prudent measures are taken to suppress the feuds and jealousies, that have already arisen.' (To Major General Greene, September 1, 1778.)

Chapter XXXI

THE NEW SITUATION AT THE END OF 1778

AT THE end of 1778 the British had admitted the defeat of their attempts to subdue the Northern States. Their armies had been unable to keep the field against the Americans, and this had prevented them from occupying American territory away from the sea. At the end of the year the main British army was held on the defensive at New York and Newport, where they could be supplied by sea. And this was actually the end of serious British operations in the Northern States, for the whole war. It was a military situation that would have been unbelievable for the British leaders at the outbreak of the Revolution.

Yet, in 1778, it was a situation accepted without question by the British leaders, as the result of bitter experience. The mere statement of this military situation is praise enough of Washington. For it was the concrete and visible product of Washington's labors in command of the American Army, a command so personal that it included the creation of the American forces which had curbed the British armies. After three years of offensives with superior British forces, the King's Ministers had been forced to the point of acknowledging their military failure in the North, and of preparing to shift the scene to the South.

From this time on, in the North, British military operations were confined to expeditions along the coast, and to raids on the frontier with the assistance of the Indians. These forays of the British and Indians were a tragic feature of the year 1778. After the failure of the Loyalists and Indians in the Mohawk Valley, at the time of the Burgoyne invasion, the Johnsons and the two Butlers withdrew to Fort Niagara, where their Loyalist followers were joined by Brant and his Mohawks. Fort Niagara became a base from which Loyalists and Indians made frequent raids upon the frontier settlements. And they were able to do this for a long time unpunished, as they could make a safe retreat to their distant stronghold. These incursions could not affect the general result of the Revolution. In fact, they served to inflame the Americans against the British and Indians. But the desolation and suffering caused by them went beyond description.

In 1778 the destruction of two settlements stood out among these horrors. In July Colonel John Butler, with a company of his Rangers, a regiment of Johnson's Greens, and a large body of Seneca Indians, descended upon Wyoming, in Pennsylvania on the Susquehanna. This was a massacre of men, women, and children, with revolting tortures of the hapless settlers. In November the same scenes were repeated at Cherry Valley, in central New York. Throughout the frontier settlements, there was a constant war of raiding Tories and Indians. It was like the border warfare of the French and Indian War, only on a scale of greater depredations. As in the former war, Washington was greatly moved by the tale of these atrocities of 1778, and he planned an expedition to aid these settlers in 1779.

But, in 1778, there had been the start of one expedition which was destined to achieve important results. This was the expedition of George Rogers Clark,[1] of less than two

[1] With the endorsement of Patrick Henry, Jefferson, Wythe, and Madison.

274

hundred men at first, which left Pittsburgh (May, 1778) in a flotilla of boats, proceeded down the Ohio to the Mississippi, and gained possession of Illinois, which was annexed to Virginia as a 'county.' This was the beginning of the 'winning of the west.'

The British raids along the coast, and marauding detachments sent into New Jersey in the fall of 1778, also aroused the resentment of the Americans — and also could not have any effect upon the course of the war. Martha's Vineyard was despoiled, and the whaling towns of New Bedford and Fair Haven were burned. All this was an ignominious lapse from the original British schemes of conquest, but the Southern campaign projected by Germaine was a serious matter.

The King's Ministers, after their disappointment in the North, had resolved to shear off the Southern States, in order that these might be retained by Great Britain, even if the Northern States should break away from the Crown. The King's Ministers believed that the conquest of the South would be far easier than that of the North, and they planned to concentrate troops for this object. The first move was to strengthen the British forces in Florida, under General Prevost, and to send raiding detachments into Georgia. The British followed this up by an expedition of thirty-five hundred troops from New York under Colonel Campbell, which captured Savannah (December 28) after easily overwhelming the weak American force under General Howe. This was the situation at the end of 1778, with the British preparing for further aggressions in Georgia and South Carolina. As the winter season was favorable in the South, their operations against South Carolina were to begin early in the year of 1779.

In the North, 'the rigour of winter suspended all military

275

operations between the two great armies in the province of New York, until the return of spring.' ¹ In December, 1778, Washington disposed his troops for the winter in lines of strong intrenchments, extending from Danbury, where Putnam was in command, to New Jersey. His object was to provide for the safety of the countryside, in addition to holding Clinton in check from the American strongholds on the Hudson. Washington's headquarters were near Middlebrook in New Jersey, and he was free from the hardships and keen anxieties of the two preceding winters.

It was true that his army would shrink again in the winter months, and the low ebb of American finances made it difficult to maintain the army. But, this time, Washington could feel sure that the British were reduced to inactivity, and that he was safe from any serious attack. In addition, his army at last had attained a stable organization, as has been explained, and was not in danger of losing its existence, as in the past. The preceding narrative has made it clear that Washington's untiring exertions had given the form of an organized army to the American troops. The statement of this achievement of Washington, which was a fundamental factor in the military situation, should be reiterated as to this stage of the Revolution.

In regard to this stage of the war, another statement of fact should be made so clear that there can be no possibility of misunderstanding. This military situation at the end of 1778, in itself, was proof positive that Washington actually had accomplished his whole military object against the British — which must be the measure of his success in his task throughout the most dangerous period of the Revolution. The record of this success will be a surprise to many Americans. Yet it is the truth.

¹ Stedman: *History of the American War.*

As has been explained before in this work, and there can be no dispute in this respect, the whole object of Washington's campaigns must be considered an attempt to offset the main British army, and to ward off the conquest which at first had seemed the inevitable result of the strong forces given to General Howe. All Washington's aims were bound up in this one hope — and many times this had seemed a forlorn hope indeed. Yet, with weaker forces, in the face of difficulties and discouragements that seemed unsurmountable, Washington had won his case. In the three and a half years of his command, he had baffled and beaten off the superior British main army, until it lay huddled on the coast, after giving up all efforts to overrun the country.

This acid test, the actual military situation at the end of 1778, did not leave room for question. Yet its self-evident verdict has not been grasped in histories of the Revolution, because the great result achieved has been obscured by making the histories merely accounts of battles. At this stage, it must be emphasized again that the course of the American Revolution cannot be described in these European terms of set battles. Much more decisive than a series of battles, after the European fashion, was this record, plain for all to read, that Washington's campaigns had compelled the British to abandon their attempts to conquer the Northern States. This went far beyond any mere matter of the events of battles. It marked an actual decision won by Washington over the British main army — for it meant the defeat of the whole object of the main British army in the Revolution.

Many 'famous victories' of history cannot stand the comparison with Washington's shabby campaigns of hardships, when subjected to this exacting test of being judged only by their resultant military situations. It was not often that

277

Europe's splendid and dramatic battlefields brought results as decisive as those won by Washington's nondescript and ill-equipped troops. They never were strong enough to hope to destroy their enemy, but they had compelled their enemy to fall back, vanquished, to their overseas support.

This situation, at the end of 1778, also meant that the decisive result won by Washington had spanned the period of the war most threatening to the Americans. For, from this time on, the British were no longer free to use all their forces against the Americans. Great Britain at the beginning of 1779 was involved in a general European war, as early in that year Spain joined France in war against Great Britain.[1] Consequently, it was necessary that British naval and military forces should be diverted from America, to carry on the war against France and Spain. This was a new element in the Revolution, greatly in favor of the Americans throughout the rest of the struggle.

The adverse situation on the sea was also continuing to score heavily against Great Britain. The depredations wrought by the Americans upon British commerce were increasing all the time. The British public saw that the British military forces in America had been brought to a standstill, and at the same time they realized that losses of British shipping were mounting to unprecedented figures, and insurance rates had been raised as never before. Most of this damage to British shipping was inflicted by American privateers.

As all American commerce had been interrupted by the Revolution, privateering had become the occupation of seafaring Americans. Owners and crews made profitable ventures out of cruises against British commerce. For these

[1] Spain, however, did not enter any alliance with the United States.

privateering cruises the American ships and their crews were well suited, as the qualities of both, needed for the raids upon British commerce, had been acquired in the Colonial wars, and Americans were no novices in fighting on the seas. The alliance with France had increased the facilities of the American privateers for capturing British shipping, as the French ports were available for refitting and for sending in their prizes. Consequently they grew more daring in carrying their depredations into British waters, and there was consternation akin to a panic among British shipping interests.

In addition to the privateers which cruised under letters of marque issued in America, Franklin had been authorized by Congress to issue letters of marque in France. Franklin exercised this power in a way that increased the dangers to British shipping in British waters. The year 1778 had also seen the appearance of the infant United States Navy in British waters. As was natural, the scattered small craft commissioned in the new Navy had not stood much chance against the powerful British Navy. But Captain Paul Jones in the little *Ranger* (eighteen guns) had actually raided the British coast by destroying shipping at Whitehaven.

Jones added to this sensational exploit the still more dramatic feat of capturing the British sloop of war *Drake* (twenty guns), after a fierce engagement in British waters. Jones brought the captured *Drake* and several British merchantmen as prizes into Brest. These totals of losses of shipping on the seas, with the object lessons of depredations that had spread to British waters and even to the British coast, were creating a profound impression in England. As this warfare on the sea continued to be increasingly harmful to the British, it must always be kept in mind as a factor in deciding the war. Its details are outside the scope of this book, but its effects must be counted as a strong influence upon the course of the events which figure in the text.

In the situation that has been described, it must be evident that an entirely different phase of the American Revolution was to begin in 1779. In regard to this new phase of the war, it is of interest to note that the influence of Washington was strong in preventing the consideration of a scheme for an expedition against Canada, in which a French army of five thousand was to take part. This scheme, which had been advocated by Lafayette, was brought before Congress, and Washington opposed it in a remarkable letter,[1] which contained the following: 'I have an objection to it, untouched in my public letter, which is, in my estimation, insurmountable, and alarms all my feelings for the true and permanent interests of my country. This is the introduction of a large body of French troops into Canada.... I fear this would be too great a temptation to be resisted by any power actuated by the common maxims of national policy.' This was a notable example of the wise outlook of Washington. For it was a statement prophetic of the future policy of the United States, as it contained the essentials of the Monroe Doctrine.

[1] To the President of Congress, November 14, 1778.

Chapter XXXII

THE FIRST MONTHS OF 1779

AT THE beginning of 1779 the British were planning to extend their operations from Georgia into South Carolina. The Southern members of Congress had realized the impending dangers, and, at their request, General Lincoln had been sent to command in the Southern field. Early in January Lincoln collected what forces he could to oppose the British. Lincoln had only some six hundred Continental troops, and it was difficult to call out the local militia, as the inhabitants were afraid of an uprising of the slaves and wished to remain at home on guard. But, with two thousand militia sent from North Carolina under General Ashe, Lincoln felt strong enough to take position on the Savannah River (January 3, 1779).

On the part of the British, Prevost and Campbell united their forces at Savannah (January 17, 1779), and made dispositions to safeguard the British positions in Georgia. However, Lincoln saw that it would be important to oust the British from Augusta, in order to gain the moral effect of freeing the seat of government of the State, and he sent forward General Ashe, with fifteen hundred militia, for this purpose. Prevost retreated from Augusta before this detachment, and then, in the words of a British historian, 'taking a leaf out of Washington's own book,' [1] Prevost made

[1] Fortescue: *History of the British Army*.

a surprise attack upon Ashe at Briar Creek (March 3, 1779). By his sudden onslaught, Prevost utterly defeated this American detachment, with a loss of four hundred killed and wounded, and two hundred prisoners. The Americans were dispersed, and less than five hundred straggled back to rejoin Lincoln.

Prevost then reoccupied Augusta, and reinstated the Royal Governor in control. By great exertions Lincoln gathered enough militia to repair his losses, and in April he again advanced upon Augusta. Thereupon, Prevost, at the head of two thousand British troops, made a push toward Charleston, driving before him Moultrie with one thousand Americans, left to guard the lower Savannah. At first Lincoln had kept on his way against Augusta and had occupied that place, not thinking that Prevost would make a serious attempt to take Charleston. But, whatever his original intention had been, Prevost was attacking Charleston in earnest and Moultrie was in danger.

Upon this news, Lincoln, 'after establishing a post at Augusta,' [1] hastened back to the defense of Charleston. At the first of June the American forces were united against Prevost. At this time Pulaski's Legion, from the Northern army, had joined the Americans at Charleston. It was obvious to Prevost that there was no chance for him to capture Charleston, and, after two weeks, he withdrew the British troops to Savannah. There had been attacks upon the British, as they were about to evacuate their post at St. John's Island, but they were repulsed, and the British made good their retreat. Prevost's main army occupied Savannah, and a British post was established at Beaufort on Port Royal Island.

The contemporary British historian thus described the

[1] Stedman: *History of the American War.*

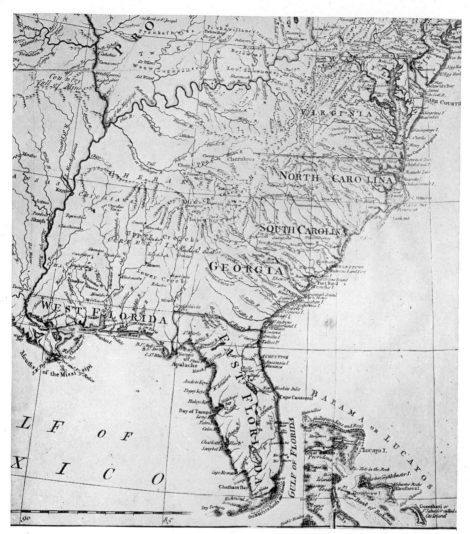

THE SOUTHERN STATES IN THE REVOLUTION

situation in the South: 'Although General Prevost had been obliged to retire from Charleston without reducing it, and although all the upper country of Georgia was now in the possession of the Americans; yet so long as the British troops maintained a footing in the lower parts of that province, with a post at Beaufort, the inhabitants of South Carolina were exposed to incursions similar to that we have already related, and could not be free from the most uneasy apprehensions.' [1] This remained the situation during the summer. But Governor Rutledge of South Carolina, who had shown much energy in organizing the defense of the State, conceived the idea of calling upon the French to join in an attack upon the British.

Count d'Estaing's force had been engaged in the fighting in the West Indies. But the hurricane season would force a suspension of all operations there, and Governor Rutledge proposed that the French should use this interval for a joint attack with the Americans on Savannah. Count d'Estaing willingly agreed to undertake this expedition, and prepared the French fleet to sail for the American coast. There was no danger of opposition from British naval forces, and the operation gave every promise of success.

As to affairs in the North, a British historian has bluntly stated: 'Meanwhile, since the end of 1778, Clinton had remained practically impotent at New York. It is true that Washington had no more troops than himself; but if New York with all its outlying posts was to be securely held, hardly a man could be spared for service in the field.... It was of course certain that, wherever the main body of the British might go, Washington and his regular troops were bound to follow; but outside the Continental Army there was always that incalculable factor the American militia....

[1] Stedman: *History of the American War.*

283

It was therefore imperative that New York should be held; and this being so, it was plain that any expeditions undertaken from thence, with the forces at Clinton's disposal, could be no more than predatory.' [1]

This British estimate is interesting, as reflecting the respect of the British leaders for the new efficiency Washington had given to the American army. 'His regular troops' in combination with 'that incalculable factor the American militia' had astonished his enemies. And for a British historian to state that the operations of the main British army 'could be no more than predatory' was significant of the great change, in three years, that had imposed so limited a strategy upon the enemy.

For Washington himself, the advent of the new year of 1779 was a time of important consultation with Congress. After establishing his army in winter quarters, Washington went to Philadelphia and remained three weeks in consultation with the 'Committee of Congress appointed to confer with the Commander in Chief.' In the first place, Washington's clear vision had brought about the rejection of the mistaken plan for the invasion of Canada, as outlined in the last chapter.[2] At the last of December, 1778, Lafayette was to leave for France, on an indefinite leave of absence granted to him at the request of Washington. In his last letter to Lafayette before he sailed (December 29, 1778), Washington wrote, 'This will be accompanied by a letter from Congress, which will inform you, that a certain expedition, after a full consideration of all circumstances, has been laid aside.'

After this unsound project had been put out of the ques-

[1] Fortescue: *History of the British Army*.

[2] 'The Committee of Congress appointed to confer with General Washington, reported against the Canada plan, after a mature discussion of the subject.' (Secret Journal.)

tion by the influence of Washington, his clear vision was also in evidence in his recommendation of the ensuing plans of operations against the British. As to the main British army, he stated, 'In reasoning upon a plan of operating for the next campaign, we ought, in my opinion, to suppose that the enemy will hold their present posts.' [1] He recognized that the expulsion of the British from New York and Newport was to be desired, but, with able common-sense, he went to the root of the matter by insisting that, 'as to the force on our part sufficient to carry the point against the whole, double the number is the least it could be undertaken with....'

After considering other plans, Washington wrote: 'It is much to be regretted, that our prospect of any capital operations is so slender, that we seem in a manner to be driven to the necessity of adopting the third plan, that is, to remain entirely on the defensive; except such lesser operations against the Indians, as are absolutely necessary to divert their ravages from us.'

This military policy was adopted by Congress, and Washington at once began his preparations against the Indians. Here he was on familiar ground, from his experience in the French and Indian War. Washington knew that the only way to prevent a repetition of the atrocities of 1778 was to give the Indians a dose of their own medicine, to carry the war into their own country and lay waste their villages. With this purpose he devoted his attention to organizing expeditions to ravage the settlements of the tribes that had joined the Johnsons and Butlers in the forays on the border.

At this time the finances of the Americans were in a deplorable state. They were drifting along, with makeshift issues of paper money that sank day by day to lower figures

[1] To the Committee of Congress, January 15, 1779.

of depreciated values. This was no wonder, as there was no national government in the true sense of the word, and the issues of currency were of doubtful paternity. Congress was representative of the States, and the right principle was there. But the powers of Congress had not become defined, and Congress was in a state of chaos. Again we must be reminded that we must not think of the Congress of the Revolution in the terms of the Congress of to-day. The newly born infant had to feel its way to the light, in its feeble struggles to play a part that had never been known before.

It was Washington's lot to be obliged to contend with this weakness of Congress throughout his command. And at this stage, he was tried to the limit of his endurance. At the time of his conferences with Congress at Philadelphia, he was exasperated by the inefficiency of Congress, and his letters, written at this time, are full of complaint — and Washington was a master in writing his denunciations when he saw that things were wrong. At Philadelphia he found 'abundant reason to be convinced, that our affairs are in a more distressed, ruinous and deplorable condition than they have been since the commencement of the war.' [1] He saw 'that party disputes and personal quarrels are the great business of the day; while the momentous concerns of an empire, a great and accumulating debt, ruined finances, depreciated money, and want of credit, which in its consequences is the want of everything, are but secondary considerations, and postponed from day to day — from week to week as if our affairs wear the most promising aspect.' [2]

As a matter of course, the effect of the depreciation of the currency was especially severe upon Washington, in his effort to hold together the American army. With his recom-

[1] To Benjamin Harrison, December 18, 1778.   [2] *Ibid.*

mendations to Congress for military operations, Washington also urged an increase of the Continental bounty, and he emphatically stated: 'The great impediment to all vigorous measures is the state of our currency.' [1] He wrote an earnest warning to the Committee, 'that the most unhappy consequences are to be apprehended.' [2] And Washington urged Congress to make more favorable terms in the provisions for half pay after active service.

There was an object lesson of this feeling of dissatisfaction among the officers, when Washington was gathering his forces for the expeditions against the Indians. And this might have led to serious results, if it had not been for the good offices of Washington. A New Jersey brigade had been ordered for service against the Indians, and its officers drew up a memorial to the New Jersey Legislature stating their distresses, as their families were starving, and declaring that unless they were given relief they would resign in a body. This caused great distress to Washington, who wrote to Congress: 'It shows what is to be apprehended, if some adequate provision is not generally made for the officers.' [3] But Washington, knowing the circumstances, had the good sense not to treat the affair as a case of military insubordination. He reported to Congress: 'I have signified my disapprobation.... I thought best to take no direct notice of it.... I contented myself with writing a letter to General Maxwell. I have this moment received information that the Assembly has made some provision for their troops.... The officers withdrew their remonstrance, and the Assembly went into the business.' [4] Upon this, the New Jersey troops responded to the call for their services.

[1] To the Committee of Congress, January 15, 1779.
[2] Ibid., January 20, 1779.
[3] To the President of Congress, May 1, 1779.   [4] Ibid., May 11, 1779.

The command of operations against the Indians was first offered to General Gates, as was his due. But this was a matter of form, as it was evident it would not be to his taste. And Gates wrote a characteristic note in refusal: 'The man, who undertakes Indian service, should enjoy youth and strength; requisites I do not possess. It therefore grieves me, that your Excellency should offer me the only command to which I am entirely unequal.' Washington had expected this refusal, and had written in his letter to Gates: 'I have enclosed a letter for General Sullivan, on whom, if you decline, it is my intention the command shall devolve.' [1]

The energetic Sullivan at once accepted this appointment, and went to Washington's headquarters. The first move against the Indians was an expedition from Fort Schuyler, which surprised the Onandaga towns, and destroyed all their settlements, without any loss for the Americans. But the main effort was to be an expedition under General Sullivan himself, who was well suited to this task. Washington evinced an intense interest in this expedition, and his letter of instructions to Sullivan stands as probably unique among such letters from a commanding general. Every line is instinct with Washington's intimate knowledge of the Indians, derived from his experience in the French and Indian War.

Washington wrote: 'The expedition you are appointed to command is to be directed against the hostile tribes of the Six nations of Indians, with their associates and adherents. The immediate objects are the total destruction and devastation of their settlements, and the capture of as many prisoners of every age and sex as possible.' [2] These were ruthless words from the humane Washington, but he knew

[1] To Major General Gates, March 8, 1779.
[2] To Major General Sullivan, May 31, 1779.

the Indians. The scenes of murder and devastation on the border, in the French and Indian War, were before his eyes, and he knew that the only safety lay in remorseless destruction. He added, 'I would recommend that some post in the centre of the Indian country, should be occupied with all expedition, with a sufficient quantity of provisions; whence parties should be detached to lay waste all the settlements around, with instructions to do it in the most effectual manner, that the country may not be merely overrun, but destroyed.'

His knowledge of Indian warfare prompted the following advice as to the tactics to be used: 'I beg leave to suggest as general rules that ought to govern your operations, to make rather than receive attacks, attended with as much impetuosity, shouting, and noise, as possible; and to make the troops act in as loose and dispersed a way as is consistent with a proper degree of government, concert, and mutual support. It should be previously impressed upon the minds of the men, whenever they have an opportunity, to rush on with the war-whoop and fixed bayonets. Nothing will disconcert and terrify the Indians more than this.' And his instructions as to terms of peace were very wise: 'When we have effectually chastised them, we may then listen to propositions for peace, and endeavour to draw further advantages from their fears. But, even in this case, great caution will be necessary to guard against the snares, which their treachery may hold out. They must be explicit in their promises, give substantial pledges for their performance, and execute their engagements with decision and despatch. Hostages are the only kind of security to be depended on.'

Chapter XXXIII

THE LAST PART OF 1779

THE most serious of the British forays along the coast, in the early months of 1779, had been an expedition to the Chesapeake, with a strong fleet and twenty-five hundred troops. Norfolk and Portsmouth had been sacked and destroyed (May, 1779) with great sufferings for the inhabitants. Upon this news, Washington had written to Congress: 'The predatory war, which the enemy now seem resolved to carry on, will be very distressing. Little aid can be afforded from the army, in its present situation, and the militia appear too ill provided with arms to defend themselves. How this can be remedied, and the army supplied, I know not. But it ought to be an essential object of policy with the particular States, to put the militia on a respectable footing, and under such regulations as will enable them to assemble with rapidity on sudden emergencies.' [1]

This letter from Washington went to the root of the whole question. His army was holding the main army of the enemy at bay, and preventing incursions into the country. Washington was accomplishing this with weak forces, and he could not detach troops to defend the cities and towns on the coast from British raids. The only remedy was to arouse the local militia, to be ready to defend the places attacked by the enemy. This was also the only practical way to

[1] To the President of Congress, May 25, 1779.

strengthen the American forces in the South, and Washington wrote: 'It appears to me, that a reinforcement to the southern army is an indispensable object.' [1] As Washington stated, his army was restricted by 'the preparations for the Indian expedition.' [2]

These preparations were more than justified by the results, for General Sullivan's expedition gave the needed chastisement to the Indians. His main body, under his personal command, consisted of three thousand troops assembled in the early summer near Wyoming, to move up the west branch of the Susquehanna. From the Mohawk came another American force under General James Clinton. This, added to Sullivan's main body, made a total of about five thousand. The British and Indians could not rally forces sufficient to oppose the Americans. Johnson, the Butlers, and Brant were totally defeated near Newtown on August 29, and the Americans swept through the heart of the Indian country. They burned their villages, devastated their fields, and made the whole tract uninhabitable. Another expedition under Colonel Brodhead from Pittsburgh was equally destructive.

This campaign of devastation was a blow to the power of the Indians, from which they never recovered. 'The wisdom of Washington's policy of carrying the war against the Indians into their own country, and conducting it in their own way, was apparent from the general intimidation produced among the tribes by these expeditions.' [3] After returning from this arduous expedition, General Sullivan's health was impaired, and he retired from the service.

Through the summer, affairs in the South were at a standstill, with both parties watching one another, and the

[1] To the President of Congress, May 25, 1779.   [2] *Ibid.*
[3] Irving: *Life of Washington.*

Americans preparing for the attempt on Savannah in conjunction with the French. In the North, the British continued their policy of raiding the coast. In July Tryon had led an expedition which caused great destruction along the Connecticut shore. The shipping and warehouses at New Haven were burned, and also all of Fairfield, Green Farms, and Norfolk. As has been explained, Washington's army was too weak to enable him to send troops to meet these enemy attacks. But he suddenly devised a counter-offensive, which interrupted these raids of the enemy.

What was in Washington's mind was vividly expressed in a letter to General Wayne, as to a project for capturing Stony Point: 'While the enemy are making incursions to distress the country, it has a very disagreeable aspect to remain in a state of inactivity on our part. The reputation of the army, and the good of the service, seem to exact some attempt from it. The importance of Stony Point makes it infinitely desirable, that this post could be the object.' [1]

The main stronghold of the Americans was West Point, the key of the Hudson. Below, at Stony Point and Verplanck's Point, which were opposite one another on the river, the Americans were also constructing works in the spring of 1779. A strong British expedition from New York, with troops on their shipping, had captured these posts at the end of May, before they had been completed and garrisoned. There were only about thirty men at Stony Point, and they abandoned the place at the approach of the enemy. The British also easily overpowered and captured the small force of about seventy men at Verplanck's Point. Thereupon, the British constructed a strong fortification at Stony Point, and placed there a garrison of six hundred troops. They also fortified Verplanck's Point. Clinton did not ven-

[1] To Brigadier General Wayne, July 9, 1779.

ture to make any attacks against the Americans at West Point.

Consequently, these British positions were not a threat to West Point. However, Washington was very anxious to attempt the capture of Stony Point, not that this could have any important military result, but because he realized it would produce a widespread moral effect. Washington's letter to Wayne, whom he chose to carry out this favored project, showed the almost uncanny skill with which Washington planned all the details of this daring assault. And, after reading these, we can well believe the tradition that Wayne said, 'General, I'll storm hell if you will plan it.' Washington was so convinced the strong position could be carried only by surprise, that he wrote: 'Secrecy is so much more essential to this kind of enterprise than numbers, that I should not think it advisable to employ any other than light troops. If a surprise takes place, they are fully competent to the business; if it does not, numbers will avail little.' [1] This was certainly reducing the problem to its simplest terms, and in itself expressed a sound doctrine of war. In this regard, Washington's warning instructions were most original, in their departure from the usual formal tactics of the day: 'Knowledge of your intention, ten minutes previously obtained, blasts all your hopes; for which reason a small detachment, composed of men whose fidelity you can rely on, under the care of a judicious officer, should guard every avenue through the marsh to the enemy's works, which our deserters or the spies can pass, and prevent all intercourse. The usual time for exploits of this kind is a little before day, for which reason a vigilant officer is then more on the watch. I therefore recommend a midnight hour.... A white feather, or cockade, or some other visible badge of dis-

[1] To Brigadier General Wayne, July 10, 1779.

tinction for the night, should be worn by our troops, and a watchword agreed on to distinguish friends from foes.' [1]

These instructions were the foundation of the success of this undertaking. With the utmost care, the chosen American troops were brought into position on the land approach to the fortress, without arousing any suspicion of their presence. This was accomplished in the afternoon of July 15, 1779. Half an hour before midnight they made their attack in two columns. In advance of each column was a forlorn hope of twenty men to remove the abatis. One was under Lieutenant Gibbon, the other under Lieutenant Knox. Washington had directed, 'The whole of them are to advance with fixed bayonets and muskets unloaded.' [2] With this disposition, the surprise assault was successful. The garrison was thrown into confusion, and surrendered at discretion.

Washington very wisely had abandoned the idea of a simultaneous attack on Verplanck's Point, on account of 'the hazard thereby run of defeating the attempt on Stony Point, which is infinitely the most important.' [3] He had hoped to follow up the capture by the reduction of Verplanck's Point, but the American forces failed to arrive. This failure was not of any importance, as the Americans had no idea of taking up a position lower on the Hudson than the stronghold of West Point. Accordingly, the captured guns and stores were taken away, and the fortifications were destroyed.

This brilliant success [4] of the Americans had the immediate result hoped for by Washington. The contemporary British historian wrote: 'Intelligence of the capture of Stony Point, and the danger of Fort Lafayette on Verplank's Neck,

[1] To Brigadier General Wayne, July 10, 1779.   [2] *Ibid.*   [3] *Ibid.*
[4] The loss of the Americans was only 15 killed, 83 wounded; of the British, 63 killed, 554 taken prisoners.

Stoney Point 16th July 1779
2 Oclock A. M.
Dear Genl
The fort & Garrison
with Colo Johnston are ours our Officers
& men behaved like men
who are determined to be
free yours most Sincerely
Anty Wayne
Genl Washington

WAYNE'S DISPATCH ANNOUNCING THE CAPTURE OF STONY
POINT

having been brought to Sir Henry Clinton just after his
conference with Sir George Collier, the expedition against
New London was for the present laid aside, the transports
and troops were recalled from the Sound, and the army
made a forward movement to Dobbs Ferry, on the North
River.' [1]

Shortly after this, occurred the failure of an expedition
sent out from Boston, entirely without the concurrence of
Washington, to destroy a new settlement of the British on
Penobscot Bay. This district was a part of Massachusetts in
those days, and the Massachusetts men equipped a force of

[1] Stedman: *History of the American War.*

their own to eject the intruders. They laid an embargo on shipping, and equipped their expedition, which arrived in Penobscot Bay (May 25, 1779). Their only hope of success was a prompt attack, but at the first resistance, the leaders sent to Boston for reinforcements — and dallied about, waiting for them. This gave an opportunity for the energetic British Admiral Collier to assemble a force which suddenly overwhelmed the Massachusetts expedition in August. Their shipping was destroyed, and their troops were obliged to retrace their way to Massachusetts through the wilderness.

But, in the vicinity of New York, the Americans followed up the success at Stony Point by 'a bold and successful attack made by the American Major Lee upon the British post, at Paulus Hook, on the Jersey shore, opposite to New York.' [1] This was a project of 'Light Horse Harry,' in emulation of Wayne's exploit at Stony Point. Washington, at Lee's first proposal, imposed caution, 'unless it can be made in a manner less hazardous,' and that 'it might not require more than three hundred men.' [2] But Lee carried the operation through under these conditions. His force surprised and captured the British post, with almost no loss, and Lee made good his escape with one hundred fifty-nine prisoners (August 19, 1779).

After these successful diversions, Washington made his headquarters at West Point, where he fortified the American positions so strongly that the British never dared to attack them throughout the war. Even the arrival of Admiral Arbuthnot, with reinforcements, did not change this situation. Admiral Collier resigned the command to Admiral Arbuthnot. In regard to this situation, it could not be de-

[1] Stedman: *History of the American War.*
[2] To Major Henry Lee, August 10, 1779.

scribed in terms more clear than those of the contemporary British historian: 'Although it was now late, the season for action was not yet entirely over, but the appearance of the Count d'Estaing with his formidable fleet on the coast of Georgia, intelligence of which, as well as of his threatened attack against New York, was brought about this time, obliged the commander in chief to give up all thoughts of offensive operations during the remainder of the campaign, and to concentrate his force, that he might be prepared to meet the shock which he was to expect from a combined attack of the French by sea and the Americans by land. In this view, Rhode Island was evacuated, and the garrison withdrew to New York. And in this respect alone, by obliging Sir Henry Clinton to change his system and act upon the defensive during the remainder of the campaign, the expedition of the Count d'Estaing to the coast of North America, otherwise unfortunate, may be said to have been serviceable to the American cause.' [1]

Influenced by his anticipation of an attack upon New York by the French and Americans,[2] General Clinton not only abandoned Rhode Island, but he also withdrew the British troops from Stony Point and Verplanck's Point, and disposed all the British forces to defend New York. This was, in itself, an object lesson of the total failure of the British campaigns in the Northern States. Washington had hoped there would be a combined attack on New York and he reported to Congress: 'I set about concerting measures necessary for coöperation with his Excellency the Count d'Estaing, agreeably to the powers vested in me by the

[1] Stedman: *History of the American War.*

[2] 'Such were the forcible reasons for rescuing the garrison and stores from Rhode Island from an unprotected state, and giving security to the harbour of New York.' (Letter of Clinton, September 30, 1779.)

resolve of Congress. I have called upon the State of Massachusetts for two thousand militia, Connecticut for four thousand, New Jersey for two thousand five hundred, and Pennsylvania for one thousand five hundred.' [1] But there was no chance for carrying out this project, as d'Estaing's force was committed to the joint operation with the Southern army in Georgia.

This operation was a joint attack on Savannah, and it was already in progress when Washington wrote the above. On September 23 the combined forces invested the place, and a siege was pressed by regular approaches for three weeks. Then d'Estaing grew impatient, especially as the season of autumnal gales was approaching. Accordingly he determined upon an assault, although the enemy's defenses had not been impaired to any extent that justified it. This overconfident attack was decisively beaten off, with slight loss to the British (October 9, 1779). The French and Americans lost about one thousand. Count Pulaski was among the killed, and d'Estaing himself was twice wounded. Upon this unexpected defeat, d'Estaing reëmbarked his troops, and, after sending part of his fleet to the West Indies, returned with the rest to France. This obliged Lincoln's troops to withdraw into South Carolina.

It was another case of the failure of the coöperation of the new allies to accomplish military results. And it was no wonder that there was again a great deal of prejudice aroused among the people against the French. But the matter of these failures in America was no measure of the help the French were giving in the great game that was being played.

However, the withdrawal of the French fleet from America opened the way, at the last of 1779, for the British to

[1] To the President of Congress, October 4, 1779.

undertake their campaign of conquest in the South.[1] After
the news of the defeat at Savannah, Washington reported to
Congress that the British were 'preparing for a considerable
embarkation of troops from New York.' He had decided
that these troops must be destined for the South, and he detached from his army the North Carolina brigade and the
whole of the Virginia line, 'ill as they could be spared,' [2] to
reinforce General Lincoln in the South. This was the utmost Washington could do to help the threatening situation
in the South. His instinct was right, for, on December 26,
1779, 'Clinton sailed with a force of seven thousand six hundred men for the capure of his new base at Charleston.' [3]

[1] '...when the welcome news of d'Estaing's repulse left him free to form his
plans for a campaign in Carolina.' (Fortescue: *History of the British Army*.)

[2] To the President of Congress, November 29, 1779, December 7, 1779; to
Major General Lincoln, December 12, 1779.

[3] Fortescue: *History of the British Army*.

Chapter xxxiv

THE SHIFTING CONDITIONS FOR 1780

THE year 1779 ended, with Clinton's expedition on its way by sea to attack Charleston. Thus far, the efforts of the British in the South had not accomplished results of importance. In the words of the contemporary British historian, 'With the raising of the siege of Savannah ended the campaign to the southward, which, although it closed with an achievement honorable to the British arms, was nevertheless unproductive of those advantages which had been expected at the commencement of it.' [1] This expressed the lack of military results in 1779 for the British in America. Their disappointment in the South, added to their being reduced to the defensive in the North, made only a total of failure for the British Ministers in that whole year.

Abroad, the situation had grown much more serious for Great Britain. Spain also had entered the war against her, and Gibraltar was being besieged. The inevitable result was, that the resources of Great Britain must be diverted to provide forces for carrying on the war against France and Spain. This meant that the subjugation of America could no longer be the main object of Great Britain, and this new form assumed by the war was exerting a vital influence upon the Revolution.

This change in the whole character of the problem for

[1] Stedman: *History of the American War.*

Great Britain cannot be emphasized too strongly. It brought in its train a change of sentiment in Great Britain, which should be described. It was true that the alliance of the Americans with France had alienated many who, at first, had sympathized with the Americans. And all Great Britain was rising in a united effort against the coalition of enemies. Yet this very fact, that Great Britain's enemies in Europe had become the main danger, was creating a new public opinion in Great Britain.

To the public mind, the retention of the former British Colonies in America was becoming a matter of minor importance. Instead of being engaged only in suppressing a local rebellion in far-away America, Great Britain was facing a European war, with France and Spain already arrayed against her, with Holland hostile to the point of war, which was to come in 1780, with Frederick the Great hostile in every way, though he never came to open war. The natural consequence was, the British people, absorbed in their struggle against their pressing European enemies, began to be anxious to get rid of the American nuisance on any terms. This is not an exaggerated statement, for it must be admitted that, in the new phase of the war from this time to the end, Great Britain was only half-hearted in the American Revolution.

The conduct of the war in Europe had become the one great interest in the minds of the British — and this had made a minor matter of the American Revolution. The influence of this change of British public opinion, with its reaction in favor of letting the Americans go, is another thing that has not been made sufficiently clear in histories of the American Revolution. The subsequent course of the war in America for the British had been reduced to two possibilities. If the British Ministers could win a decisive victory in the South, they might hope to disrupt the new United States. But, on the other hand, as the event proved, the first serious British disaster would mean the abandonment of the war in America.

The continuation of losses at sea was another influence added to these discouraging factors, which were preventing the King's Ministers from vigorously pushing the war in America. The destruction of British commerce by the American privateers was constantly increasing. And there was always the persistent effect upon the British public mind of these losses of British shipping. This was so widespread that it was everywhere creating a distaste for the American war. In this regard the quotation from Maclay again should be given, which so well described this situation: 'In all the memorials presented to Parliament the argument used to bring about peace was the unprecedented destruction of English commerce.'

In addition to these depredations of the American privateers in 1779, American warships actually were harrying the waters about Great Britain. In September, 1779, came the most spectacular exploit of Paul Jones' career. After his successes in the *Ranger,* the French had helped to fit out a small squadron for him. Of these, Jones' flagship was an old Indiaman, the *Duras,* rechristened *Bon Homme Richard.* In this nondescript craft, laid alongside the British frigate *Serapis,* Paul Jones fought the desperate 'moonlight battle' off Flamborough Head. With his ship smashed to wreck, upon being called on to surrender, Paul Jones gave the unique answer: 'I have not yet begun to fight.' And he forced the *Serapis* to surrender, only in time to transfer his crew to her from the sinking *Bon Homme Richard.*

Of course, these raids in British waters did not mean great actual damage, but they increased the impression of the 'unprecedented destruction of English commerce,' which was growing to enormous figures.[1] As Fiske has stated, 'The moral effect, in Europe, of such a victory within sight of the British coast was prodigious.' [2]

As the result of this European situation, the outlook was very unfavorable for the British at the first of 1780. But the advent of Clinton's expedition against Charleston was the beginning of a series of disasters for the Americans. The situation at Charleston was the same as that at New York in 1776, when Howe arrived with an overwhelming force to capture the place. In 1776 Congress had insisted on an effort to defend New York. In 1780 the government of South Carolina demanded a defense of Charleston. In each case the American commander was thus obliged to make the best defense he could.

This was a disadvantage imposed upon Washington in 1776, and this same disadvantage was imposed upon Lincoln in 1780. But there was a very great difference in the conduct of affairs. At New York, Washington, after realizing the superiority of the British forces arrayed against him, had consistently maneuvered to save his weaker army from being cooped up by the enemy. The result was, the British only accomplished the barren conquest of New York. For Washington's army had escaped capture, and remained footloose in the countryside, to the undoing of all the British plans. In the case of Charleston, the result was to be very different, because Lincoln stolidly committed his army to being shut up and besieged in Charleston.

This was a fatal error. The loss of Charleston, like the loss of New York, would have been a matter of small impor-

---

[1] As has been stated, the total of destruction of British commerce grew to eighteen million dollars.

[2] Fiske: *The American Revolution.*

tance. But, when Lincoln allowed his whole army to be besieged in Charleston, it meant inevitably the loss of this whole army. And it also meant that the British would make a clean sweep, for the time being, as Lincoln's army comprised all the American troops available for the defense of South Carolina. In the case of Washington at New York, the hive had been taken, but the swarm was outside to sting the British. In the case of Lincoln, he was to allow the whole swarm to be caught in the British net.

While this situation was being developed in the South, Washington was struggling with the difficulties that always beset him when his army was in winter quarters. These perplexities were multiplied, for the reasons that have been explained. The financial affairs of the American were going from bad to worse, and again it can be stated that only Washington's personal influence held the fabric of the army from dissolution. Again there can be no question as to the effect of this personal influence of Washington in saving the army. The Continental Army had been his own creation, after overcoming every obstacle. The intriguing and hostile elements had been eliminated, by the sheer contrast of their petty and base methods with what can only be described as the magnanimity of Washington — and again he was faced by a fateful test.

Again Washington's magnanimity met the test, and this quality, innate and enduring in Washington, brought the army through the fearful winter that ensued, of unprecedented cold, and with all finances hopelessly in confusion. For always the American soldiers knew that he was one with them — that he was with them and of them in all their sufferings. In a letter to Greene, Washington wrote (January 22, 1780), after the awful grip of the winter had fastened itself upon the army: 'To share the common lot, and partici-

pate in the inconveniences, which the army, from the peculi-
arity of our circumstances, are obliged to undergo, has with
me been a fundamental ideal.' This was the source of his
strength, and the facts themselves are the proof of what
Washington accomplished in the winter of 1779–1780.

Of this winter, Irving has written one of his most graphic
descriptions: 'The winter set in early, and was uncommonly
rigorous. The transportation of supplies was obstructed; the
magazines were exhausted, and the commissaries had neither
money nor credit to enable them to replenish them. For
weeks at a time the army was on half allowance; sometimes
without meat, sometimes without bread, sometimes without
both. There was a scarcity, too, of clothing and blankets,
so that the poor soldiers were starving with cold as well as
hunger.... A rigorous winter had much to do with the
actual distresses of the army, but the root of the evil lay in
the derangement of the currency.'[1] This has drawn a better
picture of the situation than could be given in many pages
of description.

In this critical predicament of the army, Washington
found the one solution of the problem that saved the situation. He decided that the time had come when he must
commandeer supplies, and he felt at last obliged to call upon
the counties to furnish supplies in proportion to their abilities. These were to be delivered at the camp, and certifi-
cates for payment would be given in return. This act of
Washington prevented the dispersal of the army. And
Washington's way of carrying out, what in other hands
would have created prejudice as an arbitrary measure, won
success for his project.

In his instructions, for this impressment of supplies, Washington wrote: 'I am persuaded you will not forget that, as

[1] Irving: *Life of Washington.*

we are compelled by necessity to take the property of citizens for the support of an army on which their safety depends, we should be careful to manifest that we have a reverence for their rights, and wish not to do anything which that necessity, and even their own good, do not absolutely require.' This good spirit, in defining the levy of supplies, did away with any feeling of oppression, and it was greatly to the credit of the inhabitants of the State of New Jersey that they responded generously to the demands made upon them at this emergency.[1]

So successful was this measure of Washington that it was also extended to other States. Unquestionably this provided the one means of holding the army together. For, as described by Irving, the winter was one of the coldest ever known. New York Bay was frozen over. As the British warships were caught in the ice, Knyphausen, who was left in command of the British in New York, grew apprehensive of an attack across the ice. He even gathered seamen from the warships to strengthen the garrison in New York. But Washington had no forces available for any such attack. His army was inferior in numbers. For not only had American troops been sent to the South, but Washington's own forces had shrunk into a band of ill-equipped, half-starved and half-clothed men who were fighting the cold in their huts. Washington wrote, 'They have borne their distress (in which the officers have shared a common lot with the men) with as much fortitude as human nature is capable of.'[2]

Under these conditions, there was no possibility for Washington to attempt any stroke on a large scale with the

[1] 'In doing this, though you may not be authorized by the strict letter of the law, by consulting its spirit, which aims at the relief of the army, in an emergency of so pressing and peculiar a nature, you will merit the acknowledgments of your fellow-citizens.' (To the Magistrates of New Jersey, January 8, 1780.)

[2] To Governor Trumbull, January 8, 1780.

American army. The wonder was that he was able to keep it in existence at all. But Washington's letters showed that he was keenly alive to the opportunity offered by the ice bridges for an enterprise so much to his mind, and that only the condition of his army obliged him to give up the idea of an attack in force upon the British. Washington wrote: 'Our affairs are in so deplorable condition (on the score of provisions) as to fill the mind with the most anxious & alarming fears. Such a situation at all times to be lamented, is peculiarly unfortunate at this juncture, when there now is, or soon must be, a field opened for Enterprise.' [1]

In spite of the fact that any serious assault was thus precluded, Washington did his utmost to take advantage of the frozen waterways for harassing the enemy. That was all he could hope to accomplish. With this purpose, he gave to General Stirling a force of twenty-five hundred for a surprise attack across the ice against Staten Island, which was then held by a British force of about twelve hundred. This was an enterprise 'not likely to be attended with bad consequences, provided the state of the ice affords a ready and safe passage and return.' [2] This attack Stirling attempted to carry out, in the night of January 14. But the attack failed completely, as the approach of Stirling's force was discovered by the enemy, in time for the British troops to take refuge in their works, where they were too strong to be attacked. The only thing left for Stirling was to recross the ice and retreat to the Jersey shore, with what prisoners he had picked up. Stirling thus retreated with little damage, except that some of his men were frost-bitten.

But, on the other hand, as has been explained, Washington's weakened army was also safe from British attacks in

[1] To Brigadier General Irvine, January 9, 1780.
[2] Instructions from Washington, January 12, 1780.

force. For the British were committed to their defensive policy in the North. Consequently, it had been decided in advance that the British were merely to hold New York, and to make raids as opportunity offered. Throughout the winter, they did not deviate from this strategy. They raided Paulus Hook and Elizabethtown, and captured some prisoners at each place. There were also raids in Westchester County, which became known as the 'neutral ground' and was the scene of much fighting in the forays of both sides. These unimportant raids, which could not have any influence upon the military result, summed up the operations in the North for the first months of 1780.

In the South there was a very different situation. As has been stated, Lincoln was allowing his whole army to be hemmed in at Charleston. Washington was sending troops to the South to the utmost of his ability, in spite of the feeble strength of his own army. There was nothing more he could do to help Lincoln, but the following showed that he fully realized the danger of Lincoln's conduct of affairs: 'Your anxiety on the score of southern affairs cannot exceed mine. The measure of collecting the whole force for the defence of Charlestown ought no doubt to have been well considered before it was determined. It is putting much to the hazard; But at this distance we can form a very imperfect judgment of its propriety or necessity. I have the greatest reliance on General Lincoln's prudence; but I cannot forbear dreading the event.' [1]

[1] To Baron Steuben, April 2, 1780.

Chapter xxxv

DEFEAT IN THE SOUTH AND THE FRENCH
REINFORCEMENT IN THE NORTH

IN THE South, the worst apprehensions of Washington were realized, as to the plight of Charleston. He had made the right estimate, that the crux of the situation was whether the British could be kept out of the harbor.[1] Undoubtedly Lincoln and his advisers were influenced by the easy repulse of the former ill-conducted attack, under Sir Peter Parker in 1776. And they were overconfident that the British would be unable to force the passage of the bar. But it was a very different matter to cherish hopes of making a successful defense on land against the overwhelming British forces attacking Charleston in 1780. As to the possibilities of defending the bar, 'it soon appeared that these were illusory.'[2] The powerful British fleet found no difficulty in forcing its way into the harbor.

With the defense by sea thus abruptly set at nought, on land the advance of the British had been slow, and they had given Lincoln ample warning of the British superiority. But, instead of taking the sensible viewpoint of Washington,

[1] 'My apprehensions, after all, are principally for the harbor. If this is secured, the operations against you must become critical and arduous.' (To Major General Lincoln, April 15, 1780.)

[2] 'Great expectations were undoubtedly, at one time entertained of the successful defense of the bar, from the advantageous position of the American squadron; but it soon appeared that these were illusory.' (Stedman: *History of the American War.*)

who wrote, 'The impracticability of defending the bar, I fear, amounts to the loss of the town and garrison,' [1] General Lincoln only wasted this time in useless attempts to strengthen the land defenses of Charleston.[2] And he, 'instead of remaining with his army in the open country, shut himself up in Charleston, at the earnest request of the inhabitants, and with the forces under his command, amounting to seven thousand men of all denominations under arms, resolved to defend it to the last extremity.' [3]

This was only putting the American army into a trap, as the British were allowed to invest Lincoln's defenses at their leisure — and then it was all over, for a successful resistance was out of the question. Lincoln's army was surrendered (May 9, 1780). To show how complete was Lincoln's failure, it is enough to realize that 'the losses of the British during the siege did not exceed two hundred and sixty-five killed and wounded.' [4]

This collapse was the most serious defeat of the Americans in the Revolution. For the South, it meant that all the American forces in South Carolina had been eliminated. The triumph of the British seemed to be complete, and Cornwallis was left with a force of five thousand to occupy what was regarded as conquered territory, and to overrun the Southern States. Washington wrote, 'There is much reason to believe the southern States will become the principal theatre of the war.' [5] This remained true of the rest of the Revolution.

[1] To Colonel John Laurens, April 26, 1780.

[2] 'The slow advance of the British army had given time to the provincials not only to strengthen, but greatly to enlarge the defences of Charlestown.' (Stedman: *History of the American War.*)

[3] Stedman: *History of the American War.*

[4] Fortescue: *History of the British Army.*

[5] To Major General Lincoln, April 15, 1780.

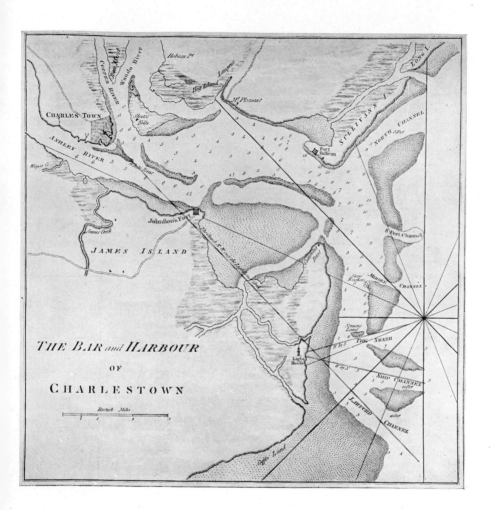

THE BAR and HARBOUR

OF

CHARLESTOWN

British Miles

For the British, it indeed meant a sudden turn for the better, after their series of defeats and disappointments. But their exultation [1] was premature. In the countryside partisan bands were being organized to wage irregular warfare against the British, under the skillful leadership of Marion, Sumpter, Pickens, Williams, and their ilk. The activity of these bands was increased by overconfident political proclamations, given out by Clinton before he returned to New York, which incensed the inhabitants. And all the familiar symptoms of a rising against the British began to be in evidence.

Beside this, Washington was still sending all the troops he could to the South. Washington himself was precluded from going to this new scene of action. Aside from the other needs of the army, which made necessary his presence in the North, the activities, which have been described for the rehabilitation of the army, demanded his personal care. In this regard he wrote explicitly: 'If it were proposed by Congress, I confess to you I should not dislike the journey, did our affairs in this quarter permit it; but unluckily the great departments of the army are now in total confusion; and Congress have just appointed a committee in conjunction with me, to new model and rectify them. Till this is done, I could not leave this army.' [2] But a strong detachment of two thousand Maryland and Delaware troops was on its way to the South at the time of the capture of Charleston.

These troops were under the command of de Kalb, and, as they did not arrive in the Carolinas until June, they were not involved in the disaster at Charleston. They were halted at Hillsborough, in North Carolina, to form the nucleus of a new army. New calls were made upon the militia of the

[1] Horace Walpole: 'We look on America as at our feet.'
[2] To Colonel John Laurens, April 26, 1780.

States south of Pennsylvania. It also became a question of appointing a new commander for the Southern Department. Washington was in favor of Greene, as the ablest general in the army. But Washington was allowed no influence in the matter. There was enough left of the false glamor of Gates' reputation, as the conqueror of Burgoyne, for Congress to make the hasty mistake of appointing Gates to this command (June 13, 1780), without even consulting Washington. This was inexcusable, for Gates' own behavior already made it apparent he had outlived his usefulness in the American army.

The result was inevitable — and probably it was for the best that the disaster was immediate. Gates found the forlorn troops under de Kalb at Hillsborough. This force was utterly destitute of equipment or service of supply. After gathering in all the available militia, Gates' army merely numbered 3052, of which only fourteen hundred were regulars. The rest were raw militia. Yet, a few days after taking command, the shallow Gates assumed a fictitious energy (July 27, 1780) and marched his army against Camden. By so doing he delivered his army into the enemy's hands, as it was an easy prey for the attacks of Cornwallis and his Regulars. The battle of Camden (August 16, 1780) destroyed Gates' army, with a loss of two thousand, killed, wounded, and prisoners. The gallant de Kalb was killed while vainly trying to stem the tide of defeat. But this ignominious and unnecessary defeat also totally destroyed the prestige of Gates. So complete was his fiasco, that he was relegated to obscurity.

It was a costly defeat for the Americans, but it removed an obstacle to success in the South. And it opened the way for Washington to carry out his original intention, to appoint Greene to the command in the South. As will be evident in the ensuing narrative, this wise choice of Greene for this command saved the whole situation. For this reason, what seemed to be the depth of woe for the Americans in the South, was actually the turn of the tide.

It required this object lesson of incapacity to make Congress turn again to Washington, and, as on previous occasions when Congress had blundered, the task of repairing the blunder was put in the hands of Washington. Upon the realization of the full extent of Gates' failure, Congress passed a resolution, which was best described in a letter from Washington to Greene: 'By a letter received yesterday afternoon from his excellency, the President of Congress, of the 6th inst. inclosing the Copy of a Resolution of the preceding day, I find it has been their pleasure to direct me to order a Court of Inquiry to be held on the conduct of Major General Gates, as Commander of the Southern army; and also to direct me to appoint an Officer to command it in his room, until the inquiry is made. As Congress have been pleased to leave the Officer to command on this occasion, to my choice, it is my wish to appoint you; and, from the pressing situation of affairs in that question, of which you are not unapprized, that you should arrive there as soon as circumstances will possibly admit.' [1]

In the mean time important events had occurred in the North. At the very time when Charleston was doomed to capture, Lafayette had returned to America with good news for Washington, who wrote on May 14, 1780: 'The arrival of the Marquis de Lafayette opens a prospect, which offers the most important advantages to these States, if proper measures are adopted to improve it. He announces an intention of his court to send a fleet and army, to coöperate effectually with us.' Upon this, Washington's first thought, warned by past experience with Congress, was to devise a simple

[1] To Major General Greene, October 14, 1780.

means by which he, as Commander in Chief, would be able to coördinate with Congress.

As has been explained, Washington was then hard at work upon the rehabilitation of the army. He wrote in this same letter: 'In the present state of our finances, and in the total emptiness of our magazines, a plan must be concerted to bring out the resources of the country with vigor and decision. This I think you agree with me cannot be effected, if the measures to be taken should depend on the slow deliberations of a body so large as Congress, admitting the best disposition in every member to promote the objects in view. It appears to me of the greatest importance, and even of absolute necessity, that a small committee should be immediately appointed to reside near headquarters, vested with all the powers which Congress have, so far as respects the purpose of a full coöperation with the French fleet and army on the continent. Their authority should be plenipotentiary to draw out men and supplies of every kind, and to give their sanction to any operations which the Commander-in-Chief may not think himself at liberty to undertake without it, as well beyond as within the limits of these States. The committee can act with despatch and energy. By being on the spot it will be able to provide for exigencies as they rise, and the better to judge of their nature and urgency. The plans in contemplation may be opened to them with more freedom and confidence, than to a numerous body, where secresy is impossible, where the indescretion of a single member by disclosing may defeat the project.'

The advantages of this well-conceived measure were so obvious that Congress appointed the committee, as advised by Washington.[1] The reader should study Washington's

[1] This 'Committee of Coöperation' appointed by Congress consisted of Philip Schuyler, John Matthews, Nathaniel Peabody.

description of this measure, as another instance of Washington's skill in writing. It would be hard to find, in so concise a form, a more complete exposition of a project. In fact, Washington's writings, in themselves, are an enduring proof of his ability — and the nonsense that has been set forth, as to his having documents 'written for him,' only shows ignorance of his actual writings.

At the first news of the promise of the French force, Washington's mind at once estimated the possibilities of an immediate attack on New York in these clear terms: 'The reasons for proceeding immediately to New York, in the present situation of the enemy there, are these. Their whole effective land force, in regular troops, is about 8,000 men, to which may be added about 4,000 refugees, and such of the militia as they would be able by persuasion or force to engage; but on the militia they can I should suppose place little reliance. Their naval force is one ship of 74 guns and three or four small frigates. If the arrival of the French succor should find them in this situation, the fleet can enter the harbor of New York without difficulty, and this is a point upon which the success of the whole enterprise absolutely turns.' [1] This was written before any news of the fall of Charleston, and Washington thus expressed the crux of the situation at New York, as he had in regard to that at Charleston. In the absence of Clinton's expedition in the South, there actually was an opportunity for a French fleet to enter New York Harbor.

But the arrival of the French fleet was delayed — and this opportunity passed away. While waiting for the French reinforcement, Washington's first plea to the newly appointed Committee from Congress was: 'The court of France has done so much for us, that we must make a decisive effort on

[1] To the Marquis de Lafayette, May 16, 1780.

our part.' ¹ He again emphasized what had been his contention from the first, 'Unless the principal part of the force can be composed of men regularly organized, and on the continuance of whose service we can rely, nothing decisive can be attempted.' ² In this appeal he advocated 'the extension of the Draught.' ³ All through this time, the correspondence of Washington showed the difficulties of keeping the machinery of the army moving at all. Washington made the expectation of the arrival of the French a new occasion for an appeal to the States: 'I am sincere in declaring a full persuasion, that this succor will be fatal to us, if our measures are not adequate to the emergency.' ⁴

All through this period of expecting the arrival of the French expedition, this was a spur which Washington plied with energy. The newly appointed Committee of Congress was a great help, and the call upon the States was producing results. Washington's hope was to gather a force that would be adequate for an attack upon New York. Washington was under no delusion on this point: 'In Europe to besiege Troops in fortified places, the proportion of men necessary is computed at six to one in favor of the besiegers. We cannot ask less than two to one against New York — allowing us the command of the water which will be a material advantage.'⁵ Upon this last element 'the command of the water' depended the issue of undertaking the attack against New York.

But, when the French expedition actually arrived at Newport (July 10, 1780), there was a great disappointment, as the French naval force was totally inadequate to establish

---

¹ To Committee from Congress, May 25, 1780.
² To a Committee of Congress, May 25, 1780.   ³ *Ibid.*
⁴ To President Reed, May 28, 1780.
⁵ To the Honorable Committee of Coöperation, May 31, 1780.

this necessary 'command of the water.' In this regard, Washington wrote: 'This makes them rather inferior to the combined naval forces of Arbuthnot and Graves; but, as a second division of ships and Land Forces (a circumstance you will keep to yourself) may be expected in a few weeks, it is probable we shall gain a superiority at sea by the time we can be ready to operate, as Count Rochambeau is of the opinion that his land forces will not be sufficiently recruited under four weeks from the 12th instant.' [1] This was putting the best face upon the matter. But, in reality, all hopes were ended of carrying out the attempt against New York. For, instead of receiving accessions to the French naval force, the French were soon blockaded in Newport by a superior British naval force. The expected reinforcement for the French never arrived, as it was also blockaded in Brest by superior British naval forces.

This situation imposed inactivity upon the French expedition. Of course, without the expected superior French naval force, the enterprise against New York was out of the question. This time, a definite arrangement had been made in France, that Rochambeau and his army would be under the command of Washington — and the French forces were at his call. But, on the one hand, Rochambeau was unwilling to leave the inferior French naval force, under Admiral Ternay, unsupported at Newport, and also their weakness on the sea prevented the French troops from being available for Washington to use in an attack upon New York. The disappointment was great, but there was nothing that could be done without a strong naval force, consequently, the army of Rochambeau remained idle at Newport.

[1] To Major General Greene, July 19, 1780.

Chapter XXXVI

ARNOLD'S TREASON
THE TURN OF THE TIDE IN THE SOUTH

IN THIS interval of enforced inactivity in the North, Washington had left West Point (September 18, 1780), with Lafayette and Hamilton, for a conference at Hartford with Count Rochambeau and Admiral Ternay. On Washington's return to West Point (September 25, 1780) he met the news of the treason of Benedict Arnold. There is no need to go into details as to this wretched story. The facts are too well known. But it is necessary to brush aside all the romantics that have been written of Arnold as a fallen Lucifer. There was nothing of that glamor in the story of Arnold. He was for sale, and he was bought and paid for. That summed up his case.

Arnold, on the field of battle, was a brilliant and inspired soldier. He had a flashy personal attractiveness, which won his wife, the Tory belle of Philadelphia who was the one tragic figure in the drama. But, beyond this, Arnold was only a despicable character. He was devoid of principle or honor, and in money matters grasping and dishonest. This sordid character of Arnold was known in the army. One of the American officers, on duty at West Point at the time, has left the following record. His suspicions of Arnold had been aroused by 'seeing the cannon disconnected making new carriages and the men sent out to cut wood and timber so

that we had scarce enough to man the guard, and recollect-
ing what my father told me when Arnold was appointed
Col. to go to Quebec, he said he was sorry to hear it. I asked
him why and he said that he was so avaricious that he would
sell his country for money enough. Arnold had been in the
commissary department in the French war and my father
belonging to the General Court was concerned in the settlement of his accounts.' [1]

Arnold had been long in correspondence with the British,
before the military court had censured him for his conduct
in Philadelphia. This court had directed Washington
(January 26, 1780) to write a reprimand to Arnold, which
Washington did, in the mildest terms possible. And there
was no doubt left of the fact that Arnold would be given
honorable command in the American Army. In March,
Arnold advocated a project for an expedition with shipping,
but there were no ships available. In July, Arnold sought
from Washington the command of West Point — with the
deliberate intention of betraying this key to the Hudson
into the hands of the enemy.

Washington had great confidence in Arnold's ability, and
had intended to give him a command in the field. In the
disposition of the army, published in the general orders of
August 1, 1780, Arnold was assigned to the command of the
left wing of the army. This fact, that he had been nominated for this important duty, should be enough to dispose
of the theatrical figure of a man embittered by injustice and
driven into a frenzy. On the contrary, Arnold was already
a scheming traitor, and he urged his wound as an excuse for
his request to command West Point, instead of being as-

---

[1] Narrative of Captain Benjamin Gould, of Topsfield, Massachusetts. Manu-
script in possession of George A. Hopkins, of Boston. Captain Gould was 'ordered with a number of other officers to guard André.'

signed to active duty in the field. In compliance, Washington changed Arnold's assignment, and gave him the command of West Point.[1]

The foregoing has described the facts — and all the tawdry tinsel can be discarded. Arnold was a bribed traitor, intent only on obtaining the price of his treachery. Then he found his nemesis. For, although Arnold was undoubtedly a skillful soldier, he proved to be a most unskillful and clumsy plotter. Arnold had the whole situation in his hands. As commander of West Point, he was able to make treacherous dispositions of his troops, and to weaken the defenses of the place. These things he had done, until, in the words of the homely narrative which has been quoted, the defenses were stripped, 'so that we had scarce enough to man the guard.' The British expedition had been prepared, with strong naval forces to go up the river, and the traitor had removed a link from the great chain that obstructed the passage of the river, under pretense of repairs, so that it was only held by a rope and could be broken at any time.

Yet, with everything ready for the success of this foul plot, the plotters chose to put on the stage the old melodrama of the 'spy and the papers' — and this was their undoing. On the part of the British, their emissary was actually the Adjutant General of Clinton's army, Major André. And he with Arnold went through all the conventional forms of meeting by stealth in a secluded house, and stuffing the unnecessary 'papers' into André's boots, where they were promptly found by the American patrols — and the whole plot was foiled.

As to the unfortunate Major André, there was much sympathy for him in America. He was an officer of engaging personality, and it seemed a hard fate that he should

[1] Letter of instructions, August 3, 1780.

Head Quarters Robinsons
House Sepr 22d 1780

Permit Mr John Anderson to pass the
Guards to the White Plains. or below
if He Chuses. He being on Public
Business by my Direction

B. Arnold M Genl

MAJOR ANDRÉ'S PASS

meet death, when the guilty Arnold escaped. But it is now universally admitted that there could have been no other verdict. By deliberately going to Arnold, to arrange the details for the traitor to betray the fortress, André put himself outside military law. When he was captured, in disguise and with the traitor's papers concealed in his boots, André's standing was only that of a self-convicted spy. Any remission, by Washington, of André's well-deserved sentence was out of the question.

For Washington, the revelation of Arnold's treason was a great shock. It is enough to quote Washington's letter, written when he first heard this heart-rending news: 'I arrived here yesterday, on my return from an interview with the French general and admiral, and have been wit-

321

ness to a scene of treason, as shocking as it was unsuspected. General Arnold, from every circumstance, had entered into a plot for sacrificing West Point. He had an interview with Major André, the British adjutant-general, last week at Joshua H. Smith's, when the plan was concerted. By an extraordinary concurrence of incidents André was taken on his return, with several papers in Arnold's handwriting, that proved the treason. The latter unluckily got notice of it before I did, went immediately down the river, got on board the *Vulture*, which brought up André, and proceeded to New York. I found the post in the most critical condition, and have been taking measures to give it security, which I hope will be to-night effectual.' [1]

In the matter of the defense of West Point, the thoroughly aroused Washington acted promptly, and with great efficiency, to correct the treacherous dispositions of the American troops, which Arnold had devised to make the place an easy prey for a British attack. The result was, West Point was soon in a state to make a strong defense, and the British expedition never dared to undertake an attack. Thus fortunately was the peril averted. Washington wrote: 'That overruling Providence, which has so often and so remarkably interposed in our favor, never manifested itself more conspicuously, than in the timely discovery of his horrid intentions to surrender the Post and Garrison of West Point into the hands of the Enemy.' [2]

And Washington showed that he rightly estimated the sordid character of Arnold. Laurens had written that Arnold must be suffering the 'torment of a mental Hell.' But, in reply ,Washington wrote: 'André has met his fate, and with that fortitude, which was to be expected from an

[1] To Governor Clinton, September 26, 1780.
[2] To President Reed, October 18, 1780.

accomplished man and gallant officer; but I am mistaken if at this time "Arnold is undergoing the torment of a mental Hell." He wants feeling. From some traits of his character, which have lately come to my knowledge, he seems to have been so hackneyed in villany, and so lost to all sense of honor and shame, that, while his faculties will enable him to continue his sordid pursuits, there will be no time for remorse.' [1] This was relegating Arnold to his proper level of infamy.

At this time, Washington was occupied in plans for calling out troops to meet the new situation. As to the South, he wrote: 'Should a further extension of their Conquest in that quarter be their object, I am in hopes that the force, collected by the exertions of North Carolina, Virginia, and Maryland, will keep them confined to the limits of South Carolina, at least till a better disposition of our Affairs can be made, or until we may receive more effectual assistance from our Allies; a measure which they have most seriously in view, and of which an unlucky coincidence of circumstances has hitherto deprived us. The French Fleet has been blocked up in the harbor of Newport almost ever since its arrival there by a superior British squadron; which superiority has been lately increased by the arrival of Admiral Rodney from the West Indies with ten ships.' [2]

Affairs in the South constituted the most pressing problem for the Americans at this time. Yet, even after the incompetent Gates had sacrificed at Camden the only American force that could be considered in any sense an army, the overconfident Cornwallis was faced by the dilemma, so incomprehensible to the British, that a defeat in the field did not mean the end of the resistance of the American country-

[1] To Lieutenant Colonel John Laurens, October 13, 1780.
[2] To Major General Gates, October 8, 1780.

side. It was true that Gates' army was a thing of the past. From the European point of view, armed resistance had been put down — and to the European mind, this meant the end of the matter. But, on the contrary, the very presence of the enemy was inspiring the Americans to new resistance, and the whole countryside was rising against the invader. This was the always recurrent factor in the American Revolution — but the British leaders were never able to cope with it. This cannot be stated too often.

To the mind of Cornwallis, his was to be the easy task of occupying conquered territory. As the British contemporary historian stated, 'the provincial force to the southward seemed for the time being entirely annihilated; and nothing prevented earl Cornwallis from proceeding immediately on his long-projected expedition into North Carolina, but the want of some supplies for the army.' [1] These were soon obtained and (September 8, 1780) Cornwallis began his march to subdue North Carolina. Moving wide of his main army were the commands of Ferguson and Tarleton, Cornwallis' best partisan leaders. It is interesting to continue the British account: 'The previous measures appeared well adapted to the end. And the reduction of the province of North Carolina was undoubtedly at this time confidently looked for. But to confound human wisdom, and set at nought the arrogance and presumption of man, unexpected incidents daily arise in the affairs of human life, which, conducted by an invisible hand derange the best-concerted schemes, as will be exemplified in the event of the present expedition.' [2]

This rhapsody, in the best style of the day, expressed the British surprise at 'unexpected incidents,' which were

[1] Stedman: *History of the American War.*   [2] *Ibid.*

merely repetitions in 1780 of what began on April 19, 1775 — and had been going on ever since! The passage, in itself, was a complete sermon on the inability of the British to conquer America. The sequel, in the British account, left no doubt in this respect: 'But whilst he (Cornwallis) was taking measure for this purpose, the unwelcome news arrived of the defeat of major Ferguson; the fall of that officer, and the destruction, captivity, or dispersion of his whole corps. The total loss of so considerable a detachment, from the operations of which so much was expected, put a stop, for the present, to the farther progress of the commander-in-chief, and obliged him to fall back into South Carolina, for the protection of its western borders against the incursions of a horde of mountaineers, whose appearance was as unexpected as their success was fatal to the prosecution of the intended expedition.' [1]

The defeat of Ferguson was nothing but a repetition of the same story, of which Lexington and Saratoga were the outstanding chapters. Ferguson with a strong detachment of twelve hundred was in a region where he did not conceive it possible a force could be raised that would put him in danger. He had turned aside to attempt to intercept a small body of American partisans, but he suddenly found that enemies were springing up all about him. He started to retreat to Cornwallis (September 30), but was hemmed in by the Americans, and took position on King's Mountain, which he said was 'a place from which all the rebels outside of hell cannot drive us.' But the Americans stormed this position. Ferguson was killed, and, after losing 389, the rest of his force surrendered.

This was the Battle of King's Mountain (October 7, 1780). And it was another event of the American Revolu-

[1] Stedman: *History of the American War.*

tion that was of a decisive importance, far greater than was indicated by the numbers involved. As described in the British account, the result at once ended all ideas of Cornwallis that he was a conqueror overrunning the country at his will. Instead, he saw nothing to do but to retreat to South Carolina, 'for the protection of its western borders against the incursions of a horde of mountaineers.' [1] There could not have been a more complete overturn of a military situation.

On the part of the Americans, the moral effect was equally great. It gave new life to the rising in South Carolina also, and the bands of Marion, Sumter, and the other partisan leaders, increased in numbers and in activity. When Cornwallis retreated into South Carolina, the remnants of the American army, which had been collected after the defeat at Camden, advanced to Charlotte. When Greene arrived to take command (December 2, 1780) these had increased to twenty-three hundred, about half of which were militia. It was a forlorn force, ill-equipped and ill-found in every way, but in the hands of Greene it was destined to accomplish great things.

Greene's conception of his task was nothing less than inspired. Instead of ignoring the partisan bands, as Gates had done, he made them important in his strategy. Greene's scheme of strategy must be stated in advance, in order to understand the change at the new year of 1781. He constituted his army the nucleus for rallying all these American forces, for the irregular harassing warfare, which was always most effective against the British of that formal school. He made the country what Cornwallis called a 'hornets' nest.' At times Greene's army was united. At other times it was divided into partisan bands. But it was always attacking

[1] Stedman: *History of the American War.*

and harassing the Regulars. Yet Greene's most daring moves were always controlled by the resolve never to put his army in a position where it might be sacrificed in a set battle. This was what underlay all Greene's wonderful conduct of the ensuing campaign, which was on the point of beginning at the first of 1781.

For this campaign, in addition to the skillful coöperation of the local leaders, Washington was sending to him Morgan the ablest partisan leader of them all, the engineer Koskiusco, and 'Light Horse Harry' Lee with his legion. Steuben had also been sent to command in Virginia, to defend the State against a raid by Arnold, and to maintain Greene's communication with the North. Greene had thus the advantage of being able to rely upon some of the best American officers, but the credit for the conception and execution of the ensuing campaign must be given to Greene's own ability. Washington was in complete accord with Greene's scheme of campaign.[1]

In the North, as the inferiority of the French naval forces continued, it was impossible to undertake the much-desired attack on New York. With Washington making every effort to send reinforcements to the South, the army went into winter quarters at the end of November. At this time Washington supplemented his pleas for a permanent force, which have been described. He wrote: 'But I will take the liberty in this place to give it as my opinion, that a foreign loan is indispensably necessary to the continuance of the war. Congress will deceive themselves, if they imagine that the army, or a state that is a theatre of war, can rub through a second campaign as the last. It would be as unreasonable as to suppose that, because a man had rolled a snow-ball

[1] 'I entirely approve of your Plan for forming a flying army.' (Washington to Major General Greene, November 8, 1780.)

till it had acquired the size of a horse, that he might do so till it was the size of a house.' [1]

On November 28 Washington reported to the President of Congress from Morristown: 'I arrived at this place to-day, having yesterday broke up the camp near the Passaic Falls, and detailed the Troops to their different places of Cantonment. I shall repair to New Windsor, where I propose to establish my Winter-Quarters, after having made some necessary regulations here and visited the Hospitals.'

At this time came the plea of Lafayette for a command in the Southern theater of the war. Washington rightly made this the test of 'European and Southern advices, wch. ought & alone can determine you with propriety —— These you are more in the way of receiving than I am.' Washington wrote to Lafayette that, 'if there is a prospect of naval superiority in these seas,' he advised Lafayette not to go to the South. But he added: 'On the other hand, if we are likely to remain in a state of inactivity in this quarter, your seeking service to the Southward, where there is a more fruitful field for enterprise, is not only an evidence of your zeal, but will be supported by every rule of military reasoning.' [2] For the time being, Lafayette abandoned his idea of going to the South. He wrote to Washington of 'intelligence of ships and troops having been put in readiness at Brest.' These hopes were to prove illusive.

This situation left Washington in winter quarters, struggling with the problems of the upkeep of his army. But, on the part of the British, Clinton's main army in the North had become a force 'always apprehensive' and confined to New York. The detachment under General Leslie (three thousand) which Clinton had sent to Virginia (October, 1780)

[1] To John Sullivan in Congress, November 20, 1780.
[2] To the Marquis de Lafayette, December 8, 1780.

had been diverted to reinforce Cornwallis in South Carolina. To replace this, Clinton sent (December, 1780) a force of sixteen hundred under the traitor Arnold, constituted a Brigadier General in the British Army, to operate against Virginia.

This situation, at the end of 1780, was gloomily summed up, as follows, by a British historian: 'Such, therefore, was the position in America at the close of 1780. Cornwallis had been forced back to Winnsborough in South Carolina, with his communications everywhere threatened, and with his whole plan of invasion wrecked by the defeat of Ferguson; while Clinton, always apprehensive as to the movements of Washington and of the French at Rhode Island, was weakening his force by constant detachments to the south, for inland operations which at heart he disapproved. So far superiority at sea had enabled him to carry on the war on these terms; but how long that superiority might endure was another question.' [1]

[1] Fortescue: *History of the British Army*.

General Wayne, with two officers,[1] had shown great courage and good judgment in going to the mutineers, to attempt to bring them back to their service. The men insisted on marching off to seek redress from Congress, but protested that they were ready to be led against the enemy at any time. And, when Clinton sent two emissaries to them, to tempt them with offers of high pay to join the enemy, they declared they were 'not Benedict Arnolds,' and delivered the wretched spies to Wayne, to be hanged as they deserved. It was so unmistakably evident that the men did not mean any treason, that President Reed of Pennsylvania met them near Princeton, and an agreement was made which gave them justice in the matters of enlistments and pay. This ended the mutiny (January 7, 1781) — and it also ended what seemed a very great danger for the Army. There was another minor outbreak among the New Jersey troops, which was easily put down (January 20, 1781). But the 'revolt,' which 'for a time had spread alarm among the friends of American liberty, and excited the highest hopes of its foes,'[2] was of no help to the enemy. On the contrary, it gave proof that discontent did not mean the American soldiers would go over to the enemy.[3]

In spite of this first ill augury of the new year, Washington was steadfast in his resolution to adhere to his own scheme of strategy, and to think of the military situation only in terms of preparing for a crushing attack upon the British, whenever the means might be available. Washington's

[1] 'Colonels Butler and Stewart, two officers popular with the troops.' (Irving: *Life of Washington.*)

[2] Irving: *Life of Washington.*

[3] 'It is somewhat extraordinary, that these men, however lost to a sense of duty had so far retained that of honor, as to reject the most advantageous propositions from the enemy.' (Washington to Count de Rochambeau, January 20, 1781.)

letters were convincing evidence of this. But always he clearly saw that 'a Naval Superiority through the next Campaign' [1] was the absolutely necessary factor. In January, Laurens was about to leave for France on an important mission to the French Government, carrying urgent letters from Rochambeau and Lafayette, in order to arouse the French Ministry to the wise course of sending aid to the Americans in 1781, and to urge the importance of strong French naval forces in America.

France was faring none too well in the European war, and the arguments of Lafayette and Rochambeau, with a statement from Washington, convinced the French Government that sending money to America would do a great deal of harm to the enemy at comparatively small cost. Franklin had already been promised a grant of six million livres and a loan of four million. In addition, 'Necker consented to a loan of ten millions more, to be raised in Holland in the name of the King of France.' [2] In this way the pressing financial needs of the Americans were alleviated.

But, as to the vital matter of 'superior naval forces,' Washington's clear vision was expressed in a paragraph of his statement, given to Laurens, before leaving for France: 'That next to a loan of money, a constant naval superiority on these coasts is the object most interesting. This would instantly reduce the enemy to a difficult defensive, and, by removing all prospect of extending their acquisitions, would take away the motives for prosecuting the war. Indeed, it is not to be conceived how they could subsist a large force in this country, if we had the command of the seas, to interrupt the regular transmission of supplies from Europe. This

[1] Private Instructions to Brigadier General Knox, February 16, 1781.
[2] Bancroft: *History of the United States.*

superiority, (with an aid in money,) would enable us to convert the war into a vigorous offensive.' [1]

This was another example of Washington's skill in writing. His insistence on this point was the foundation of the success of the campaign of 1781. And Washington also showed his wisdom by ending all ideas of having the French naval assistance encumbered by bringing the second reinforcement of French troops for Rochambeau. This was a disappointment for Rochambeau, who was anxious for more troops. But Washington was right in seeing that there would be sufficient troops to attack the British, if only the French naval force could be assured.

This decision of Washington, to abandon the plan of additional French troops, made the question of the French naval forces much simpler. And, with this complication out of the way, the American representatives won their point. It was agreed that Admiral de Grasse was to receive orders to sail from the West Indies to the American coast, to be at the disposition of Washington and Rochambeau. Of course, at the beginning of 1781, this was still far off beyond the horizon. But the mere recital of this course of events is enough to show Washington's foresight, and his intuitive grasp of the one possible solution of the problem.

It is no exaggeration to state, that, at the forlorn beginning of 1781, Washington's scheme for a decisive attack on the British seemed an impossible dream. There were no means in sight to make it a reality. However, to the mind of Washington, it was a vital reality — and the event was to justify his faith. But it was astonishing to read Washington's 'private instructions' to Knox, his Chief of Artillery and trusted confidant. These bear the date of February 16, 1781 — long before Laurens had even arrived in France with his

[1] To Lieutenant Colonel John Laurens, January 15, 1781.

missives for the French Government. Yet Washington confidently announced to Knox his scheme, with 'a naval superiority through the next Campaign,' [1] for 'a capital operation against New York, or against Charleston, Savannah, Penobscot &c., in case of inability to undertake the siege of the first and principal object.' [2]

And Washington instructed Knox, to 'take your measures accordingly by making such estimates and demands, and other arrangements as may appear to you best calculated to produce what we want.' [3] Naturally, even to the astute Knox, these instructions, given at the time when the American Army was at a low ebb, seemed to ask him to wave a Prospero's wand. Knox wrote to Washington, telling him of the nakedness of the land, but promising to do the best he could. But Washington had gazed far into the crystal, and, from this time on, he and his chosen officers were intent on plans for this offensive against the British, even though there seemed to be no means in sight for its execution.

In the South, at the first of 1781, there was soon no doubt of the fact that Washington's appointment of Greene to the command had changed the whole situation. And here it should be noted, that Congress, after the object lesson of the blunder in giving Gates an independent command in the South, had made Greene 'subject to the control of the commander-in-chief.' [4] Greene would have been a loyal subordinate to Washington in any case, from his own attachment to his chief. But it was a good thing to have Congress make the acknowledgment, that at last the American Army was coördinated under its Commander in Chief. There was

---

[1] To Brigadier General Knox, Private Instructions, February 16, 1781.
[2] Drake: *Life and Correspondence of Henry Knox.*
[3] To Brigadier General Knox, Private Instructions, February 16, 1781.
[4] Journals of Congress.

no longer any fear of dissensions. The ensuing campaign was to be Washington's own.

With the approval of Washington, as has been quoted, Greene did not delay in making his force a 'flying army.' He boldly divided his army into two partisan bands. The larger (1100) Greene commanded in person, and kept it on the Pedee River to coöperate with Marion. The other force (900) was given to Morgan, to operate to the westward and to keep active the mountain militia who had won King's Mountain. These dispositions were at once effective, and Cornwallis suddenly found that his 'hornets' nest' was disgorging swarms that stung him on all sides. Bewildered and harassed, Cornwallis was at a loss. In desperation, he detached Tarleton, with a force of eleven hundred, to attack Morgan. But Morgan led Tarleton into the Battle of Cowpens (January 17, 1781) and destroyed the British force, with almost no loss to himself.[1] It was in this action that Colonel William Washington so distinguished himself, in command of the cavalry.

Morgan's remarkable victory at Cowpens was another event in the Revolution that won results, 'unexpected by Lord Cornwallis,'[2] and of far reaching importance. The contemporary British historian wrote: 'The defeat of his majesty's Troops at the Cowpens formed a very considerable link in the chain of circumstances which led to the independence of America.'[3] For Cornwallis, it was the beginning of the end, as, from this time, he was all abroad, and drawn hither and thither by Greene's bewildering tactics. After Cowpens, Cornwallis allowed himself to be

[1] The American losses were 12 killed, 61 wounded. The British losses in killed, wounded, and prisoners, were 830.

[2] Stedman, *History of the American War.*

[3] *Ibid.*

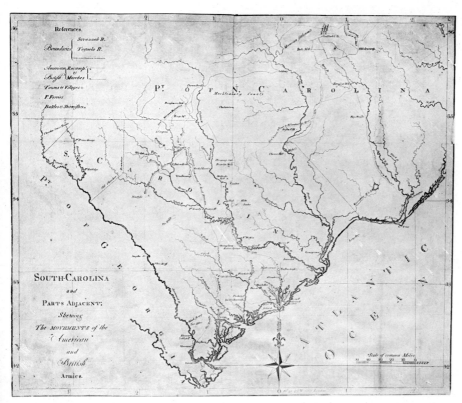

OPERATIONS IN THE SOUTH

led into a fruitless pursuit of the Americans far into the northern part of North Carolina.

The expedition of Leslie, sent to the South from New York, had been absorbed into Cornwallis' army, but Arnold's force, also sent from New York (December, 1780), was raiding Virginia. Steuben, who was in command in Virginia, rallied the militia in sufficient numbers to compel Arnold to fortify himself at Portsmouth, opposite Norfolk. After this situation had developed, Washington appointed Lafayette to a command 'to act against the corps of the enemy now in Virginia, in conjunction with the militia, and some ships from the fleet of the Chevalier Destouches, which he informed me sailed on the 9th instant from Newport.' [1] This hope of French naval forces in the Chesapeake was not realized, as the French detachment from Newport was obliged to return, after an action with the superior forces of Admiral Arbuthnot, which entered the Chesapeake.

But sending the American force under Lafayette to Virginia was of real value, as it arrived in season to balance the British reinforcement under General Phillips (2000) sent from New York. At this time Washington wrote to Laurens, citing the failure of Destouches, to enforce his contention for a superior French naval force: 'The observations contained in my letter to you of the 15th of January last are verified every moment; and, if France delays a timely and powerful aid in this critical posture of our affairs, it will avail us nothing, should she attempt it hereafter.' [2]

[1] To the Marquis de Lafayette, Instructions, February 20, 1781.
[2] To Colonel John Laurens at Paris, April 9, 1781.

Chapter xxxviii

THE DEVELOPMENT OF THE SITUATION OF 1781

WITH Washington intent on his scheme for attacking the British, whenever the French naval force should be available, Greene's brilliant campaign against Cornwallis was winning extraordinary results in the South. And these were destined to change Washington's objective from New York to the Southern field. In February, Greene had led Cornwallis a chase to the borders of Virginia, where the British general gave up his pursuit, after Greene had crossed the Dan River. From there, Cornwallis withdrew to Hillsborough, but Greene promptly proved that he had not abandoned North Carolina, by recrossing the Dan and renewing his harassing tactics against Cornwallis.

After days of elusive maneuvering, Greene offered battle to Cornwallis (Battle of Guilford Courthouse, March 15, 1781). After a stubborn contest, the Americans were forced to retreat from the field. But this was of small moment to the Americans, in contrast to the effect of the battle upon the British.[1] Cornwallis' army was so weakened, that he actually was compelled to retreat to the sea.[2] He thus abandoned his whole campaign, and Greene's efforts had ac-

[1] 'Phillips truly described the engagement as the sort of victory that ruins an army.' (Fortescue: *History of the British Army*.)

[2] 'Leaving his sick and wounded to the care of the inhabitants, with many assurances that he would speedily return to them.' (Fortescue: *History of the British Army*.)

338

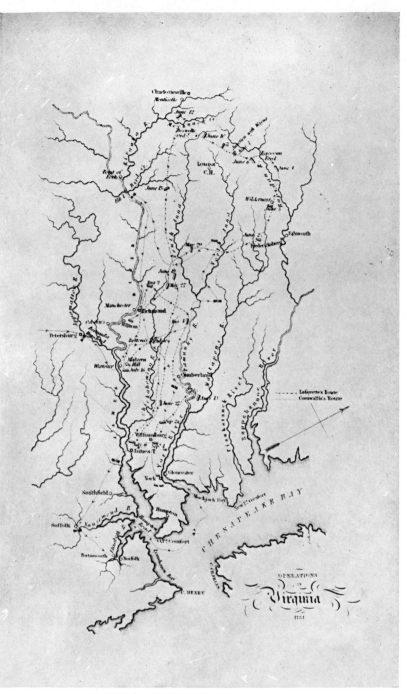

SCENE OF OPERATIONS IN VIRGINIA

complished a complete and surprising success. Cornwallis drew off his army to Wilmington, the nearest point on the coast where he could rely on the support of the British shipping (April 7, 1781).[1]

This unexpected overturn of the situation, which brought disappointment to all Cornwallis' confident expectations of an easy conquest, totally discouraged the British commander. Instead of an assured occupation of the country, he had only met a revolt of the countryside against him.[2] And Greene's skillful control had given to this uprising the two elements which made it formidable. Greene not only constituted the partisan bands a factor in his army organization, but he provided a leadership that made use of all these forces in a constant harassing offensive against the British. The 'hornets' were always stinging the British — yet the wily Greene never gave the British the opportunity to destroy the swarm, in contrast to the unfortunate mistakes of Lincoln and Gates.

Greene's masterly conduct of this campaign in the Carolinas, against Cornwallis, had been a convincing experience for the British general. It had made Cornwallis despair of winning results in these States — and he suddenly made the unexpected decision to undertake a campaign in Virginia. Accordingly, he moved his army from Wilmington (April 25, 1781), and effected a junction with the British forces of Phillips and Arnold at Petersburg (May 20, 1781). These troops had been raiding the Virginia country. Before Cornwallis arrived, Phillips had died, and Arnold was left in command. Their joint forces gave Cornwallis over five thousand.

[1] 'Under such circumstances, although a victory had been gained, a retreat became necessary toward that quarter from which supplies could be obtained.' (Stedman: *History of the American War.*)

[2] 'Lord Cornwallis was greatly disappointed in his expectations of being joined by the loyalists.' (Stedman: *History of the American War.*)

339

Undoubtedly Cornwallis hoped to redeem his discomfiture in the Carolinas by a brilliant success in Virginia. There is also no question of the fact that Cornwallis made this fatal decision on his own authority. Cornwallis was high in the favor of Germaine, and he wrote to Clinton, the British Commander in Chief: 'I cannot help expressing my wishes that the Chesapeake may become the seat of war, even, if necessary, at the expense of abandoning New York.' [1] And without waiting to hear from Clinton, Cornwallis moved into Virginia. This was afterwards, in England, a matter of bitter controversy between Clinton and Cornwallis. Clinton proved that he opposed this project.[2] But it was also shown that the British Ministers approved Cornwallis' move into Virginia. Germaine wrote, 'Lord Cornwallis' opinion entirely coincides with mine of the great importance of pushing the war on the side of Virginia with all the force that can be spared.' [3] The responsibility was thus fixed.

In the mean time, the resourceful Greene had appreciated the opportunity offered by the withdrawal of Cornwallis, and he had led his army into a raid of South Carolina. Greene had followed the retreat of Cornwallis, until he realized that the British general was to establish himself on the coast. Greene at once understood what this meant — that Cornwallis could be ignored as an active force for the time being. Greene's sudden move into South Carolina won as complete and unexpected a success as his campaign against Cornwallis. His arrival in April had the immediate moral effect of proving that the British were not overrun-

---

[1] Cornwallis to Clinton, April 10, 1781.

[2] 'Had you intimated the probability of your intention, I should certainly have endeavored to have stopped you.' (Clinton to Cornwallis, May 29, 1781.)

[3] Germaine to Clinton, June 6, 1781.

ning the country.[1] And Lord Rawdon, who had been left in command of the British forces in the Carolinas, soon was being subjected to the same harassing tactics that had ended the hopes of Cornwallis. Greene had pushed for Camden, and he had also detached Lee to coöperate with Marion against Fort Watson, which was an important link in Rawdon's chain of communications. The American partisans captured this fort (April 23, 1781) by the novel device of erecting a huge tower of lumber, which dominated the place and forced its surrender.

At this time Greene fought Lord Rawdon at Hobkirk's Hill (April 25, 1781). This was another defeat on the field, like Guilford Courthouse, but it produced the same result — the abandonment of the whole area by the enemy! Rawdon found himself so beset that he retreated toward Charleston. Greene's partisan bands quickly overran the country. Camden was taken, and the other British posts were soon captured. The climax was the taking of Augusta (June 10, 1781), which meant the loss of Georgia. Of all the inland posts of the British, only Ninety-Six was left in their hands. Rawdon made an obstinate attempt to hold his place, but he was forced to evacuate it (June 29, 1781), and Greene had thus won the whole interior country of the Southern States. It was another case of the extraordinary results obtained in the American Revolution, without dramatic battlefields of victory, but with gains obtained that were more decisive than often happened in formal European campaigns of set battles.

This had been the object lesson of Washington's campaigns, as has been explained in this text. And Greene showed that he had become an apt disciple of the Washington doctrine, of winning results against the British under

[1] 'People began to look for victory.' (Fiske: *The American Revolution.*)

conditions so disadvantageous that they were prohibitive of victories on the battlefield. Washington had won his case in the North, and Greene accomplished the same end in the South.

All through the spring, there is no question of the fact that Washington was intent on New York, for his projected attack. The trend of events in the South had not yet developed to the extent of changing his purpose. On May 22, 1781, Washington had an important interview with Rochambeau at Weatherfield, and it was agreed that the French army should march to the North River to join Washington's army for a combined operation. This operation was to depend upon the presence of the French fleet, under de Grasse, from the West Indies.

The essentials of Washington's plans were: 'To form a junction of the French and American armies upon the North River as soon as possible, and move down to the vicinity of New York, to be ready to take advantage of any opportunity, which the weakness of the enemy may afford. Should the West Indies Fleet arrive upon the Coast, the force thus combined may either proceed in the operation against New York, or may be directed against the enemy in some other quarter, as circumstances shall dictate.'[1] But, at this time, Washington still adhered to 'the preference, which an operation against New York seems to have in the present circumstances over an attempt to send a force to the southward.'[2] Rhode Island was to be protected by militia — to guard against raids upon the French squadron and Rochambeau's heavy impedimenta, which had been left at Providence.

Two days after the adoption of this project, Washington

[1] 'Substance of Conference at Weatherfield,' May 22, 1781.
[2] *Ibid.*

sent a Circular Letter to the States, stating: 'The accomplishment of the object, which we have in contemplation, is of the utmost importance to America....The operation in view will require, in addition to the French army, all the Continental battalions from New Hampshire to New Jersey inclusive to be completed to their full establishment. ... I should hope that by proper exertions in collecting and sending forward the men that have been already raised, and compelling by vigorous and decisive methods the delinquent towns to furnish their quotas, the greater part of the men may be collected by the 1st of July.' Washington also urged the States to raise forces of local militia, for use while this main army would be occupied in its offensive against the British.

Rochambeau did not delay in carrying out his part of the agreement, and the French army joined Washington on the Hudson in July. Then ensued a tense period of waiting for news of the destination of the French fleet from the West Indies, upon which depended the execution of Washington's plan of attack.

In the mean time, Cornwallis' campaign in Virginia failed to fulfill any of the high hopes of the British general. Upon his first arrival in Virginia in May, Cornwallis' army of five thousand veterans was opposed only by Lafayette's force, which was at Richmond. Lafayette had been sent to Virginia to check the depredations of Arnold,[1] and he had but three thousand troops, two thirds of which were raw militia. To the mind of Cornwallis, Lafayette seemed no obstacle to success, and the British general stated, 'The boy cannot escape me.'

In this conviction, Cornwallis moved at once against Lafayette, in full confidence that he would destroy this

[1] Arnold did not remain with Cornwallis, as he was recalled to New York.

343

inferior American force. But Lafayette also proved that he was a pupil of Washington, and he showed real ability in retreating before Cornwallis. Without giving the British general any opportunity to do serious damage to his force, Lafayette led Cornwallis through the difficult country, until the Americans safely crossed the Rapidan on June 4. Cornwallis, thereupon, gave up the pursuit as hopeless. He launched a raid under Tarleton. This failed in its object to capture the members of the Virginia Assembly and Governor Thomas Jefferson. Some stores were destroyed, but Tarleton was compelled to rejoin Cornwallis by a new advance of Lafayette, who had been reinforced (June 10) by Wayne with one thousand of the Pennsylvania line.

Cornwallis then found himself in the same predicament as in the Carolinas. All his expectations of assistance from the Loyalists had proved vain. Although Lafayette was still too weak to join battle, yet he was harassing Cornwallis. Consequently the British general again was being beset in a hostile country, where his movements were accomplishing nothing. Again Cornwallis gave up the problem and withdrew to his sea communications. He moved his army to Williamsburg, while Lafayette 'hung continually on Cornwallis's flanks and rear during the march.' [1]

At Williamsburg (June 26) 'Cornwallis's wanderings were abruptly ended by the receipt of new orders from Clinton. Enclosing an intercepted letter from Washington to Lafayette, the Commander in Chief directed Cornwallis to establish a defensive post at Williamsburg or Yorktown, and to send back to New York every man he could spare as soon as the operations in train should have been completed.' [2] This was only a part of the information the British had received as to Washington's real intent at the time to make

---

[1] Fortescue: *History of the British Army.*   [2] *Ibid.*

the attack on New York, as has been described. For all the American and French preparations then were openly being made for this project.

The British leaders, the two generals in America and Germaine in England, remained at helpless cross-purposes, irresolutely vacillating as to details, but with no clear conception of any plan. It dribbled down to a situation where Cornwallis was to retain all his troops, but 'that it was the opinion both of Clinton and Admiral Graves, who had lately superseded Arbuthnot, that a defensive post must be established at Old Point Comfort in York River for the protection of the British cruisers.' [1] Old Point Comfort was rejected by the British engineers, and, upon their recommendations, Cornwallis proceeded to fortify Yorktown and Gloucester, on the opposite banks of York River.

Cornwallis, thus established at Yorktown, had an army of seven thousand after the garrison of Portsmouth had been withdrawn to join his forces, and all the British troops had been concentrated under his command (August 22, 1781). Lafayette had also been reinforced by Steuben, and his force had been increased to five thousand. After pressing upon Cornwallis whenever he could, he placed his forces at Malvern Hill. There he remained to hold the troops of Cornwallis in check, although Lafayette was not strong enough to venture any attack upon Cornwallis.

This whole military situation in America was helplessly unsound for the British, and was the culmination of their mismanagement of the war. But the danger of keeping Cornwallis in Yorktown was not suspected, for two reasons. In the first place, the British never conceived it possible that their naval superiority off the American coast would be threatened. They could not imagine that de Grasse's whole

[1] Fortescue: *History of the British Army.*

fleet would be ordered to America.[1] In the second place, the British were equally blind to the possibility of Washington's moving his army into the South. But while the British were thus passive in fancied security, these two assumed impossibilities were on the way to accomplishment.

[1] 'No one ever dreamed that he would carry all his ships with him to America. Rodney reckoned that he would take at most ten.' (Fortescue: *History of the British Army*.)

Chapter xxxix

WASHINGTON'S MOVE TO THE SOUTH

IN THE North, after the French army had joined Washington's army on the Hudson, the first weeks were spent in active preparations for the attack on New York. Troops were moved down to King's Bridge, and Washington and Rochambeau made reconnoissances of the British positions. This open activity of his enemies about New York confirmed Clinton's information that New York was to be the point of attack. As has been explained, the alternative of taking his army to the South had been present in the mind of Washington, in spite of his preference for the New York attack. And all of Washington's careful preparations included the scheme of transporting the army thither. It was not until July 30 that Washington definitely expressed his change of plan. In a letter to Lafayette, of that date, he wrote: 'Our views must now be turned towards endeavoring to expel them totally from those States, if we find ourselves incompetent to the siege of New York.' [1]

Consequently, the change of plan did not imply that means of carrying out the operation must be improvised hastily. For measures had been taken in advance for the execution of the operation of moving the army to the South.

---

[1] In his diary of the same date, Washington, in reference to the question of the movements of Barras from Newport, used the phrase, 'blocking up those now in Virginia.'

347

Knox had been zealous in his mission, and, most important of all, Robert Morris, the newly appointed Superintendent of Finance, had pledged his own credit for transportation and supplies. This was a great public service, at the time of dire need, and it always will be remembered with gratitude by his countrymen.

Washington's secret letter of instructions to Robert Morris (August 2, 1781) showed how far things had advanced. Washington wrote, 'The principal difficulty, which occurs, is obtaining transports at the moment they may be wanted; for if they are taken up beforehand, the use for which they are designed cannot be concealed, and the enemy will make arrangements to defeat the plan.' And Washington directed Morris to obtain information, 'without making a direct inquiry,' as to the vessels for transport service obtainable at Philadelphia, Baltimore, 'or other places in Chesapeake.' Everything was now in train — and Washington only waited for news from de Grasse. At last, on August 14, 1781, came the expected message: 'The Concorde frigate has arrived at Newport from Count de Grasse. He was to leave St. Domingo the 3d of this month, with a fleet of between twenty-five and twenty-nine sail of the line, and a considerable body of land forces. His destination is immediately for the Chesapeake.' [1]

Upon this, Washington at once put his plan into action. He wrote to de Grasse (August 17): 'For this purpose we have determined to move the whole of the French army and as large a detachment of the American as can be spared, to the Chesapeake, to meet your Excellency there.' [2] And de Grasse was instructed: 'We would observe, that it will be very essential to the dispatch of the business in contempla-

[1] Washington to Lafayette, August 15, 1781.
[2] This letter was signed by Washington and Rochambeau.

348

tion, for you to send up to Elk River, at the head of Chesapeake Bay, all your frigates, transports, and vessels proper for the conveyance of the French and American troops down the bay. We shall endeavor to have as many as can be found in Baltimore and other ports secured, but we have reason to believe they will be very few.'

To de Barras, in command of the French squadron at Newport, Washington wrote (August 15, 1781): 'I cannot avoid repeating therefore in earnest terms the request of Count Rochambeau, that you would form the junction, and as soon as possible, with the Count de Grasse in Chesapeake Bay.' To Lafayette Washington sent instructions: 'Under the circumstances, whether the enemy remain in full force, or whether they have only a detachment left, you will immediately take such a position as will best enable you to prevent their sudden retreat through North Carolina, which I presume they will attempt the instant they perceive so formidable an armament.... You will take measures for opening a communication with Count de Grasse the moment he arrives, and will concert measures with him for making the best use of your joint forces until you receive aid from this quarter.' [1] And to Robert Morris Washington wrote, confirming the alteration of his plan, 'in confidence imparted to you,' with instructions: 'Besides the provisions necessary at the Head of the Elk to carry the troops down the bay, a very considerable quantity will be wanted in Virginia.... I have written to the Count de Grasse, and have requested him to send up his light vessels of every kind to Elk; but I would nevertheless wish to have all that may be at Baltimore and the upper parts of the bay secured.... I shall direct the quartermaster in due season to take up all the small craft in the Delaware for

[1] Washington to Lafayette, August 15, 1781.

349

the purpose of transporting the troops from Trenton to Christeen.' [1]

Merely to read the foregoing will be sufficient to bring conviction that the ensuing victory was no matter of luck. Washington's far-reaching *coup* won one of the greatest surprises in military history, but the foundation of its success was Washington's own skill in planning the details of his combination. Washington did not allow any delay in putting his forces in motion, as he knew that rapidity of execution was the one essential. On August 17 Washington himself mapped out the line of march for the French army, which provided for its arrival at Trenton in the evening of August 29. The Americans proceeded by a different route to Trenton.

About four thousand American troops were left under the command of Heath, with the instruction from Washington: 'The security of West Point and the posts in the Highlands is to be considered the first object of your attention.' [2] Washington was sure that this force would be able to make a stout defense of West Point, but he shrewdly ordered Heath to take station 'above the Croton,' for the purpose of 'annoying the enemy and covering the country,' with use of his troops 'to hold the enemy in check, and carry on the *petite guerre* with them.' Washington explained the purpose of this: 'The uncertainty, which the present movement of the army will probably occasion with the enemy, ought to be increased by every means in your power, and the deception kept up as long as possible.'

In addition to these ingenious dispositions to deceive the enemy, great pains were taken to disguise the departure of the troops. A column was marched through Chatham,

[1] To the Superintendent of Finance, August 17, 1781.
[2] Instructions to Major General Heath.

Springfield, and Brunswick, to give the appearance that the movement into New Jersey was against Staten Island and Sandy Hook. A French bakery was actually set up at Chatham, as a blind. So successful was this well-conceived system of deception, that the British had not the slightest suspicion of any unusual movement, and the American and French troops actually marched across New Jersey, while Clinton thought they still were hovering about New York.

At Trenton the baggage and stores of the army were put on board shipping. But there were not enough additional transports to carry the troops, and only one regiment went by water. Washington and Rochambeau left Trenton on August 30 for Philadelphia. The French and American troops followed, and marched through Philadelphia on their way to the Head of the Elk.

At Yorktown, Cornwallis remained totally unconscious of the deadly combination of forces moving against him. The utter inability of the British to grasp the fact, that de Grasse was taking his whole fleet to America, was summed up in their confidence that the dispatch of fourteen ships of the line would be ample to take care of the French naval forces. Admiral Hood commanded this British naval force sent from the West Indies, as Rodney had left for England, on account of ill health. The following from Germaine showed the British satisfaction in the situation: 'As Sir George Rodney knows the destination of de Grasse, and the French acknowledge his ships sail better than theirs, he will get before him and be in readiness to receive him when he comes upon the coast. I see nothing to prevent the recovery of the whole country to the King's obedience.' [1]

Hood actually did outsail de Grasse, and the British fleet

[1] Germaine to Clinton, August 2, 1781.

351

arrived off the Chesapeake (August 25, 1781). Hood found no signs of de Grasse, and proceeded to New York, where he came under the command of Admiral Graves. The British received information that de Barras had sailed from Newport for the Chesapeake, and Graves put to sea (August 31) with eighteen ships of the line to intercept de Barras. In the mean time, de Grasse had arrived in Chesapeake Bay with twenty-eight ships of the line. He at once detached four ships, to convoy the troops from his fleet up the James River to Lafayette. With his remaining twenty-four ships of the line he anchored in Lynhaven Bay, just inside the southern cape of Chesapeake Bay.

Consequently, Graves, when he arrived off the Chesapeake (September 5), was surprised [1] to find himself in the presence of a superior naval force. Graves engaged the French fleet, but he was overmatched. After five days of maneuvering, he found many of his ships so damaged [2] that he was forced to return to New York to refit. And de Barras made good his junction with de Grasse, bringing eight ships and transports carrying a heavy siege train. The powerful French fleet thus had established at once the required naval superiority in the Chesapeake.

Cornwallis remained inactive, and he was losing whatever chance he had of breaking away before Washington arrived. Lafayette, after receiving the reinforcement of three thousand French troops of Marquis de St. Simon, brought in de Grasse's fleet, advanced to Williamsburg on September 7, and took post there to oppose any attempt of

---

[1] 'His appearance in such overwhelming strength was a surprise to every English commander, and upset all calculations.' (Fortescue: *History of the British Army.*)

[2] One ship of the line, the *Terrible*, was so shattered that she was abandoned and burnt.

352

Cornwallis to escape.[1] But the British general, who did not dream of the advent of Washington, 'decided, however, to hold his hand, and busied himself with the strengthening of his position.'[2]

In this tragedy of errors for the British, it was not until September 2 that Clinton first ascertained the departure of Washington for the South. Even then, he did not realize the full peril of Cornwallis, for he believed that Graves' fleet was far superior to any French naval force in American waters.[3] The only action taken by Clinton was to send Arnold on a raid of the Connecticut coast, 'with a view of making a diversion in Connecticut, and drawing general Washington's attention that way.'[4] But the contemporary British historian continued: 'It was not of sufficient importance to stop general Washington in his progress to Virginia. The enterprise in which he was now engaged was of the utmost moment. If successful, it would have a material influence in shortening the duration of the war, and was not therefore to be abandoned for any partial consideration whatsoever.'[5]

At this same time, Greene was giving the last blow to the hopes of the British in the Carolinas. Lord Rawdon had broken down in health, and had left for England.[6] Colonel Stuart had taken command of his troops. On September 8 Greene fought Stuart, in the Battle of Eutaw Springs, and Stuart was forced to retreat to Charleston, where the British

[1] 'Obviously, Cornwallis could have attacked this force and beaten it before the arrival of Washington's army.' (Fortescue: *History of the British Army.*)

[2] *Ibid.*

[3] 'Adding, in tragic ignorance of the true state of affairs, that as Graves had sailed Cornwallis need fear nothing.' (Fortescue: *History of the British Army.*)

[4] Stedman: *History of the American War.*   [5] *Ibid.*

[6] Lord Rawdon was unlucky in being captured on his way by de Grasse and brought a prisoner to Chesapeake Bay.

were cooped up for the rest of the war, depending upon their shipping for support. All self-government had been restored in the Southern States, as in the North. In both North and South, the military situation was the same. Of all the overpowering British armies, which at times had seemed about to conquer America, there remained only these isolated British forces huddled on the coast.

Each of these British forces, outside its pent-up lines, had no more control, even over the adjacent country, than if it had been stationed on an island off the coast. This was the result of all the years of British efforts to overrun rebellious America. And this military situation, at the time the final blow was to fall, should be set forth unmistakably. It has been too often obscured in controversies over details, but, strangely enough, it has never been better described than in the words of the contemporary British historian: 'It came as a surprise upon the world; and men were obliged to conclude, either that the force of Great Britain was ill-directed, or that no invading army, in the present enlightened period, can be successful, in a country where the people are tolerably united.' [1]

[1] Stedman: *History of the American War.*

Chapter XL

THE SIEGE OF YORKTOWN

FROM Philadelphia the American and French troops marched to the Head of the Elk and from there they were to be taken in the transports down the bay to Williamsburg. Washington had gone on in advance, and September 14 arrived at Williamsburg, to take over the command from Lafayette. The next day Washington reported to the President of Congress: 'I have the honor to inform Congress, that I arrived at this place last evening; that soon after my arrival, I received the pleasing intelligence, that the Count de Grasse, who had put to sea on the 5th in pursuit of the British fleet, had returned to his former station at Cape Henry, having driven the British from the coast, and effected a junction with the squadron of the Count de Barras.'

Washington explained the danger that had existed for transports in the bay, until it was certain that the French fleet was on guard. 'Orders are this morning gone on to press them forward with every despatch possible.' [1] With the French fleet at the entrance of the Chesapeake, nothing could interfere with this transportation of troops, and on September 26 the joint forces were all concentrated at Williamsburg. Some of the French troops had marched to Annapolis, and were taken on board transports there. The

[1] 'Hurry on then, my dear Sir, with your troops on the wings of speed.' (Washington to Major General Lincoln.)

355

united American and French forces were over sixteen thousand — and the doom of Cornwallis was sealed.

In his diary (September 17) Washington recorded: 'In company with Count Rochambeau, the Chevalier de Chastellux, General Knox, and General Duportail, I set out for an interview with the Admiral, and arrived on board the Ville de Paris (off Cape Henry) the next day about noon; and having settled most points with him to my satisfaction, except not obtaining an assurance of sending ships above York, I embarked on board of Queen Charlotte, the vessel I went down in; but, by reason of hard blowing and contrary winds, I did not reach Williamsburg again till the 22d.'

The record of this interview has been preserved, in the form of questions propounded by Washington and answers given by de Grasse, signed by each, and constituting a working agreement. The main question was in regard to the length of the stay of the French fleet on the American coast, as Washington had been informed this would be limited to a short period. In this respect, de Grasse made the following explicit pledge: '1st, The instructions of Count de Grasse fix his departure to the 15th of October, and some engagements which he has made for other operations oblige him to be punctual; but having already taken much upon himself, he will also engage to stay until the end of October.' As to the troops of Saint-Simon, de Grasse also promised, 'You may count upon those Troops to that Period for the Reduction of York.'

As to the third question, 'to force the passage of the York River,' de Grasse replied: 'But I suspend my definitive answer until I can reconoitre the local situation and force of the enemy.' But this was of minor importance, and de Grasse also wrote, 'I have offered, and I again offer 1,800 or 2,000 men from my ships; but I wish that these Troops may

not be employed but in a Coup de Main.... I can give some Cannon and powder.'

This agreement meant that Washington could rely upon the French fleet for the time required to besiege Cornwallis. But Washington had one grave anxiety in this regard. Admiral de Grasse had received information that the reinforced British fleet was approaching, and he planned to take the French fleet to sea to meet them. Washington at once sent an urgent plea: 'That the enterprise against York, under the protection of your ships, is as certain as any military operation can be rendered by a decisive superiority of strength and means.... I most earnestly entreat your Excellency farther to consider, that, if the present opportunity should be missed, that if you should withdraw your maritime force from the position agreed upon, that no future day can restore to us a similar occasion to strike a decisive blow.' [1]

This eloquent appeal was sent to de Grasse by the hand of Lafayette, and Lafayette's arguments were added to those of Washington. They convinced de Grasse, who wrote in reply: 'The result has been, that the plan I had suggested was the most brilliant and glorious, but it would not fulfil the views we had proposed. It is consequently decided, that a large part of the fleet shall anchor in York River, that four or five vessels shall be stationed so as to pass up and down the James River, and that you shall aid us with the means to erect a battery on Point Comfort, where we can place cannon and mortars. We shall immediately proceed to execute this arrangement, and I hasten to give you notice, that we may act in concert for the advancement of our operations.' [2]

This reply of de Grasse touched Washington deeply, and

[1] Washington to de Grasse, September 25, 1781.
[2] De Grasse to Washington.

he replied: 'The resolutions that you have taken in our circumstances prove, that a great mind knows how to make personal sacrifices to secure an important general good. Fully sensible of those, which you have made on the present occasion, I flatter myself that the result of the operations, conducted under your auspices, will compensate them by its utility to the common cause. Your Excellency may depend on every assistance, that the allied armies can give, relatively to the battery which you propose at Point Comfort, and that our utmost exertions will be used in hastening the investment of the enemy.' [1]

With every doubt removed as to the coöperation of the French naval forces, Washington proceeded with great energy to 'the investment of the enemy.' It would be impossible to give a better account, of the first stages of the siege of Yorktown, than that in Washington's report to the President of Congress (October 1, 1781): 'I have now to acquaint your Excellency, that I marched from Williamsburg with the whole army on the 28th, and approached within about two miles of the enemy, at York, at which distance a show was made of some opposition on the left; but, upon the Count de Rochambeau, who commanded that part of the army, his moving a few pieces of field-artillery, under direction of the Baron Vioménil, and giving a few shots the enemy retired. On the 29th, the American troops moved forward, and took their ground in front of the enemy's works on their left; no opposition, save a few scattered shots from a small work by Moor's Mill, on Wormley's creek and a battery on the left of Pigeon Quarter. A small fire all day from our riflemen and the enemy's Yagers. 30th in the morning, we discovered that the enemy had evacuated all their exterior line of works, and withdrawn themselves to those near the body of the town.

[1] Washington to de Grasse, September 27, 1781.

By this means we are in possession of very advantageous grounds, which command in a very near advance almost the whole remaining line of their defence. All the expedition, that our circumstances will admit, is using to bring up our heavy artillery and stores to open our batteries. This work I hope will be executed in a few days, when our fire will begin with great vigor.

'The investment of the enemy is fully completed and drawn very near to their lines, except on the river above the town where their communication is still open. To prevent this and to complete the blockade, a request is gone to the Count de Grasse, desiring him to push if he thinks it practicable one or more ships above the town; this, if effected, will answer many very valuable purposes. The position of the Count de Grasse is judiciously taken, the main fleet keeping their station in Lynhaven Bay, and detachments made to secure the rivers; the determination of the Count is favorably disposed to comply with our wishes in every necessary co-operation.'

It has been difficult to find any excuse for the act of Cornwallis in abandoning his outer line of defenses.[1] As stated by Washington, this gave the Americans and French 'very advantageous grounds' which commanded 'almost the whole remaining line of defence.' It hastened the fall of Cornwallis, as it permitted his enemies to establish their first parallel (October 6) 'within six hundred yards.' [2] The allied guns opened their bombardment October 9, and it was at once so destructive 'that the enemy withdrew their cannon from their embrasures, placed them behind the merlins,

---

[1] 'Thereupon, for no apparent reason, Cornwallis abandoned the outer line of defenses and retired within the works of the town, though these were commanded by the outer line.' (Fortescue: *History of the British Army*.)

[2] To the President of Congress, October 12, 1781.

and scarce fired a shot during the whole day.' [1] A frigate and two transports were burned by hot shot in the bombardment.

This was accomplished by Washington's army, with almost no loss, and, in the evening of October 11, the allies 'advanced our second parallel within three hundred yards of the enemy's works, with little or no annoyance from them. Only one man was killed, and three or four wounded.' [2] The feeble resistance of Cornwallis astonished Washington, who wrote: 'I shall think it strange indeed, if Lord Cornwallis makes no vigorous exertions in the course of the night, or very soon after.' [3] But Cornwallis had put himself in a hopeless position for defense.

On the British left there were two advanced redoubts, and, upon the report of Washington's engineers that they were 'sufficiently injured by our shot and shells to make them practicable, it was determined to carry them by assault on the evening of the 14th.' [4] In friendly emulation, it was decided that one redoubt was to be stormed by the French under Baron de Vioménil, the other by the Americans under Lafayette, with Hamilton leading the advance. Both assaults were successful, and, in the words of the contemporary British historian, 'by the unwearied labour of the enemy both redoubts were included in their second parallel before the morning.' [5]

The loss of these redoubts made Cornwallis' situation 'almost hopeless.' [6] The only retort he was able to make was a

[1] To the President of Congress, October 12, 1781.

[2] *Ibid.*   [3] *Ibid.*

[4] *Ibid.*, October 16, 1781.

[5] Stedman: *History of the American War.*

[6] 'On the 14th the capture of two advanced redoubts made the British position almost hopeless.' (Fortescue: *History of the British Army.*)

feeble sortie,[1] before the break of day on October 16. At the first attack, the British penetrated the lines at two places, but they were soon driven back, without accomplishing any damage of importance. 'At this time not a gun could be shown by the garrison on that side of the works attacked by the enemy, and the shells were nearly expended; Lord Cornwallis was therefore reduced to the necessity of either preparing to surrender, or attempting to escape with the greater part of the army; and he determined to attempt the latter on the Gloucester side of the river.'[2]

Whatever possibility of escape there might have been in this last resort of Cornwallis,[3] was ended by a storm that night. On October 17 the situation was thus vividly pictured by the British historian: 'In the mean time, by the force of the enemy's cannonade, the British works were tumbling into ruin: Not a gun could be fired from them, and only one eight-inch and little more than an hundred cohorn shells remained. They were in many places assailable already; and if the same fire continued a few hours longer, it was the opinion of the engineer and the principal officers of the army, that it would be madness to attempt to maintain them with the present garrison, exhausted by the fatigue of constant watching, and reduced in its numbers by sickness even more than by the enemy's fire. Under such circumstances his lordship, on the seventeenth of October, unwilling to expose the remains of his gallant army to the danger of an assault, which, from the enemy's numbers and the ruined

---

[1] 'The British troops having been weakened by sickness, as well as by the fire of the besiegers, Lord Cornwallis could not venture to make so large sorties as to hope from them much success.' (Stedman: *History of the American War*.)

[2] *Ibid.*

[3] 'Undoubtedly the attempt was beyond calculation hazardous, and the issue totally precarious; but, if it afforded even a glimpse of hope, it was preferable to an immediate surrender.' (Stedman: *History of the American War*.)

state of the works, could not fail to be successful, made proposals for a capitulation.' [1]

Accordingly, on that day, Cornwallis sent a note to Washington, proposing a cessation of hostilities, and a meeting 'to settle terms for the surrender of the posts of York and Gloucester.' [2] On October 18, Articles of Capitulation [3] were drawn, on the basis of the terms granted to General Lincoln at Charleston.[4] Accordingly, on October 19, 1781, the troops of Cornwallis marched out of their works, piled their arms, and filed off as prisoners of War. The losses of the garrison in the siege were 552. The total of prisoners amounted to 7073, of whom about 6600 were troops. 'The blow was, on the whole, perhaps the heaviest that has ever befallen the British Army, and to all intents it put an end to the war in America.' [5]

On the day of the surrender, Washington reported to the President of Congress: 'I have the honor to inform Congress, that a reduction of the British army, under the command of Lord Cornwallis, is most happily effected. The unremitted ardor, which animated every officer and soldier in the combined army on this occasion, has principally led to this important event, at an earlier period than my most sanguine hopes had induced me to expect.' Washington cited, 'with the warmest sense of acknowledgment, the very cheerful and able assistance received in the course of our operation from his Excellency the Count de Rochambeau and all his officers

[1] Stedman: *History of the American War.*

[2] Earl Cornwallis to Washington, October 17, 1781.

[3] 'Which, though not altogether agreeable to earl Cornwallis's wishes or proposals, were nevertheless such as his desperate situation obliged him to accept.' (Stedman: *History of the American War.*)

[4] 'The same honors will be granted to the surrendering Army as were granted to the garrison of Charleston.' (Washington to Cornwallis, October 18, 1781.)

[5] Fortescue: *History of the British Army.*

of every rank in their respective capacities.' Washington wrote in equally warm terms of the services of de Grasse and the officers under his command. To de Grasse Washington sent a personal acknowledgment, that was characteristic of the magnanimity of the American Commander in Chief: 'The surrender of York, from which so much glory and advantage are derived to the allies, and the honor of which belongs to your Excellency, had greatly anticipated our most sanguine expectations.' [1]

On the day of the surrender, Clinton had at length sailed from New York to the assistance of Cornwallis. He brought with him seven thousand of his best troops. This British fleet arrived off Chesapeake Bay October 24, and was met by reports of Cornwallis' surrender. After lingering off the mouth of the bay until October 29, the fleet returned to New York. Of course it is useless to speculate on what would have happened if it had arrived before the surrender. But it should be stated that the total strength of the British fighting fleet was twenty-five ships of the line. The French fleet of de Grasse, reinforced by the squadron of de Barras, consisted of thirty-six ships of the line. This greatly superior French fleet was guarding Chesapeake Bay, throughout the siege of Yorktown and until after the surrender of Cornwallis. Consequently we must realize that, as in the case of Clinton's tardy move up the Hudson when Burgoyne was hemmed in by swarms of enemies, an earlier arrival would have been no guaranty of a rescue.

[1] Washington to de Grasse, October 20, 1781.

pean war continued to absorb the interest of the British. The antagonism to the American war had grown to an extent that meant an open revolt against continuing it, at the first unfavorable turn of events.

At the news of the surrender of Cornwallis, the British historian stated, the American war 'was reprobated, together with the incapacity and misconduct of ministers, as the cause of all our misfortunes.' [1] That had become the prevailing opinion of the American war in Great Britain. The national spirit of Great Britain was arrayed against the European enemies. It was no longer a matter of national pride to conquer America. The American war was merely 'a favorite measure with the court.' [2] Its opponents became too strong to resist: 'The misfortunes of the last campaign gave them advantages which all the influence and power of the administration were unable to surmount.' [3] And the contemporary British historian has left no doubt of this situation: 'The murmurs of the people had been hitherto suppressed, from the hopes held out of a speedy and successful termination of the war; and with the recovery of the revolted colonies, accompanied by the monopoly of their trade, they were taught to expect such an influx of wealth as would speedily compensate for the present expenditure. But after the events of the last campaign, no one could be found so sanguine as to expect that the revolted colonies could be recovered by the force of arms. The experience of nearly six years had served to show, that although a province might be overrun and subdued, it could not be secured and preserved without the concurrence of the inhabitants; and the war waged in the southern colonies for the two years past, established this fact beyond contradiction.' [4] It should be

[1] Stedman: *History of the American War.*
[2] *Ibid.*   [3] *Ibid.*   [4] *Ibid.*

noted that this statement, from one who served through the Revolution, presented a picture much more true than the recent superficial theses on its history.

The losses at sea from the depredations of the American privateers were still growing and all the commercial interests of Great Britain were being arrayed against the American war. These demands became outspoken. The city of London petitioned the King to put an end to 'this unnatural and unfortunate war.' And there were many public meetings for the same purpose. This trend of public opinion in Great Britain must be realized, in order to understand the ending of the American Revolution.

In America, Washington had been anxious to follow up the capture of Cornwallis' army by a similar *coup* against Charleston.[1] But de Grasse already had prolonged his stay beyond his instructions. He felt obliged to depart for the West Indies [2] — to engage in the series of operations, which ended in his utter disaster. With no possibilities of further offensives against the enemy, Washington sent back his army to their old positions about New York. The French army of Rochambeau remained encamped in Virginia. Wayne and St. Clair were sent with reinforcements for Greene in the south.

But the real fighting of the American Revolution was at an end. Only dying embers smouldered. Wayne found no difficulty in driving the last remnants of the British from the countryside of Georgia into Savannah. Even this seaport

[1] '...Opened to a combined attack, and might be carried with as much certainty as the place which has just surrendered.' (Washington to de Grasse, October 20, 1781.)

[2] 'My ulterior operations require my return to an appointed place at a fixed day. That day approaches, and it would be impossible for me to break my engagement voluntarily.' (De Grasse to Lafayette, October 26, 1781.)

the British did not long retain, as it was evacuated July 11, 1782, and all the British troops in the South were shut up in Charleston. In the North they remained hemmed into New York. These British forces on the American coast confessed themselves impotent, and remained inactive. Bancroft has noted, as 'the last blood shed on the field during the war,' the loss of the valuable life of John Laurens[1] (August 27, 1782) in a skirmish with a British foraging party from Charleston. To these small dimensions had hostilities shrunk. Young Laurens was only twenty-seven, and he left behind him a record of gallantry in the field, in addition to his able conduct of his mission to France.

Yet, even under these victorious conditions, Washington was beset with new difficulties. The very assurance of victory, among the Americans, made it a harder task to procure maintenance for the army. Even under the spur of menacing dangers, it had been uphill work to induce the States to perform their parts. But now, with the peril over, the States lapsed back into an indifference that was starving the army. Washington had given warning against the danger of this attitude. After Yorktown, when he was on his way to appear before Congress, he wrote: 'My greatest fear is, that Congress, viewing this stroke in too important a point of light, may think our work too nearly closed, and will fall into a state of languor and relaxation.'[2] But Congress at last had learned its lesson, from sad experience, and was one with Washington in this matter. To Washington was given the assurance (November 28, 1781): 'It is their fixed purpose to draw every advantage from it, by exhorting the states in the strongest terms to the most vigorous and timely

---

[1] Washington stated: 'He had not a fault that I could discover, unless it were intrepidity bordering upon rashness.'

[2] Washington to Greene, November 16, 1781.

exertions.' There could be no mistaking this 'best disposition imaginable in Congress.' [1]

After this endorsement by Congress, Washington's anxiety was in regard to the States. He sent out a Circular Letter to the States, calling upon their aid, in which he wrote: 'Whether we consult our true interest, substantial economy, or sound policy, we shall find that relaxation and languor are, of all things, to be avoided. Conduct of that kind, on our part, will produce fresh hopes and new exertions of the enemy.' [2] This was followed up by a second Circular Letter,[3] in which Washington reiterated, that he was 'apprehensive, the prosperous issue of the combined operation in Virginia, may have (as is too common in such cases) the pernicious tendency of lulling the country into a lethargy of inactivity and security.'

But, in spite of the efforts of Washington, the different States were backward in furnishing what was necessary for the troops. For this reason, both in the North and in the South, the winter after winning the victory was filled with hardships for the American soldiers, as had been the case when their cause seemed hopeless. There was much dissatisfaction, and, as before, it spoke volumes for them that the troops held together as well as they did. On his last page the contemporary British historian praised this quality, in generous terms: 'The Americans had neither money nor credit; but they learned to stand in need only of a few things; to be contented with the small allowance that nature requires; to suffer as well as act. Their councils, animated by liberty, under the most distressing circumstances, took a grand and high-spirited course, and they were finally trium-

[1] Washington to Lafayette, January 4, 1782.
[2] January 22, 1782.
[3] January 31, 1782.

phant.' [1] This was a tribute, in which the ring of sincerity cannot be mistaken, from a British officer who was in active service against the Americans throughout the Revolution.

It was not until March that Washington felt he could re-assure Greene as to the danger of a resumption of the offensive on the part of the British. In a letter to Greene expressing his 'pain to hear of your distress for want of clothing and other necessaries,' he wrote; 'By late advices from Europe, and from the declarations of the British ministers themselves, it appears that they have done with all thoughts of an excursive war, and they mean to send small, if any reinforcements to America.' [2]

This was in recognition of the course of events in England, which were unmistakably leading to the repudiation, on the part of Great Britain, of the war against the Americans. With the coming of the new year of 1782, the opposition in Parliament had continued to press this question upon the North Ministry. At each exchange the supporters of Lord North fell away, and the opposition increased in numbers. 'At last, on the twenty-seventh of February, they succeeded in carrying a vote [3] for addressing his majesty to direct his ministers no longer to wage an offensive war against the revolted colonies, and to assure him that they would most cheerfully concur in such measures as may be found necessary to accelerate the blessing of returning peace.' [4]

As there was an attempt to evade this address, Conway, on March 4, brought forward a second address, which declared that the House would consider enemies to the King and country all who would attempt to continue the war to

[1] Stedman: *History of the American War.*
[2] Washington to Greene, March 18, 1782.
[3] Carried by a vote of 234 against 215.
[4] Stedman: *History of the American War.*

subdue the revolting Americans. After a debate, this was adopted without a division. There was no mistaking this verdict. It meant the fall of Lord North's Ministry — and the end of the personal government of the King. This was a gain for Great Britain as great as that for America. Never again were the King's Ministers to ignore their responsibility to the nation.

Upon the passing of Lord North, a new Ministry was formed with Lord Rockingham as Prime Minister. Lord Shelburne was Home Secretary, and thus was in charge of all measures relating to America. He and Franklin were old friends. When Franklin saw that Shelburne was to be in the cabinet, the far-seeing American wrote a personal letter to Shelburne, expressing the hope that the change of sentiment in Great Britain would 'tend to produce a general peace, which I am sure your lordship, with all good men, desires.' In the same spirit, Shelburne replied (April 6, 1782): 'I have had a high opinion of the compass of your mind and of your foresight. I have often been beholden to both, and shall be glad to be so again, so far as is compatible with your situation. Your letter, discovering the same disposition, has made me send to you Mr. Oswald.... He is fully apprised of my mind, and you may give full credit to any thing he assures you of. At the same time, if any other channel occurs to you, I am ready to embrace it. I wish to retain the same simplicity and good faith which subsisted between us in transactions of less importance.' In this friendly and direct manner began the negotiations which were to lead to the treaty that acknowledged American independence.[1]

[1] 'The key to the treaty that followed.' (Bancroft: *History of the United States*.)

Chapter XLII

THE ACHIEVEMENT OF INDEPENDENCE

ALTHOUGH the actual treaty of peace was far away, yet, in the spring of 1782, there no longer could be any question of the fact that the new British Government was on the way to acknowledge the independence of the United States. A most significant sign of this was the appointment of Sir Guy Carleton (April 4), to supersede Clinton in the command at New York. Immediately upon his arrival at New York, Carleton sent a letter to Washington (May 7, 1782), inclosing the resolutions of Parliament, which were cited in the preceding chapter. Carleton described himself, as 'appointed by his majesty to the command of the forces on the Atlantic Ocean, and joined with Admiral Digby in the commission of peace.'

He wrote: 'I transmit to your Excellency certain papers, from the perusal of which your Excellency will perceive what dispositions prevail in the government and people of England towards those of America, and what effects are likely to follow. If the like pacific disposition should prevail in this country, both my inclination and duty will lead me to meet it with the most zealous concurrence.' He also asked a passport for one of his aides, to convey to Congress 'a similar letter of compliment' with copies of the resolves of Parliament.

This communication from the newly appointed British

Commander in Chief at once put the war on a different basis in America. And, throughout his service in New York, Carleton adhered to the spirit of this message. As has been stated in regard to his conduct in Canada, he was a humane man of high standards. There were no more raids of the Arnold type,[1] and Carleton made every effort to put a stop to the petty warfare, which he stigmatized as 'equally calamatous and dishonorable to both parties.'

This remarkable letter from the British Commander in Chief, officially transmitted, was, to all intents and purposes, an appeal for a cessation of hostilities, under promise that the British Government no longer would attempt to deny the independence of America. On August 2 Carleton gave an additional assurance to Washington: 'We are acquainted, Sir, by authority, that negotiations for a general peace have already commenced at Paris, and that Mr. Grenville is invested with full powers to treat with all parties at war, and is now at Paris in the execution of his commission. And we are likewise, Sir, further made acquainted, that his Majesty, in order to remove all obstacles to that peace, which he so ardently wishes to restore, has commanded his ministers to direct Mr. Grenville, that the independency of the thirteen Provinces should be proposed by him in the first instance, instead of making it a condition of a general treaty.' This letter was signed by both General Carleton and Admiral Digby.

But, although Washington realized, in regard to the British, that 'their commanders in this country are in a manner tied down to a defensive war only,'[2] yet he believed it necessary to keep up a concentration of troops against them. Washington feared that the negotiations might break down,

[1] Arnold was kept out of the country.
[2] Washington to Rochambeau, August 16, 1782.

373

or that the British interpretation of independence for America might mean 'that the King of England should have the same kind of supremacy here as in Ireland.' [1] Washington knew how strongly the King was opposed to letting go his hold on America, 'The whole tenor of his conduct, as well as his proroguing speech on the 11th of July, plainly indicates it, and shows in a clear point of view the impolicy of relaxation on our part. There is nothing, which will so soon produce a speedy and honorable peace, as a state of preparedness for war.' [2]

The French army of Rochambeau was brought to the Hudson. The first division arrived at King's Ferry September 15. Soon afterwards, the whole French force was quartered on the left of the American army in the region of Verplanck's Point, 'and the two armies rejoined with the most lively demonstrations of reciprocal satisfaction.' [3] But the French army was soon ordered to the West Indies. They marched from the Hudson to Boston, and sailed December 24, 1782, having been in America two and a half years.

Washington accepted the 'assurances from Sir Guy Carleton, that the incursions of savages are stopped by authority,'[4] and Washington withdrew the Continental troops from the Northern frontier. In addition to this humane action on the part of Carleton, the British Commander in Chief rendered his good offices in the vexed questions of exchanges of prisoners. These were put on a liberal basis, as the result of Carleton's efforts, who thus repeated his generous conduct at the time of the invasion of Canada.

For the rest of the year the cessation of military activity

[1] Washington to Greene, August 6, 1782.
[2] Washington to James McHenry, September 12, 1782.
[3] Memoirs of Rochambeau.
[4] Washington to Governor Clinton, October 19, 1782.

continued. But this very circumstance contributed to increase the discontent of the army. On the whole, the American soldiers had endured their hard lot with extraordinary fortitude. But, at this last stage, they lacked the spur of service against an active and threatening enemy. It was growing evident to them that the fighting of the war was over, and, in addition to their present hardships, they feared that the neglect of their well-being, on the part of their States, would go to the extent of sending them back to civil life without any resources for a new beginning.

On October 2, 1782, Washington made a special plea to the Secretary of War, in behalf of his troops: 'The evils of which they complain, and which they suppose almost remediless, are the total want of money or the means of existing from one day to another, the heavy debts they have already incurred, the loss of credit, the distress of their families at home, and the prospect of poverty and misery before them.' [1] And, to the end, Washington was indefatigable in striving to mend this situation. It was more due to the personal efforts of Washington, than to any other cause, that serious trouble was avoided.

General Knox had been placed in command of West Point.[2] The army moved from the encampment at Verplanck's Point, and on November 28 went into winter quarters in huts at New Windsor. Washington's headquarters were at Newburg. He wrote that he had thought of asking for a leave to go to his home in Virginia, 'for everything else seemed to be in a state of inactivity and almost tranquility,' but one 'consideration alone prevented' Washington from making this visit. This was the 'temper of the army,' which rendered his presence necessary. Washington explained this

[1] General Lincoln was Secretary at War for Congress.
[2] Instructions, August 29, 1782.

375

situation, in regard to an address sent by the troops to Congress. He wrote: 'This address, though couched in very respectful terms, is one of those things, which, though displeasing, is just now unavoidable. For I was very apprehensive once, that matters would take a more unfavorable turn, from the variety of discontent which prevail.' [1] This must be the picture of Washington's task, as the war was ending — a constant endeavor to adjust the troubles of the American soldiers.

But, at the beginning of the year of 1783, Washington first saw the negotiations for peace reach a stage that implied the independence of the United States. On January 8, 1783, Washington wrote to Livingston, Secretary of Foreign Affairs: 'The power given to Mr. Oswald, to treat with any commissioner or commissioners properly authorized from the United States of America is more than I expected would happen before the meeting of Parliament. But, as the gentlemen on the part of America could not treat with him unless such powers were given, it became an act of necessity to cede them to effect their other purposes. Thus I account for the indirect acknowledgment of our independence by the King, who, I dare say, felt severe pangs at the time he put his hand to the letters patent. It is not, however, less efficacious or pleasing on that account; and breaking the ice is the great point gained.'

But, when he wrote these words, the question already had been decided. Neither in Europe nor in America had the leaders comprehended how completely Washington's phrase 'breaking the ice' had been accomplished by the friendly exchanges between Shelburne and Franklin. They soon had put the recognition of the independence of the United States in a special category, so that it was not endangered by

[1] To Joseph Jones, in Congress, December 14, 1782.

all the fluctuations of the terms of the general treaty of peace. It had happened most fortunately that the other American commissioners [1] were busy with the Dutch treaties at The Hague, and for a long time the American negotiations were in the hands of Franklin alone. Under the care of this ablest of American diplomatists, the American terms were well established, and a treaty recognizing the independence of the United States was being prepared far in advance of the treaty with the other nations.

Strangely enough one event in the war, apart from America and a great disaster, actually had an influence to hasten the independence of America. After leaving the United States, de Grasse for a time was successful in the West Indies. But, on April 12, 1782, his fleet was crushed by the British fleet under Rodney. No more complete naval defeat has ever been recorded, and de Grasse was carried away a prisoner from the seas where he had hoped to win victory. It was a pathetic finale, after the great accomplishment in America, and it had the effect of ending the European war. The sudden recovery of the dominion of the seas gave Great Britain an unexpected chance to obtain an advantageous peace, and the British leaders were eager to avail themselves of this opportunity.

To their minds, and to the minds of the British public, America merely stood as an obstacle in the way of peace — to be thrown aside on any conditions, no matter what, if only that boulder could be removed from the path of the settlement of the European war. This is the true statement of the view taken of America by Great Britain in 1782, when the British only were excited over the outcome of the Euro-

[1] Adams, Franklin, Jay, and Laurens were the American commissioners. Jefferson had also been appointed, but he at first refused, and afterwards was too late to go abroad.

pean war. This was the situation that made clear the course of Franklin, and with consummate skill he took advantage of the British eagerness to get America out of the way. As a result, he accomplished one of the greatest achievements in all diplomacy, and, when the other American commissioners joined him in Paris, it was only a matter of discussing the details. On November 30, 1782, the provisional articles of peace between Great Britain and the United States were signed at Paris, granting complete independence.

This ended the American Revolution, so far as concerned the United States. And this act, of granting the independence of America 'in the first instance,' brought about a general peace. It proved an inducement to lead France and Spain to make terms with Great Britain, which was the main object of the British in agreeing to the treaty with America in advance. There were many negotiations, especially on the part of Spain, but at last agreements were reached, and on January 20, 1783, the preliminary articles of the treaty of peace were signed in Paris.

But, before this news came to America there were disturbances in the army, which Washington's presence and personal influence barely kept within bounds. The letter from the army to Congress in December, 1782, of which Washington had written, had only caused debates in Congress, as to whether Congress should act upon it or should refer it to the States. The feeling in the army grew more bitter, until an anonymous address was sent about through the camp, calling for a mass meeting of the officers 'to obtain that redress of grievances which they seem to have solicited in vain.' Thereupon Washington took the wise course of issuing general orders, disapproving 'such disorderly proceedings,' and calling a meeting of his own for the officers.

Head Quarters Newburgh
15th of March 1783.

Gentlemen,

By an anonymous sum-
mons, an attempt has been made to con
vene you together ———— how inconsis
tent with the rules of propriety! ——
how unmilitary! ———— and how subversive of all order and discipline
—— let the good sense of the army
decide. ——

In the moment of this summons, another anonymous product-
on was sent into circulation; addressed more to the feelings & passions, than to the reason & judgment
of the army. ———— The author of the
piece, is entitled to much credit for
the goodness of his Pen: —— and I could
wish he had as much credit for the
rectitude of his Heart —— for as men
see thro' different Optics, and are
induced by the reflecting faculties
of the Mind, to use different means
to attain the same end; —— the author
of the address, should have had
more charity, than to mark for
Suspicion

FIRST PAGE OF WASHINGTON'S NEWBURGH ADDRESS

He thus put the matter on a proper basis, and under proper control. This meeting assembled March 15, 1783, with Gates presiding as senior officer. Washington came into the room, as soon as the officers had gathered, and made a moving speech, urging his officers to act with moderation, and promising to continue his efforts on their behalf: 'While I give you these assurances, and pledge myself in the most unequivocal manner to exert whatever ability I am possessed of in your favor, let me entreat you, Gentlemen, on your part, not to take any measures, which, in the calm light of reason, will lessen the dignity, and sully the glory, you have hitherto maintained. Let me request you to rely on the plighted faith of your country and place a full confidence in the purity of the intentions of Congress.'

After his address, Washington went out of the room and left the officers free to proceed as they thought fit. All were greatly moved by Washington's appeal, and their first act was to pass a unanimous resolve, to thank him and 'to assure him that the officers reciprocate his affectionate expressions, with the greatest sincerity of which the human heart is capable.' They then passed resolves giving a most moderate statement of their case, and professing 'unshaken confidence in the justice of Congress and their country.' They requested Washington 'to write to his Excellency the President of Congress, earnestly entreating the more speedy decision of that honorable body upon the subject of our late address' And they 'resolved unanimously, that the officers of the American army view with abhorance, and reject with disdain, the infamous propositions contained in a late anonymous address to the officers of the army, and resent with indignation the secret attempts of some unknown person to collect the officers together in a manner totally subversive of all discipline and good order.' It would be difficult to

379

find a record of so complete a personal influence as that exerted by Washington on this critical occasion. It changed a meeting, that promised to be insubordinate to a dangerous degree, into a gathering of officers who reaffirmed their loyalty.[1]

At length the news of actual peace came to America from France. Soon afterwards (April 6, 1783) General Carleton wrote to Washington announcing the signing of the preliminary articles of peace on January 20: 'The King, Sir, has been pleased in consequence of these events, to order proclamations to be published, declaring a cessation of arms as well by sea as land; and his Majesty's pleasure signified that I should cause the same to be published in all places under my command, in order that his Majesty's subjects may pay immediate and due obedience thereto; and such proclamation I shall accordingly cause to be made on Tuesday next, the 8th instant. In consequence thereof, and in conformity to the articles of peace, all our prisoners of war are to be set at liberty and restored with all convenient despatch, entertaining no doubt that similar measures will be taken on the part of the United States of America.'

And General Carleton ended his letter with the following generous message: 'Upon this great occasion, Sir, I am to offer my strongest assurances, that, during the short period of my command here, I shall be ready and earnest to cultivate that spirit of perfect good will, which, between the United States of America and the King of Great Britain, and the subjects and citizens of both countries, will, I trust always remain.' Under Carleton in New York was the only

[1] 'The meeting was had yesterday. The occasion, though intended for opposite purposes, has been one of the happiest circumstances of the war, and will set the military character of America in a high point of view....' Washington's comment.

British force of any importance remaining in the United States,[1] as Charleston had been evacuated December 14, 1782.

The American proclamation of the cessation of hostilities was made April 19, 1783, the anniversary of Lexington and Concord. It then became a question of disbanding the army. A suggestion from Washington did much to promote good feeling. He proposed: 'that at the discharge of the men engaged for the war, Congress should suffer those men, non-commissioned officers and soldiers, to take with them as their own property, and as a gratuity, the arms and accoutrements they now hold.' [2] Another great help was the result of this letter to Congress. The ruling was made that enlistments of 'men for the war' did not end until the definite treaty of peace. But Congress resolved: 'That the Commander-in-Chief be instructed to grant furloughs to the non-commissioned officers and soldiers of the United States enlisted to serve during the war, who shall be discharged as soon as the definitive treaty of peace is concluded.' [3]

Washington availed himself of this authority and great numbers of furloughs were granted, and the men were never called back. By this means a great part of the army was sent home, as there was a long interval before the final treaty was drawn up. This gradual dispersal of the American soldiers averted much of the trouble that might have happened. For there was still a great deal of discontent, as the soldiers were paid off in notes due in the future. There was one outbreak of a few Pennsylvania troops in June. These forced themselves into the hall of Congress.

[1] There were only a few other small posts on the outskirts, nothing in the States themselves.

[2] To the President of Congress, April 18, 1783.

[3] Journal, May 26, 1783.

But they were raw recruits, and Washington skillfully took advantage of this fact, to hold up their conduct as the text of a steadying sermon to the army: 'For when we consider, that these Pennsylvania levies, who have now mutinied, are recruits and soldiers of a day, who have not borne the heat and burdens of the war, and who can have very few hardships to complain of; and when we at the same time recollect, that those soldiers, who have lately been furloughed from the army, are the veterans who have patiently endured hunger, nakedness, and cold, who have suffered and bled without a murmur, and who, with perfect good order have retired to their homes without a settlement of their accounts, or a farthing of money in their pockets; we shall be as much astonished at the virtues of the latter, as we are struck with horror and detestation at the proceedings of the former; and every candid mind, without indulging ill-grounded prejudices, will undoubtedly make the proper discrimination.' [1]

While the army was 'being thus reduced to merely a competent garrison for West Point,' [2] Washington made a tour of the northern and western posts with a view to ascertaining what should be done when the British evacuated the outlying regions ceded by the treaty. The evacuation of New York was delayed from time to time, not at all through the fault of Carleton, who was anxious to take his forces away. But, because there were so many people and their goods to be removed, he had much difficulty in collecting the great quantity of shipping needed. It was a repetition on a large scale of the pathetic tragedies of Boston and Philadelphia. From each of these there had been an exodus of Loyalists with the Royal troops. In the case of New York,

[1] To the President of Congress, June 24, 1783.
[2] *Ibid.*

during the long British occupation, a separate population had gathered of those who cast their lot with the British. These had to be taken away, with their effects, and the fall of 1783 passed before General Carleton was able to accomplish this.

Chapter XLIII

THE FINAL SCENES

IN THE interval, when it had become evident that the dissolution of the American Army of the Revolution was approaching, General Knox made a proposal 'to perpetuate the friendships formed by the officers of the army, so soon to be disbanded, and at the same time to create a fund for their indigent widows and orphans.' [1] From this suggestion came the founding of the Society of the Cincinnati. The membership was to consist of officers of the American Army, who, like the Roman Cincinnatus of old, had been called suddenly from the tasks of peace, and were to return to their communities to resume these tasks.

Meetings were held, and this idea was carried into effect. The membership was to be passed on to the posterity of the officers, in order to perpetuate their ties of friendship. Its objects were: 'to preserve inviolate the rights and liberties for which they had contended; to promote and cherish national honor and union between the States; to maintain brotherly kindness toward each other, and extend relief to such officers and their families as might stand in need of it.' [2] In order to secure funds for this last purpose, each officer was to contribute one month's pay. Washington was unanimously chosen President of the Society of the Cincinnati,

[1] Drake: *Life and Correspondence of Henry Knox.*
[2] Irving: *Life of Washington.*

ORIGINAL DIPLOMA OF MEMBERSHIP IN THE SOCIETY OF THE CINCINNATI

and General Knox its secretary. The first meeting of the newly organized society was to be in May, 1784. The leading French officers who had served in America were also to be members.

The postponements of the evacuation of New York continued, from time to time, but there was no longer any question of the fact that the British were anxious to leave. In view of this, Congress appointed November 2, 1783, the day for disbanding the army. Only a small force was to be retained in service, until the peace establishment could be constituted. The large numbers, who were on furlough, were discharged at their homes.

Washington, in his farewell orders to the army, published November 2, 1783, made an earnest plea to his soldiers, 'that they should prove themselves not less virtuous and useful as citizens, than they had been persevering and victorious soldiers.... Let it be known and remembered, that the reputation of the federal armies is established beyond the reach of malevolence; and let a consciousness of their achievements and fame still incite the men, who composed them, to honorable actions; under the persuasion that the private virtues of economy, prudence, and industry, will not be less amiable in civil life, than the more splendid qualities of valor, perseverance, and enterprise, were in the field.'

This was one instance in history, when a successful military leader was deeply in earnest in his desire to send back his soldiers to civil life, without a thought of using his military forces for any personal ambition of his own. There was not a trace of Cæsar in George Washington.[1] That was self-evident, in thought, word, and deed.

[1] Some of the officers had gone to the length of having it suggested to Washington that he should grasp the rule of the country. This met an indignant blast from Washington, which ended it forever; 'No occurrence in the course of the

385

On November 18, Washington was able to write to the President of Congress: 'I have at length the pleasure to inform your Excellency and Congress, that Sir Guy Carleton has fixed upon the time at which he proposes to evacuate New York.' Carleton had been apprehensive of 'a deliberate combination to plunder the city of New York' [1] at the time of the evacuation by the British. Washington assured him 'that such arrangements have been made, as will, in my opinion, not only utterly discountenance, but effectually prevent, any outrage or disorder.' [2] As a matter of fact, there never was any serious danger in New York.

But Washington had consulted with Governor Clinton, as to the best means of establishing at once civil government in the evacuated city. For two days the departure of the British was farther delayed by bad weather, but, in the morning of November 25, the British troops were being moved away, and the American troops came down to the Bowery, which was then the upper part of the city of New York. At one o'clock the British had left, and the American troops marched into the city. Then followed the formal entry of General Washington and Governor Clinton, on horseback with their suites and escorted by a troop of cavalry. In procession with them, came the Lieutenant Governor and members of the Council, with the Speaker and members of the Assembly. This was typical of the immediate restoration of American civil government.

Washington's task was ended, and he only asked Congress

war has given me more painful sensations, than your information of there being such ideas existing in the army, as you have expressed, and I must view with abhorrance and reprimand with severity.... Let me conjure you, then, if you have any regard for your Country, concern for yourself or posterity, or respect for me, to banish these thoughts from your mind.' (Washington to Colonel Nicola, May 22, 1782.)

[1] Washington to Carleton, November 22, 1783.

[2] *Ibid.*, 1781.

to designate the time and place for resigning his commission. Congress was to assemble at Annapolis, and they asked Washington to go there and appear before them for this purpose. Washington wrote, that 'after seeing the backs of the British Forces turned upon us, and the Executive of the State of New York put into peaceable possession of their Capitol,' he was to 'proceed to Annapolis and get translated into a private Citizen.' [1]

This characteristic description was illuminative of the mind of Washington, of his freedom from taint of personal ambition to gain anything for himself. But, in the largest sense also, it summed up his service. He had fought the good fight. He had won his war — and it must be called *his war* — with a dauntless courage [2] that had prevailed against every disadvantage and discouragement. For the American Commander in Chief, 'seeing the backs of the British' meant the victorious end of campaigns, waged always with lack of the resources of war, yet always curbing the enemy. And, when Washington put the civil government 'into peaceable possession of their Capitol,' it meant constituting representative government for his country without a trace of military dictatorship.

No argument in the case will be given in this book. The recital of the facts in the case is all that is necessary. For the record of the American Commander in Chief, the true George Washington, stands on these facts, which have been stated in the text of this book.

In conclusion, there should be quoted Irving's description of Washington's farewell to his officers, one of the most

[1] To James McHenry, December 10, 1783.

[2] '...And, on all great occasions, not a little animated by the courage of general Washington, who has been proverbially called a Fabius, but in whose character courage, in fact was a feature still more predominant than prudence.' (Stedman: *History of the American War.*)

moving passages in our literature [1]: 'In the course of a few days Washington prepared to depart for Annapolis, where Congress was assembling, with the intention of asking leave to resign his command. A barge was in waiting about noon on the 4th of December at Whitehall ferry to convey him across the Hudson to Paulus Hook. The principal officers of the army assembled at Fraunces' Tavern in the neighborhood of the ferry, to take a final leave of him. On entering the room, and finding himself surrounded by his old companions in arms, who had shared with him so many scenes of hardship, difficulty, and danger, his agitated feelings overcame his usual self-command. Filling a glass of wine, and turning upon them his benignant but saddened countenance, "With a heart full of love and gratitude," said he, "I now take leave of you, most devoutly wishing that your latter days may be as prosperous and happy as your former ones have been glorious and honorable."

'Having drunk this farewell benediction, he added with emotion, "I cannot come to each of you to take my leave, but shall be obliged if each of you will come and take me by the hand."

'General Knox, who was nearest, was the first to advance. Washington, affected even to tears, grasped his hand and gave him a brother's embrace. In the same affectionate manner he took leave of the rest. Not a word was spoken. The deep feeling and manly tenderness of these veterans in the parting moment could find no utterance in words. Silent and solemn they followed their loved commander as he left the room, passed through a corps of light infantry, and proceeded on foot to Whitehall ferry. Having entered the barge, he turned to them, took off his hat and waved a

[1] Irving followed the account in Marshall's *Life of Washington*, and it is notable that Thackeray reverently gave the same version in *The Virginians*.

silent adieu. They replied in the same manner, and having watched the barge until the intervening point of the Battery shut it from sight, returned, still solemn and silent to the place where they had assembled.' [1]

[1] Irving: *Life of Washington.*

THE END

Index

Abercromby, Gen., attack on Ticonderoga, 26

Adams, John, endorsement of Washington as Commander in Chief, 51, 52; member of Naval Committee, 86; member of Board of War and Ordnance, 123; one of the American Commissioners, 377

Adams, Samuel, 56

Albany, N.Y., 161

Alexandria, Virginia, Washington ordered to, 14

Allegheny and Monongahela, Fort at, 14, 15

Allen, Ethan, leader of the Green Mountain Boys, 54, 55

Amboy, Howe at, 174, 192, 194, 259

American Army, 70, 83, 116, 117, 118; in the vicinity of New York, 123, 124, 125, 126; at Long Island, 131, *et seq.*; withdrawal to the New York side, 138, 139; evacuation of, 144, 145, 146, 147, 148; abandonment of all Manhattan Island, 149; *et seq.*; in New Jersey, 158, *et seq.*; in the first half of 1777, 182, 183, 184, 185, 186, 192, 198; at Philadelphia, 203, *et seq.*; at Brandywine Creek, 213, *et seq.*; at Germantown, 224, 225, 226, 227; at Valley Forge, 234, 236, 237, 238, 239, 240, 241, 248, 249, 252, 258; at Newport, 267, 268, 269, 270; at the end of 1778, 273, 276, 277; during the first months of 1779, 281, *et seq.*; at the end of 1779, 290, *et seq.*; the condi-

tions for 1780, 300, *et seq.*; defeat in the South and French reinforcements in the North, 309, *et seq.*; Arnold's treason, 318, *et seq.*; beginning of 1781, 330, *et seq.*; development of the situation, 338, *et seq.*; Washington's move to the South, 347, *et seq.*; the Siege of Yorktown, 356, *et seq.*; the results, 365, *et seq.*; achievement of Independence, 372, *et seq.*; the final scenes, 385, *et seq.*

American Colonies, cleavage with Great Britain, 29, *et seq.*; General Congress of, 35, 36, 37, 39; opponents of the ministerial policies, 49, *et seq.*

American Commissioners, 377

American Navy, 85, 86, 110, 116, 279, 280, 302, 303

American privateers, 176, 278, 279, 302

American Revolution, origin in cleavage with Great Britain, 29, *et seq.*; outbreak of, 37, *et seq.*; events of, 42, 43, 44; uprising, 45, *et seq.*; situation at Boston, 68, *et seq.*; siege of Boston, 80, *et seq.*; expulsion of the British from Boston, 96, *et seq.*; military situation, 104, *et seq.*; after the evacuation of Boston, 112, *et seq.*

Amherst, Lord, 107

André, Major, involved in plot of Benedict Arnold, 320, 321, 322; capture and execution, 322

Annapolis, 355, 387, 388

391